Backyard
PROBLEM
SOLVER

www.jerrybaker.com

Backyard
PROBLEM
SOLVER

2,168 Natural Solutions for Growing
Great Grass, Super Shrubs, Bright Bulbs,
Perfect Perennials, Amazing Annuals,
Vibrant Vegetables, Terrific Trees,
and Much, Much More!

by Jerry Baker,
America's Master Gardener®

Published by American Master Products, Inc.

Executive Editor: Kim Adam Gasior
Published by American Master Products, Inc.
Contributing Writers: Barbara Pleasant and Vicki Webster
Project Editor: Vicki Webster
Editor: Arlene Bouras
Cover Design: Kitty Pierce Mace
Text Design: Mark Bergin and Susan Bernier
Text Layout: Susan Bernier
Illustration Editor: Ilona Sherratt
Indexer: Nanette Cardon

Pleasant, Barbara.
  Jerry Baker's backyard problem solver: 2,168 simple solutions for super soil, great grass, amazing annuals, perfect perennials, vibrant vegetables, terrific trees, bad bugs, wicked weeds, and much, much more — / author, Barbara Pleasant; editor, Kim Adam Gasior . — 1st ed.
       p.   cm.
     Includes index.

     1. Gardening.   I. Baker, Jerry.   II. Gasior, Kim Adam.
III. Title.   IV. Title: Backyard problem solver
SB455.P 54   2002   635
              QBI01-201235

Printed in the United States of America
       12 14 15 13   hardcover

CONTENTS

To: All of those folks who've ever gone toe-to-toe with a bad bug, crafty critter, or dastardly disease in their own yard. Keep those cards and letters comin', so I can continue to help you solve your backyard problems for another 50 years. God bless you all, and God bless America!

It Sure Doesn't *Feel* Like Work!

A s most of you know, there's nothing I love better than putterin' around the old backyard. Whether I'm mowing the lawn, digging up a new flower bed, or picking the world's sweetest corn from my vegetable garden, I'm in "hog heaven," as my Grandma Putt used to say. Why, I even get a kick out of coming face-to-face with those little challenges that Mother Nature offers up from time to time. I welcome chances to outwit ornery critters, fend off dastardly diseases, and batten down the hatches when heavy weather heads my way — they're great opportunities to exercise what Grandma Putt called "the old gray cells."

Grin 'em Down

There's no doubt about it, Grandma Putt had some mighty powerful "gray cells" and when she set out to battle a problem in her yard, there wasn't any doubt about the outcome! Over the years, I've come up with my own methods for grinnin' down garden-variety varmints and sending yard problems packin'. And in my travels around this great land of ours, I've picked up more than a few ideas from folks with some pretty impressive gray cells — and great-looking yards — of their own.

In this book, I've combined it all — Grandma Putt's good old-fashioned grow-how with some newfangled ideas and, of course, my own special tips, tricks, and tonics. The result: an arsenal of surefire weapons that'll help you win your yard and garden battles hands down.

Head 'em Off at the Pass

The old saying goes that an ounce of prevention is worth a pound of cure. Well, when it comes to yard problems, I believe that an ounce of prevention is worth about a ton and a half of cure! That's why, in Part I of this book, I'll tell you how to get your plants off to a good, healthy start. That way, Old Man Trouble is less likely to come a-callin' — and if he does decide to pay a visit, you can send him packing pronto.

Guarding the Green

In Part II, we'll get down to particulars: I'll share my secrets for solving specific plant problems. I'll cover every kind of plant in your yard, from one-summer annuals to trees that, given a little TLC, could live to see your great-grandchildren climbing their branches. I'll also answer the most common questions I've heard in my travels, because chances are, they'll help you and your yard, too.

The Invasion Forces

Believe you me, yard problems come in all shapes, sizes, and forms. In Part III, I'll give you the lowdown on a whole bunch of 'em, from the teeny, tiniest terrors to the biggest of the four-legged brigade. I'll even clue you in on what to do when Mother Nature throws a curve ball your way in the form of fierce winds, too little or too much rain, or frosts that play the old game of now you see me, now you don't.

Hard Knocks

Then we'll move on to one of the most important parts of your yard, what we professionals call the "hardscape." All that refers to is the solid, nonliving, and more or less permanent fixtures such as fences, walls, and walkways. In Part IV, I'll pass along some helpful hints for keeping your current hardscape in tip-top condition. I'll even tell you how to use new fences, walls, and walkways to solve some big outdoor problems.

It's a Date

Finally, if you're anything like me, you get so wrapped up in your daily duties that you tend to forget those little seasonal chores that can fend off big-time trouble. But don't worry: Just turn to Part V, where you'll find my Calendar of Care that reminds you what to do and when to do it. I've also gathered all of my terrific tonics together so at the first sign of trouble, all you need to do is reach for a recipe and bid your problems adieu!

Go for It!

So with this arsenal at hand, you'll be able to tackle any problem your yard can dish up. But don't get me wrong, folks — I'm not trying to make your backyard sound like one woe after another. On the contrary! As Grandma Putt used to say, "There's no greater fun a body can have than tendin' this great green earth." And, as always, she was right as rain. So get out there and, above all else, have fun, folks!

Part I
SOLVING PROBLEMS FROM THE GROUND UP

Creating a yard that works as good as it looks is an art, but it's also a craft. Like any other craft, from cooking to sewing or building model ships in bottles, you first need to know about the basics.

In this section, I'll begin by telling you what you need to know about soil, which is to a gardener what a blank sheet or canvas is to a painter. It's the basis upon which all gardens are built, and the better your soil is, the better your plants will be able to fend off trouble. So the more you know about your soil, the better off you'll be! We'll also talk about planting things large and small, from long-lived trees to tiny seeds. Finally, we'll look at feeding, watering, and a few other ways to keep your plants growing the way they should. So what are we waiting for? Let's get growing!

CHAPTER 1

Super Soil and Other Secrets

There is only one place to begin making a trouble-free yard, and that's the earth beneath your feet. You have to work from the ground up, because the foundation of any good lawn or garden is good, reliable soil. Or, as my Grandma Putt put it, even if you get a plant for free, give it a $10 hole!

SETTING THE GROUNDWORK

I like working in soil, because it's very responsive, predictable stuff. I know that when I spend some time digging, cultivating, working in organic matter, and mixing in just the right timely tonics, the soil will become soft and porous, and my plants will be delighted. Yes, it's hard work, but the rewards are both immediate and long lasting. So what if it takes you an hour to prepare a planting hole for a crabapple tree and get it nicely situated in its new home? If you've done the job right, the tree will prosper for many years to come, and every time you look at it, you'll glow a little inside, knowing that you've done a small thing to make this great green world just a little bit more beautiful.

Let's Talk Dirty

Unimproved soil makes me think of little boys who start out life as little hellions, then gradually settle down, respond to their parents' nurturing, and grow into fine young men. That's how it is with soil. No matter how balky or contrary it is to start with, it will become richer and more agreeable when given a little tender loving care.

When it comes to the TLC of soil, we're basically talking about two simple things — air and organic matter. Lighten up soil with air, and buck it up with organic matter, and, like magic, you get what's called loam. Once soil gets loamy, plant roots can thread through it with ease, and all the water and fertilizer you provide go exactly where you want them to go.

Put It to the Test

The easiest way to get a fix on soil type is to squeeze a ball of damp dirt in your hand. If it's so loose and unsticky that it won't form a ball, you've got sand. Clay soil will form a ball right away, and you can even flatten it into a pancake before it falls apart. Loam will form a ball, but the ball will shatter easily if you tap it with your finger.

Soil Types and Textures

Soil type really refers to the size of the soil particles. Sandy soil has a light, gritty texture, because its particles are large; clay particles are very small, so clay soil is tight and heavy. But it's what's between the particles that counts. That brings us back to air and organic matter. When you cultivate soil, you create pockets of air for plant roots and earthworms to move through. And when you add compost or other materials made from decomposed plants, the tidbits wedge themselves between soil particles and — presto! — you end up with sandy loam, clay loam, or, if you're lucky, rich loam that's a mixture of large sand particles, small clay particles, and lots of midsize particles.

So What Difference Does the Difference Make?

Both sand and clay soils are improved the same way, by adding air and organic matter, but understanding your soil texture tells you ahead of time how you can expect your soil to behave once you put it to work growing plants.

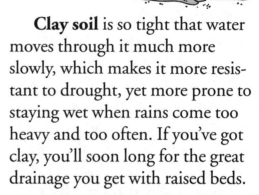

Sandy soil drains fast and dries out quickly, so it tends to need more water and fertilizer. Gardeners with sandy soil are therefore destined to become big-time mulchers with special interest in water conservation.

Clay soil is so tight that water moves through it much more slowly, which makes it more resistant to drought, yet more prone to staying wet when rains come too heavy and too often. If you've got clay, you'll soon long for the great drainage you get with raised beds.

What's Under There?

So far, we've been talking about topsoil, which is the soil you find when you dig around at the surface. The layer of topsoil may be measured in feet (if you're lucky) or inches (if you're like most of us). Beneath the topsoil lies subsoil, which is often a different color than topsoil, and is much harder, because it's so compacted.

Dig Down Deep

If chipping away at subsoil with a sharp shovel and digging fork just doesn't work, call a halt to the struggle and run some water into your half-dug planting holes. After the water percolates in for a few hours, the digging gets much easier!

You know you've hit subsoil when your shovel doesn't want to go any deeper. If subsoil starts less than a foot below the surface, you can expect that plant roots will have a hard time with it, too. Although there are exceptions, most plants need a foundation of soil at least 14 inches deep.

Sweet or Sour?

Care for a little taste of soil? I'm kidding, though back in Grandma Putt's day, many wise farmers decided whether or not they needed to lime their fields and gardens by

taking a handful of soil, sniffing it, and touching their tongues to it to see if it tasted a little sweet or a little sour. This is a learned skill that's been all but forgotten, because today we have better ways to tell whether our soil is sweet (alkaline) or sour (acid).

Your Soil's Potential

The letters pH stand for "potential of hydrogen," and the pH scale runs from 1.0 to 14.0, with 7.0 being neutral. A measurement above that signifies alkaline soil; below is acid. You can test your own soil with an inexpensive kit from the garden center. Or, if you want a detailed analysis of the nutrients in your soil, as well as an accurate pH reading, send a soil sample to a private testing lab or your local Cooperative Extension Service. It'll take longer to get the results, but you'll wind up with some valuable information that could head off a lot of problems down the road.

Jerry Baker Says . . .

"So why should you care what your soil's pH is? I'll tell you why: The pH level determines, in part, how well nutrients in the soil can be absorbed into your plants' roots. If your soil is either too sweet or too sour to suit their needs, you'll wind up with malnourished plants. If your plants aren't well fed,

they'll be easy prey for any pest or disease that comes their way. And that'll mean big-time trouble for you!"

Tinkering with Acidity

Adjusting your soil's pH one way or another is easy. Here's all there is to it.

✔ **To raise the pH of acid soil,** add lime in the form of powdered limestone, which is sold at all garden centers. Because how much lime you need varies with your soil type and climate, either get expert local advice or start small, with a 50-pound bag per 1000 square feet of soil area.

✔ **To lower the pH of alkaline soil,** use powdered soil sulfur. Start small (20 pounds per 1000 square feet) or check with local master gardeners or your Co-operative Extension Service for guidance.

✔ **After adding either lime or sulfur,** mix it in well, water the site, and test your soil again in a few months. Soils tend to revert to their natural pH over time. If you find that native soil in your area is either strongly acid or very alkaline, check your pH at least once a year, and keep a watch on plants that have peculiar tastes in soil pH.

LANDSCAPE LINGO

Anything you add to your soil to make it better is a **soil amendment,** but when gardeners use the phrase, they usually mean various sources of organic matter, such as compost, composted manure, humus, peat moss, or leaf mold. Lime and sulfur, used to adjust the soil's pH, are amendments, too.

How Much Is Enough?

You never want your soil to end up being more than 50 percent amendment. So, if you are digging a 10-inch-deep bed, you would add less than a 4- to 5-inch-deep layer of any soil amendment. Half that amount may do nicely if your soil is in pretty good shape.

Use the same rule of thumb when preparing planting holes. I like to dig out the soil, place it in a wheelbarrow, and mix it with a soil amendment, allowing about 2 parts soil to 1 part amendment. Then I use this mixture to line the bottom of the hole and backfill around the roots after the plant is in place.

Compost: from Garbage to Black Gold

While we're talking about amendments, believe you me, whatever ails your soil, adding plenty of compost is the best way I can think of to improve it! What's more, this "gold mine in a pile" is sort of like nature's garbage disposal: It takes leaves, sticks, banana peels, coffee grounds, tea bags, grass clippings, and just about any other type of plant material you toss into it, and transforms it all into soft, black humus, which plants crave like I crave chocolate.

WATCH IT ⚠️

Give 'em Time

Sawdust, weathered mulch material, and wood chips are dandy soil amendments, too, but while they're decomposing, they tie up a lot of soil nutrients. So before you use them in your yard, let them mellow out in the compost heap for a while.

Timely Tonic ⏱️

Bedtime Snack

Fall is a fine time to break new ground, because the soil has all winter to digest slow-acting amendments. This rich mixture works miracles in heavy clay soil.

25 lbs. of gypsum
10 lbs. of natural organic garden food (either 4–12–4 or 5–10–5)
5   lbs. of bonemeal

Mix these ingredients together, then apply them to every 100 square feet of soil with your hand-held broadcast spreader. Work them into the soil, and cover with a thick blanket of leaves, straw, or other organic mulch.

It's Alive!

But it would be a mistake to think of your compost pile as a purely chemical deal. Actually, it's very much alive. First, moisture helps leach out tannins and other substances that are natural preservatives, then fungi move in and complete the next phase. Next, bacteria get into the act, and, finally, what began as a pile of leaves and kitchen trimmings becomes a much smaller pile of black gold.

Green + Brown = *Compost*?

It's important to get the right balance of high-nitrogen ingredients (what gardeners call "greens") and high-carbon ones (a.k.a. "browns"). That's because if your pile is too high in carbon, it'll take a coon's age to decompose. If it's too high in nitrogen, it'll smell to high heaven.

Don't worry yourself into a frazzle over the equation, though. Just make sure you add roughly 3 parts of brown stuff (such as dried leaves, sawdust, wood chips, and sticks) for every 1 part of green (as in freshly pulled weeds, vegetable trimmings, fresh manure, and grass clippings).

Timely Tonic

Compost Feeder Tonic

Just like your plants, your compost pile needs a boost now and then. Once a month, spray it with this Tonic.

½ can of beer
½ can of regular cola (not diet)
½ cup of liquid dish soap

Mix these ingredients in the jar of your 20 gallon hose-end sprayer and apply generously.

WATCH IT

Smelly Compost

Too much nitrogen can turn a compost heap into a real nosesore, but so can lack of air: When the pile becomes too wet or too compacted, foul-smelling bacteria will give the heap a sewagelike aroma. To set things right, fluff the material with a pitchfork or digging fork, and work in some brown material, like dry leaves.

Quick Fix for Slow Compost

It's normal for leaves, sticks, wood chips, and sawdust to take several months to decompose, but you can speed things along toward the end by mixing a little high-nitrogen organic fertilizer into your heap. Microorganisms that have been waiting for a good supply of nitrogen will get busy, and you should have finished compost in only a few weeks. And don't forget to feed your compost pile; my Compost Feeder Tonic works wonders.

Hold That Gold!

There are all kinds of ways to contain your black gold in the making. They all serve the same purpose: To hold the stuff in while providing constant exposure to fresh air. You will also need a way to stir or turn the compost from time to time, so that everything gets a chance to be near the center and bottom of the mass, where decomposition tends to go fastest. Make sure you can easily add water, too. You want to keep the pile lightly moist, but never sopping wet. Here are some good container options:

- **A simple enclosure made from boards** with hardware cloth or chicken wire nailed onto it. It's a snap to build, but it's usually not all that attractive.

- **A special metal drum** that you spin on a cylinder to mix the stuff. These things are convenient as all get-out, but they tend to rust over time.

IT'S A MIRACLE! Grandma Putt made sure that her plants had a steady supply of good compost. As little as a ½-inch layer, worked into the soil in spring and fall, will ensure that your plants never run short of crucial nutrients such as zinc, selenium, and boron. Your soil will also drain better, and that's *really* important!

- **Plastic compost bins.** In my book, this is *the* way to go if you care at all about appearances — they look like plastic trash cans, and they're easy to tuck out of sight or to screen with a vine-covered trellis. Plus, they last for years and keep your compost out of grabbing range of all kinds of pesky pests.

Is It Done Yet?

Compost is done, or finished, when it becomes dark and crumbly. When a batch nears this point, start a new one, and dole the good stuff out to your plants in generous servings. Compost is not a fertilizer, but it is very rich in enzymes and beneficial bacteria — and it's a first-class banquet of trace nutrients. That's why I call it black gold!

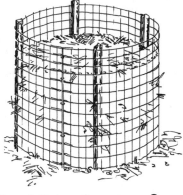

CHAPTER 2

Planting Tips and Tricks

My Grandma Putt taught me that the best time to solve a problem in your yard is before it gets a toehold. And I'll let you in on a little secret: Every last one of your plants wants to grow and prosper in your yard. It's not hard to make that happen, but you do need to make sure your plants get started on the right root. In this chapter, I'll walk you through the whole process of planting, whether you're starting from seed or from container-grown plants.

HEAD OFF TROUBLE

Let's start small, with seeds, and work our way up to long-lived trees and shrubs. It may be but a short drive from the garden center to your yard, but if you want to head off problems before they start, there is much to know about selecting, planting, and caring for the plants you call your own.

Sow or Transplant?

When you're setting out to grow annual flowers, most vegetables, and many herbs, you have two choices: You can start from seed or you can buy transplants at the garden center, all ready to be popped into the ground. There's no doubt about it, using transplants makes the job go more quickly, but to my way of thinking, there are three great reasons to start with seeds:

#1 Broader choice. Seed catalogs offer a much greater variety than any garden center could hope to carry. For example, starting from seed may be the only way you can have a dozen hot pink zinnias, or grow beloved heirloom tomatoes like the ones you remember from your grandma's garden.

#2 Rooting success. Some flowers, like morning glories, and a fair number of vegetables, including corn, beans, and all root crops, prefer to spend their lives right where they start out. In fact, some veggies resent root disturbance so much that you'll rarely, if ever, find them offered for sale as transplants.

#3 Fun. Tinkering with seeds is great, because it's inexpensive, easy, and fun. In fact, some plants are so easily grown from seed that there is no reason to start them any other way.

Make 'em Sizzle

When you're getting a new site ready for planting, digging up weeds can be a real pain in the grass. So don't dig — cook 'em out. Just water the plot well, then stretch a sheet of clear plastic over it. (An old plastic drop cloth will work fine.) In about 4 weeks — with old Sol's cooperation — those weeds will be history!

Picking Packets

The larger the seeds, the easier they are to sow and grow. If you're new to gardening, the best plan is simply to learn the size of the seeds: Seeds that feel big and knobby are usually easy to handle, while tiny seeds require more time, patience, and know-how.

WATCH IT

Slow Going Ahead

It is technically possible to start many flowering perennials, shrubs, and even trees from seed, but in most cases, it takes a lot of time and a lot of patience. Believe me, it's *not* a fast, easy route to a great-looking yard!

LANDSCAPE LINGO

Hybrid varieties are the result of carefully planned breeding projects, in which the pollen of one variety is used to fertilize the flowers of another. This crossing results in a single special generation of seeds, often coded as F1 on seed packets and in catalog descriptions.

Hybrids are usually very vigorous plants, and often feature special colors, flavors, or resistance to disease. The downside is that, although F1 hybrids do produce seeds, those seeds won't have the same great characteristics as the parent plants. To get those, you'll have to buy more seeds.

Sizing Up Seeds

The smaller the seeds, the easier it is for them to get lost in the rough-and-tumble world of the garden. Take it from me: You can avoid a lot of frustration by starting the little guys in the great indoors. Don't worry: It's easy to do, and a lot of fun besides. (To see how simple it is, see page 14.)

On the other hand, big seeds have no trouble muscling their way to the surface. In fact, many large seeds, such as beans, peas, corn, and squash, just hate having their roots tampered with. To get the best results, you need to plant them directly in the spots where you want them to grow up.

Direct Sowing Savvy

If you want to feel like a real down and dirty gardener, let yourself experience the excitement of sowing seeds directly into prepared ground. Nasturtiums, beans, and peas are great for beginners, and those beans and peas don't have to be the kind you eat. Scarlet runner beans and sweet peas will color up your yard and give you a chance to prove yourself as a champion sower of seeds.

Plant any seed at twice the depth of its size. Big beans go an inch deep, while smaller marigold seeds need shallower planting. Most seed packets list planting depth and spacing, along with the best time of year for sowing.

You can plant seeds by poking them into the soil or by making shallow furrows with a hoe, stick, or your fingers. After that, I like to cover seeds with compost or potting soil, which doesn't form a crust at the surface the way regular soil often does. That way, you'll ensure that the little sprouts will have an easy time pushing themselves up to the sun.

To promote strong germination, keep the seeded spot constantly moist by hand watering or using a sprinkler. With luck, so many seeds will sprout that you will need to pull out some of them to give the others the room they need to grow. Usually, the best time to thin is about 3 weeks after planting. And planting's easy — just follow these guidelines.

Timely Tonic

Seed and Soil Energizer Tonic

This potion will get your seeds off to a rip-roaring start.

1 tsp. of liquid dish soap
1 tsp. of ammonia
1 tsp. of whiskey

Mix all of these ingredients in 1 quart of weak tea, pour into your mist-sprayer bottle, shake gently, then once a day, mist the surface of beds planted with seeds.

Starting Seeds Indoors

You can get a head start by planting seeds indoors a few weeks to a month before the last spring frost. This is easy to do, especially if you have a grow light that you can suspend about 2 inches over the tops of your babies. To make sure your seeds get off and growing on the right root, use a high-quality, professional seed-starting mix, not regular potting soil. Seed-starting mix is a very fine, light-textured, soilless planting medium that young roots can move through easily. The good brands have also been sterilized, so there's no way your baby plants can pick up pests or diseases.

Recycling Roundup

Got an old mailbox lying around the garage? Turn it *into* a garage for your hand tools, seed packets, and other odds and ends you'll need when you're tending your garden. Just paint the box and put it on a post near your beds. Then say goodbye to running back and forth to fetch things you've forgotten!

Jerry Baker Says . . .

"To get your seeds off to a disease-free start, lightly sprinkle Jell-O powder on 'em with a salt shaker. Any flavor works, but lemon is best, because it repels some bugs. As your plants grow, feed them more Jell-O — the gelatin helps the plants hold water, and the sugar feeds the organisms in the soil."

Move 'em Out

Get your seedlings ready for the outdoors gradually by setting them outside in a protected place for a few hours a day for a day or two, working up to all day and night over a period of a week or so. Gardeners call this process "hardening off."

The Maternity Ward

You can find all kinds of seed-starting contai[...] even complete kits, at your local garden cent[...] gardening catalogs. They all work just fine. But they [...] not necessary. Anything that holds soil and has holes to let the extra water run out will work just as well. Here are some containers I like to use (after I've poked holes in the bottoms):

- Milk cartons
- Pie and cake tins
- Plastic shoe boxes
- Paper, plastic, and foam drinking cups
- Margarine, cottage cheese, and yogurt containers
- Plastic and plastic foam take-out boxes from delis and restaurants

It's in the Bag

To help your seeds germinate better, save your plastic produce bags from the grocery store and turn them into mini-greenhouses. Just wrap them loosely around your seed flats; they'll hold in just the right amount of moisture. When seedlings appear, remove the bags and place the flats under lights.

Timely Tonics

Seed Starter Tonic

Whether you start your seeds indoors or out, give them a good send-off with this timely Tonic.

1 cup of white vinegar
1 tbsp. of baby shampoo or liquid dish soap
2 cups of warm water

Mix all of these ingredients together in a bowl, and let your seeds soak in it overnight before planting them in well-prepared soil.

Damping-Off Prevention Tonic

Young seedlings are at risk for damping-off, a disease that causes their lower stems to rot. There's no cure, but you can prevent damping-off by using a sterile seed-starting medium and this quick Tonic.

4 tsp. of chamomile tea
1 tsp. of liquid dish soap

Mix these ingredients in 1 quart of boiling water. Let steep for at least an hour (the stronger the better), strain, then cool. Mist your seedlings as soon as their heads appear.

EASY BEDDING PLANTS

Plants that come in six-packs are an incredible deal! For a dollar (more or less), you get seedlings that have been babied along in a greenhouse, given exactly the amount of light and diet they need, and are now ready to strut their stuff in your garden. I always buy begonias, geraniums, impatiens, and petunias as bedding plants, because growing them from tiny seeds takes forever!

Smart Shopping

Younger is always better when it comes to bedding plants. With flowers, I look for plants that show a dense tuft of healthy green leaves and only one or two buds or flowers. With vegetables and herbs, I pick up the containers to see if the roots are so desperate for space that they've grown out through the drainage holes. Many annual flowers can recover from becoming a little root-bound, but fast-growing vegetables have a hard time with this particular form of stress.

Jerry Baker Says . . .

"Whatever you do, don't handle your seedlings by their stems or pull on them from the top. Twisting or bruising the main stem can cause serious injury to the tender young plants."

Ready for Takeoff

Most bedding plants have already waited long enough to be planted, and they are eager for roomier quarters. Still, I like to give them a few days to prepare for their transplant operation, so I water them with my Seedling Starter Tonic and busy myself getting their new home ready. This means cultivating a suitable bed and mixing an organic or timed-release fertilizer into the soil, or doing the same with planting holes, if that's what my planting plan requires.

Seedling Starter Tonic

Don't let your bedding plants go hungry! While they're still in their six-packs, treat them to this nutritious mixture.

2 tsp. of fish fertilizer
2 tsp. of liquid dish soap
1 tsp. of whiskey

Mix all of these ingredients in 1 quart of water. Feed this brew to your adopted seedlings every other time you water them, and give them a good soak with it just before you set them out.

Seedling Strengthener

Until seedlings have a little time to stretch their roots a bit, they can't make use of the ready and waiting fertilizer you've mixed into the soil. To tide them over, mist-spray bedding plants every few days with this elixir for 2 to 3 weeks after planting.

2 cups of manure
½ cup of instant tea granules
5 gal. of warm water

Put the manure and tea into an old nylon stocking, and let it steep in 5 gallons of water for several days. Dilute the brew with 4 parts of warm water before using.

Easy Does It

The actual transplanting process is best done with a gentle touch. I squeeze plants out of their containers from the bottom, and sometimes use a table knife to pry them out if they're stuck.

Quite often, I find that the roots have grown together into a tight mass at the bottom of the containers. Although it seems cruel and I can almost hear the little plants saying "Ouch" when I do it, I gently break apart the lowest inch of the root mass and spread it out, butterfly style. This little trick makes new roots grow out in different directions, which makes a big difference in the performance of the plants.

Add water and mulch, and those plants will be off and running. Then watch out!

PERENNIAL PLEASURES

To my way of thinking, flowering perennials are some of the greatest labor-savers in all of gardendom. Unlike annuals, which live for one year, set seed, and then die, perennials simply die back to the roots and go dormant in the winter. If you plant them right and give them just a little basic TLC, they'll keep coming back, filling your yard with color and fragrance year after year.

When, Oh When?

In early spring, all perennials wake up from their long winter's nap rarin' to grow. That's the best time to plant *most* of them in your garden, but *some* prefer fall planting. So how do you know when to plant what? The plant tag or catalog description will tell you. But when in doubt, just remember what Grandma Putt always said: "Great blooms come from great roots." In calendar terms, that translates into the following guidelines:

- Plant early bloomers in early fall. That will give them plenty of time to develop good, strong root structures before the first hard freeze sets in. Bleeding heart and coralbells like that head start. And poppies and peonies really need it — so don't even think of planting them in the spring.

- Plant later-blooming perennials in early spring, as soon as you can work the ground and the danger of freezing has passed. This roster includes such garden-variety favorites as asters, black-eyed Susans, chrysanthemums, and phlox. When you get them in early, they'll have all spring and early summer to put down roots before they launch their big floral display.

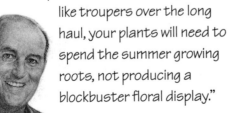

Jerry Baker Says . . .

"If early spring has come and gone, don't worry: You can still plant perennials that are actively growing. Just make sure they never dry out completely and steer clear of strong fertilizers that can encourage top growth at the expense of root development. Remember, to perform like troupers over the long haul, your plants will need to spend the summer growing roots, not producing a blockbuster floral display."

Planting Potted Perennials (Shrubs and Trees, too!)

Planting a perennial, shrub, or even a tree that's been grown in a pot is pretty straightforward. Here's how to do it in 5 easy steps:

Step 1 Prepare a planting hole that's twice as deep and wide as the container, amend the soil with organic matter, and then refill the hole halfway.

Step 2 Give the pot a few sound smacks to loosen the plant. If the soil and roots are nice and wet, the whole tangled mass should slide right out.

Step 3 Now set the plant in the hole, spread out the roots as much as possible without breaking them, and place the plant so that it's about an inch higher than it grew in its container. That's the sweet spot, because as the soil settles (and you add mulch), it will sink down about an inch. (I like to lay the handle of my shovel over the top of the hole. When the thick side of the handle lines up with

the soil in the container, I know the depth is just right.) If the plant is too low, take it out, put some more enriched soil under it, and check the depth again.

Step 4 When you know you've got the depth right, start filling in soil around the plant, stopping to add water every few inches. Putting water right into the planting hole ensures that the roots will stay moist, and helps squeeze out big pockets of air that can leave roots thirsty.

Step 5 Top off the surrounding soil with mulch, and you're done!

The State of the Union

Some roses, trees, and other woody plants are really two plants in one, because they are grafted. If you see a knobby bulge just above the soil line, you are probably looking at a graft union — the place where a cutting was grafted onto a rootstock, creating a plant that's prettier and more productive than its ungrafted counterpart. How you treat these plants when you put them into the ground depends on where you live.

✔ **In cool climates** (USDA Zone 6 and below), the graft union should be right at the soil line, or, in the case of roses, even partially buried.

✔ **In warmer territory** (Zone 7 and higher), set plants so that the graft union is an inch or two above the soil line. Otherwise, new stems may emerge from below the graft, and you'll end up with the plant used as the rootstock rather than the showier one that's been grafted onto it.

LANDSCAPE LINGO

The words **variety** and **cultivar** are often used interchangeably in catalogs and books, but there's a subtle difference between the two. A **variety** can be grown from seed, but a **cultivar** is propagated vegetatively, usually by rooting stem cuttings or dividing and replanting pieces of root taken from the parent plant.

When you buy a named cultivar, you know it will grow up to be exactly like its parent in size, leaf type, flower color, fragrance, and so forth. With a variety, all bets are off. In a seed-grown plant, any or all of those characteristics can be a little different. Named cultivars often cost a little more than plants labeled simply by their species name, but if you want to be sure of what you're getting, they're worth the price.

Give 'em Elbow Room

Keep the mature size of a plant in mind when you're planting, and you won't end up with a crowded house of a garden. The tags that come on plants often suggest proper spacing, which is based on the mature size of the plant and how much root space it needs.

It often takes shrubs 3 to 5 years to fill out and grow, and trees can take a lifetime!

TWO IN ONE

While you're waiting for slow-growing plants to reach full size, do what Grandma Putt did: Use the open space between them to grow annual flowers and spring-flowering bulbs, which make fine bedfellows for shrubs and perennials.

BARE-ROOT BABIES

Some plants go into such a deep sleep when they become dormant that they can be pulled from the soil, washed clean, and sold with their roots as bare as a baby's bottom.

Who They Are

Many of the plants that you order from catalogs come shipped bare-root. That's because, first of all, plants with no heavy soil on their roots are easier and less expensive to ship from place to place. Second, because the plants are so clean, there is little chance of shipping soilborne diseases along with them. Roses, raspberries, and other brambles are often sold with bare roots, as are many fruit trees and flowering vines. Bare-root plants are sold only in late winter and early spring.

Handle with Care

Like babies' bare bottoms, bare-root plants need delicate handling. If you can't plant them right away, lay them on the ground and pile about 4 inches of damp soil or compost over their roots so they won't freeze. (In gardeners' lingo, this process is called "heeling in.") Then, to get your babies off to a good, trouble-free start, give them a drink of Compost Tea (see page 27). When you lift out the plants a week or so later, don't be surprised if you see threadlike new roots — the first sign that the plants are emerging from their winter slumber.

When It Takes Two to Transplant

Recruit a helper when setting out bare-root plants. With two people on the job, it's fast work for one to gently pull and jiggle the plant to the correct depth, while the less fortunate one heaves in the soil alternated with sloppy slurps of water. As with container grown plants, the goal is to have the plant sitting high in the soil, so that once the soil settles, the plant will be at the same depth at which it grew in the nursery field.

PROBLEM and SOLUTION

Mangled Roots

Problem: Some roots on bare-root plants were bent and broken in shipment.

Solution: Use clean, sharp pruning shears to trim off the injured roots. As you plant, spread the remaining roots carefully to help the plant make a strong start.

PLANTING B-&-Bs

Long before there were bed-and-breakfast inns, B-&-B stood for balled-and-burlapped plants. Until the past decade or so, all shrubs and trees were sold with their roots tightly packed in soil, and the whole package was held in place with a snug wrapping of burlap. Larger trees and shrubs are still sold this way.

The Process

When setting out a B-&-B plant, use the claw end of a hammer to pull out the nails used to hold the burlap in place, along with strings of jute or wire. Set the plant in the planting hole, and then use scissors or shears to cut away most of the burlap. Because burlap is biodegradable, it's okay to leave a little bit under the plant, but I like to trim away as much as possible, so it won't become a barrier to new roots.

Before filling in soil around the root ball, thoroughly soak it with water. Add more water as you gradually fill in the planting hole, but don't worry about fertilizer at this point. Given sufficient root space and water, B-&-B shrubs and trees will get on with the first task before them, which is to grow new roots to replace the ones they lost when they were dug from the nursery field.

Your Aching Back

Every day, gardeners suffer needless injuries to their backs (and other body parts, too) by lugging heavy plants to and fro all over their yards. So before you lift that tree or tote that shrub, keep these pointers in mind:

✔ If you'll be planting a number of shrubs or trees, invest in a wheeled dolly to move them.

✔ If you grow trees or other large plants in containers, keep those pots on rolling platforms so you can easily shift them from one place to another. You can buy special plant dollies, or build your own from a board and heavy-duty casters.

✔ Before you put a heavy plant onto the ground by your planting hole, lay down an old blanket or piece of cardboard and use it to pull the plant into position.

✔ Last but not least, ask for help when you need it, because two people are always stronger than one!

HELP WANTED

CHAPTER 3

Food, Water, and Maintenance Magic

J ust like us folks, plants have certain basic needs. Fortunately for those of us who can't (or don't care to) spend all our time tending our yards, most plants don't ask for much. Just give them a little food, a little water, and a little routine care, and they'll be happy as clams — and *you* will be even happier, because you'll head off problems before they start.

PLANT FOODS AND FERTILIZERS

Some plants need little or no fertilizer at planting time, and others need a lot. Plants also differ in how often they like to be fed and the quantities of specific nutrients they need. In Part II, I'll point out the fertilizer preferences of many of the most popular plants for home landscapes. But first, let's have a look at the basics.

Which Way to Go?

There are a lot of fertilizers on the market, but each falls into one of two basic categories: chemical/inorganic or natural/organic.

Chemical/inorganic fertilizers are manufactured using synthetic substances that contain highly concentrated amounts of specific nutrients plants need, primarily nitrogen, phosphorus, and potassium (see The Plant Food Pyramid on page 26). When you apply a chemical fertilizer, you see almost instant results, because the nutrients are immediately available to your plants.

On the downside, this quick fix adds no nutrients to the soil itself. In fact, chemical fertilizers actually destroy the beneficial organisms that create the soil's natural nutrients. A pick-me-up dose now and then isn't likely to cause much harm, but used in large quantities over time, these chemicals build up in the soil and can actually hinder plant growth.

Organic/natural fertilizers, on the other hand, don't feed your plants at all. Rather, they add essential nutrients, major and minor, to the soil, where they become available to the plants. Organic fertilizers are made of naturally occurring substances, just like the ones I use in my mixes, elixirs, and tonics. When you shop for organic fertilizers, here are a few of the ingredients you may find on the label:

WATCH IT ⚠️

Don't Burn 'em Up!

If you use too much fertilizer or fail to mix it with the soil, plant roots can be destroyed and you'll see symptoms of fertilizer burn — leaves with brown, curled edges that look like they've been singed by a flame. Always err on the light side, blend fertilizer thoroughly into the soil, and follow up with a deep drench of water.

Nutrient	Source
nitrogen	cottonseed meal
	alfalfa meal
	fish emulsion
phosphorus	poultry manure
	rock phosphate
	bonemeal
potassium	granite meal
	kelp meal
	dairy manure

What's in the Bag?

Fertilizer labels always include three hyphenated numbers, such as 10-5-5, which is called the guaranteed analysis. If you remember anything from high school chemistry, perhaps your brain will be willing to hold on to the letters N–P–K, which is what the guaranteed analysis is all about. The first number stands for nitrogen (N), the second one for phosphorus (P), and the last one represents potassium (K). Low numbers — for example, 6–2–4 — mean that the fertilizer is not very concentrated, so the label will suggest using larger amounts than if the product had an analysis of 12–4–8, which contains twice as much actual fertilizer.

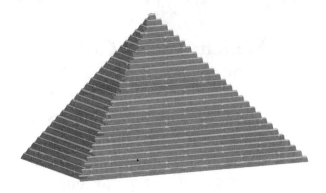

The Plant Food Pyramid

Plants make use of many nutrients, but nitrogen, phosphorus, and potassium are the biggies. Here's what each of them does for plants, nutritionally speaking:

- **Nitrogen** is the main nutrient plants use to grow new leaves and stems. A high-nitrogen fertilizer will green up a lawn quickly and cause a lot of leafy growth in other plants.

- **Phosphorus** promotes the growth of vigorous roots and the formation of flowers and seeds. Bulb fertilizers are often high in phosphorus, as are lawn fertilizers intended for use in the fall, because strong roots help these plants survive winter better.

- **Potassium** supports all phases of plant growth and helps plants stand strong when insects and diseases attack.

WATCH IT ⚠

Easy on the N!

All plants need some nitrogen in their diet, but don't overdo it. Too much of the Big N will make plants grow big and leafy, at the expense of blossoms, fruits, and seeds.

Miracle Micronutrients

Plants do not live on nitrogen, phosphorus, and potassium alone. They also need other nutrients, including calcium, magnesium, and sulfur. The best way I know to provide your plants with healthy, balanced nutrition is to give them regular doses of Grandma Putt's Compost Tea and my All-Season Green-Up Tonic. Believe me, if those green leafy guys in your yard could talk, they'd say, "Boy, that hits the spot!"

Please Pass the Calcium

Your plants will usually find the calcium they need in soil that's been amended with organic matter that has a near-neutral pH, but it doesn't pay to take chances. To avoid calcium shortages, sprinkle on a little gypsum from time to time. Besides providing this necessary nutrient, gypsum helps dissolve salts that can build up in gardens and hinder plant growth.

Another great source of calcium is probably sitting in your refrigerator: eggshells. So why not do what Grandma Putt did? Every time you cook some eggs, crush the shells, soak them in warm water overnight, and pour the water on your plants. They'll thank you by growing up to be big, strong, and beautiful.

Timely Tonics

All-Season Green-Up Tonic

1 can of beer
1 cup of ammonia
½ cup of liquid dish soap
½ cup of liquid lawn food
½ cup of molasses or clear corn syrup

Mix all of these ingredients in a large bucket, pour into a 20 gallon hose-end sprayer, and saturate your lawn, trees, flowers, and vegetables every 3 weeks throughout the growing season.

Compost Tea

Compost tea is the most healthful drink a plant could ask for. It delivers a well-balanced supply of important nutrients — major and minor — and fends off diseases at the same time.

1½ gal. of fresh compost
4½ gal. of warm water

Pour the water into a 5 gallon bucket. Scoop the compost into a cotton, burlap, or panty-hose sack, tie it closed, and put it into the water. Cover the bucket and let it steep for 3 to 7 days. Pour the solution into a watering can or misting bottle, and give your plants a good spritzing with it every 2 to 3 weeks.

Note: You can make manure tea (another wonder drink) using this same recipe. Just substitute 1½ gallons of well-cured manure for the compost, and use the finished product in the same way.

Getting Water Everywhere

I know I've been telling you to water just about everything you plant, but to tell you the truth, I'm really worried about using too much water. You should be, too. Water is much too precious to waste, and in some places it's in dangerously short supply. All plants need water when they're young, but as they develop deep and extensive roots, you should have to water them less and less.

To encourage deep roots, give plants deep water. By this I mean to really soak the soil so that water penetrates deeply, which usually takes some time. That's why soaker hoses are so handy. They release water slowly, so it has a chance to sink in and percolate down deep, where it belongs. Water that stays mostly near the surface encourages shallow roots to form, which makes plants need more water rather than less — and tends to make them weak and disease-prone besides.

Recycling Roundup

It can take a l-o-n-g time to satisfy the thirst of a tree or a big shrub. Even if you have a soaker hose, it can't be everyplace at once. That's where a big collection of plastic milk jugs comes in handy. Just use an ice pick or a big nail to poke small holes in the sides, about an inch above the bottom. Fill the jugs with water, place them all around the root zone, and let your plants drink up!

Make Merry with Mulches

No matter what you are planting, the last step, the icing on the cake, is to apply some kind of mulch over the surface of the soil. Mulches help keep the soil moist, discourage weeds, and look nice, too. And, because mulches stop rainwater from splashing up into plant leaves, they also reduce problems with some kinds of diseases.

Which Mulch for Me?

Every well-dressed landscape includes mulch, and you can choose mulches based on appearance for front-yard flower beds and shrub groupings. However, in other parts of your landscape, it's smart to base your decisions on other mulch characteristics, such as their effects on soil temperature and plant growth. Here's a quick rundown on the most popular mulches and what they can and can't do for your plants:

- **Bark mulch** is long lasting and easy to apply, so it's ideal for mulching foundation shrubs and yard trees, and you can even use it to pave woodland pathways. I like small to medium-size chunks of bark better than larger ones, which tend to float away in heavy rains.

- **Chopped leaves** are free for the raking, and they're ideal for shady areas planted with azaleas, dogwoods, and other shallow-rooted plants that prefer acid soil (oak leaves are best). A leaf mulch keeps the soil cool, too, which is an extra asset in warm climates.

- **Gravel** has a light color, fine texture, and clean appearance that make it a popular choice for mulching on soil next to houses. Gravel stops rainwater from splashing mud onto the house, and it's long lasting, too. However, weeds will push through pebbles unless you place weed barrier film over the ground before you start spreading your gravel. After a year or two, a few weeds invariably appear in gravel mulch, but any weeds will be easy to pull out or clean up with a glyphosate product if you get them when they're young.

- **Wheat straw** is unsurpassed for controlling erosion on slopes planted with shrubs, or on gentle inclines that have been sown with lawn grass seed. Wheat straw also makes a nice mulch for vegetable gardens, and, unlike hay, it contains no pesky weed seeds. When you purchase it in bales, you can easily peel off "books" of straw to lay down around your plants.

- **Wood chips** work just like bark, and nowadays you can buy them dyed in colors like rust, red, and black.

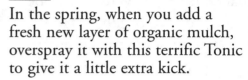

Timely Tonic

Mulch Moisturizer Tonic

In the spring, when you add a fresh new layer of organic mulch, overspray it with this terrific Tonic to give it a little extra kick.

1 can of regular cola (not diet)
½ cup of ammonia
½ cup of antiseptic mouthwash
½ cup of baby shampoo

Mix all of these ingredients in your 20 gallon hose-end sprayer, and give your mulch a nice long, cool drink.

Roll-Out Weed Barriers

Would your mulch work better with a little underwear? You bet it would! Before you spread an organic mulch beneath shrubs and trees, cover the ground with a roll-out fabric weed barrier. Weed barrier fabrics, made from spunbound or woven polypropylene, block the light weeds need to germinate and grow. A few weeds may eventually appear from seeds that blow into the top layer of mulch or get dropped there by birds, but they will have scant roots, so that you can yank them out with a gentle tug.

Local Favorites

If you want to see how dark brown cocoa shells work as mulch, visit Hershey Gardens, home of Hershey Chocolate in Hershey, Pennsylvania. You'll see pecan shell mulches around New Orleans and Mobile, and peanut shell mulch in north Florida. All of these are examples of mulches that are locally abundant, and because they're all organic, they'll break down over time, adding valuable nutrients and structure to your soil.

Take It Away!

In every part of the country, there are terrific organic mulches that are just lying around somewhere, or that somebody needs to get rid of. Here are some good-looking and nutritious mulches:

Let Tomatoes See Red

If you grow tomatoes, treat your crop to a mulch of red, reflective plastic. Scientists have found that it improves the yield and health of America's favorite vegetable. The mulch warms the soil, which tomatoes really like, and the red color deters aphids and thrips, which are common vectors of some tomato diseases.

▲ Chopped tobacco stalks

▲ Ground corncobs

▲ Mushroom compost

▲ Pine needles

▲ Seaweed

▲ Shredded bark

▲ Shredded oak leaves

SUPPORT YOUR PLANTS!

Some plants can stand on their own just fine, but many need help staying on the up-and-up. That's important for reasons besides good looks: When a plant that's meant to grow upright lies down on the job, it becomes a prime target for all kinds of pesky pests and dastardly diseases — and that can mean big trouble for you.

Support Us!

All Together

Grandma Putt liked to grow her tall plants in big masses. Instead of staking each individual plant, she'd install stakes in a random pattern among them. Then she'd weave jute or string among the stakes and stems to form a tangled network of gentle support.

Beware the Ties that Bind

No matter what kind of support you give your plants, always tie the stems in place with strips of soft cloth, old panty hose, or some other material that won't chafe against tender stems as they tremble in the wind. Remember: A bruised or cut stem leaves any plant wide open to pests and diseases.

To Each Its Own

The best way to support a plant depends on its natural growth habit. There are three major types of support:

1. Trellises, arbors, and arches not only support vines but also add to their beauty and usefulness in your yard. Just bear in mind that the bigger and heavier a vine is, the sturdier its trellis needs to be.

2. Stakes work best with tall plants like delphiniums, lilies, and monkshood. There are more kinds of stakes than you can shake a stake at — bamboo, metal, plastic, and recycled prunings. Just push the stake into the ground (very gently, so as not to damage the roots) and loosely fasten the stem to it.

3. Links, loops, and grids are tailor-made for bushy perennial flowers that tend to flop over as soon as their tops become heavy with flowers. Peonies, tall garden phlox, and good, old black-eyed Susans all fall into this category. You can buy supports made of heavy wire that you simply stick into the ground around plants in the spring, so that the stems and leaves grow up through them.

Pruning: the Shape of Things to Come

You're probably reading this section because something in your yard has grown way too big. That's the usual reason people prune, but there are better reasons to thin stems and cut back limbs. Pruning helps direct plant growth to where you want it, so the best reason to use your pruning shears is to help plants grow taller, wider, or stronger by putting more energy into a few robust branches instead of spreading it thinly to a number of little stems.

Hedge Strategies

To keep from becoming a slave to a hedge, invest in rechargeable electric pruning shears. They're great time-savers! The next step is to time your pruning to coincide with your hedge's natural growth surges. Prune it in late spring, midsummer, and again in early fall. Stop pruning when winter is still at least 6 weeks away, because tender new growth is easily injured by cold. Hedges that wear brown tips until spring are always a sad sight — and prime targets for disease and pest invasions.

The Facts of Life

Whenever you cut back a stem, you encourage another to grow somewhere else. Usually, the new growth will emerge just below where you cut. This is a simple fact of plant life, and it's one you need to carry in your head before you ever touch a plant with a tool that cuts wood.

For example, if you shear back a plant by removing all the stem tips, crew cut style, the next growth spurt will consist of a number of small stems that sprout out all over. So the next time you prune, you'll be cutting through thicker growth than you encountered the time before. That's fine if the plant in question is a hedge plant that's meant to grow that way. But with most shrubs and all trees, it's better to follow the natural shape of the plant. First remove damaged or awkward stems, and then go back and shape them up just a little bit.

Pruning to Promote Bloom

One excellent reason to prune is to help flowering plants bloom like crazy. When you "deadhead" marigolds, zinnias, and many other annual flowers by pinching or cutting off old blossoms, the plants respond by producing new stems laden with baby buds. Sometimes you can coax a second coming out of perennial flowers this way, too, or at least prolong the bloom time of those that bloom all in a rush, as peonies and chrysanthemums like to do.

TEA ANYONE?

GRANDMA PUTT'S OLD-TIME TIPS

To give her roses a postpruning pick-me-up, Grandma Putt laid tea bags onto the soil underneath each bush. The tannic acid in the tea made the soil slightly acidic, which makes roses pleased as punch!

Pep 'em Up

Some plants wear themselves out if you don't discipline them a little with your pruning shears. For example, left to their own devices, hybrid tea roses will cover themselves with blossoms and then get so exhausted that they quit cold turkey. But if you remove some of their branches after the first flush of bloom, you give them the energy to flower again. More important, you help them fend off disease by allowing air to circulate freely through the branches — and as Grandma Putt used to say, trying to grow healthy roses without good air circulation is like trying to swim without water!

'Tis the Season

To figure out when to prune any flowering plant, just think about when it blooms. To take the guesswork out of when to prune what, note which of your shrubs fall into which time slot. Then write the names on a calendar in the appropriate months. Then, bingo — you'll be a pruning wiz, and your shrubs will shower you with blossoms! Most popular landscape plants fit into one of these four categories:

▲ **Spring bloomers,** such as azaleas, forsythias, and lilacs, develop their buds by the time they become dormant in the fall. If they need pruning (which they often don't), do your cutting in late spring or early summer, right after the flowers fade. The new wood that grows during the summer will have plenty of mature buds by the season's end.

▲ **Early summer bloomers,** including many roses and spireas, often benefit from light fall pruning to thin branches.

▲ **Shrubs that produce pretty berries,** such as viburnums, can be lightly pruned in the winter after birds have consumed the fall crop of fruit.

▲ **Mid- to late-summer bloomers,** such as buddleias and crepe myrtles, are prunable anytime they are dormant, and often benefit from serious pruning in late winter or early spring. Vigorous new growth that follows on the heels of hard pruning usually leads to a heavy set of flowers.

Recycling Roundup

Anytime you prune shrubs during the growing season, as you do with spring and early-summer bloomers, you stimulate new growth — and there's nothing deer like more than those tender young shoots. To keep the brown-eyed bruisers at bay, just tie up some mothballs in old panty hose and hang the pouches from branches.

The Right Stuff

I've seen garages that have more pruning tools hanging on the walls than I've seen in some garden centers. That's fine if your aim is to own a record-breaking tool collection. But if all you want is a healthy, good-looking landscape, you don't need much in the way of hardware. These three see most of the action in my yard:

- **Hand clippers,** a.k.a. pruners, shears, or snips, are used for deadheading flowers, cutting back annuals and perennials in the fall, harvesting herbs, and pruning roses and other shrubs.

- **Loppers** are heavy-duty pruners with extra-long handles. You need a pair of these if you have high shrubs or small trees.

- **Pruning saws** come in various shapes and sizes, all designed to cut branches that are too thick for either hand clippers or loppers.

The Monsters Are Coming!

If you have an older landscape, you may have evergreens that naturally want to grow into monster-sized specimens. In that case, pruning is the only way to keep them in line. Broad-leafed evergreens (which grow mostly from Zone 6 southward) will often recover from radical pruning, but overgrown needle evergreens such as arborvitae, juniper, and hemlock never get over the shock of aggressive pruning. A haircut probably won't kill your plants, but your good intentions may lead to permanent brown "dead zones" where new growth will never appear. A better strategy is to get rid of seriously overgrown evergreens and replace them with something better — and permanently smaller!

Jerry Baker Says . . .

"Garden centers and catalogs have dozens of varieties of compact trees and shrubs to choose from. When you're shopping for woody plants, always note the mature size on the label or catalog description — and if the information is unclear, ask for help. Knowing exactly what to expect can head off a lot of problems down the road!"

Part II
PICTURE-PERFECT PLANTS IN YOUR OWN BACKYARD

Getting to know different plants is the heart and soul of gardening, and having that knowledge goes a long way toward alleviating problems in your yard. How? you may ask. Well, if you put the right plant in the right location, chances are pretty good that it'll thrive rather than fight a never-ending battle to survive. And that, my friends, means a lot fewer headaches for you.

So in this section, I'll introduce you to more than 350 of my favorite plants, and I'll explain how you can use them in your yard. I've sorted them into chapters on trees, shrubs, lawns, and so forth, so it should be easy to find your way around. Don't worry if you don't know the difference between an annual and a perennial at this point, or if you're trying to get rid of those black spots on your roses. By the time we're through with this section, I guarantee you'll have the greenest thumb in town!

CHAPTER 4

Trouble-Free Trees

My Grandma Putt used to say that if you make friends with a tree, you've made a friend for life. As usual, she was right on the button, in more ways than one. For starters, trees often outlive the folks who plant them. But beyond that, healthy, well-placed trees have more practical advantages than you can shake a branch at. And they're a snap to troubleshoot, too. In the first part of this chapter, I'll share my best secrets for choosing, using, and taking care of trees, and then we'll look at solutions to the most common problems you might have with the trees that share your home, sweet home.

AH, TREES!

It seems that all kids have special tree friends. I know I did! When I was growing up, our neighborhood was chock-full of trees that we climbed on, hung swings from, or hid behind when we didn't want to be found. I still get a little misty-eyed  thinking about a certain big old sugar maple in Grandma Putt's back-yard. In the fall, when the leaves were piled high under its branches, I'd snuggle in and lie there on my back, just gazing at the sky and dreaming about all the adventures I'd have when I grew up and became a cowboy. That particular dream never did come true, but my appreciation of trees has lasted a lifetime and just keeps on growing.

Not Just Another Pretty Face

To my way of thinking, there's no better-looking sight on earth than a tree covered with blossoming spring flowers or Technicolor® autumn leaves. But there are plenty of other reasons besides good looks to keep a few pet trees around your place. Here's a handful of the best:

✔ The right trees can cut your energy costs. They offer cooling shade in the summer, and then conveniently shed their leaves in winter so that sunlight can filter through just when you want (and need) it most.

✔ Trees' extensive roots help hold your soil in place, so it's less likely to slide away when a big storm hits.

✔ Trees help all of us breathe easier by taking in loads of carbon dioxide from the air and replacing it with oxygen.

✔ Trees offer room and board for birds, who, in turn, feast on bad-guy bugs — and treat you to loads of free entertainment!

✔ Handsome, healthy, well-placed shade trees add to your property value — just ask any real estate agent about that!

UNDER THE BIG TOP Grandma Putt used to say that she felt sorry for folks who thought of trees as just great big plants. Why, the way she looked at it, the right tree in the right place was as much fun as a three-ring circus. It gave her the music of the wind rustling through the leaves, the fresh aroma of a million spring flowers, and the antics of birds and squirrels to watch as they flitted from branch to branch. All this and a nice shady place to sit in the good old summertime!

It's Hard Work Being a Tree

Trees work harder than just about any other plants I can think of. Besides all of those other important jobs we talked about earlier, they give your yard what those garden designer folks call "structure." In plain English, that means that you can use them in all kinds of ways to make your yard into just about anything you want it to be. And they're great problem solvers, too! Here are some ways I like to use trees in my landscape:

WATCH IT !

Look Both Ways

It's great to have a shady place to park your car, but the wrong tree planted too close to your driveway will give you all kinds of trouble. Be sure you choose a tree with roots that go deep down — not out and up through your pavement (see my Top Ten Trees for Streetside Planting, page 42, for some good choices). Also, beware of trees with nuts or gooey fruit that will fall onto your car and leave dings or messy splotches.

- **Cozy it up.** Even a medium-size yard can feel as big and uninviting as the Australian outback if there's nothing to it but a grassy lawn. But add a few trees and, bingo — you've got a place that says, "Pull up a chair and set a spell."

- **Divide and conquer.** Trees make some of the niftiest "walls" you'll ever hope to find. Just by planting them in the right spots, you can make separate outdoor "rooms" in your yard — say, for instance, a vegetable garden, a badminton court, a playground for the kids, or a romping space for the pooch.

- **Frame that view.** You know how a picture frame draws your eye into a painting. Well, trees can do the same thing in a landscape, directing your gaze toward a beautiful scene, like a range of hills over yonder, or that flower garden you're so proud of.

- **Block that view.** I don't know anybody who doesn't have something around the old homestead that he'd just as soon not look at, like a busy street, the neighbors' back porch, or your own laundry line. So what do you do about it? Just plant a few fast-growing trees, and, presto, change-o — you've turned that old eyesore into a sight for sore eyes!

Jerry Baker Says . . .

"If your home turf gets too much wind to suit you, give your yard some shelter with a row or two of evergreen trees. Better yet, double up by placing a second row of flowering shrubs or small flowering trees along the inside edge of your windbreak. Any plant with white or light-colored blooms looks like a million bucks when it's backed by an evergreen screen!"

Not on *My* Doorstep You Don't!

Every tree has its place in the grand scheme of things — but for some trees, that place is far removed from any entryway. Avoid trees with messy fruit that will end up on the bottoms of your shoes, or nuts that feel (and act) like marbles underfoot. Whoops!

- **Put it in the spotlight.** If you want to call attention to something in your landscape, like the entrance to your driveway, just flank it with a couple of great-looking trees. Never again will your guests miss the turn and go flying on by!

Jerry's TOP TEN

Trees for Streetside Planting

Air pollution from cars can make a lot of trees go belly-up in a hurry. The solution? These guys, who can stand up to all the dirt and CO_2 a busy street can deliver. And there's an added attraction: They have deep, well-behaved roots that aren't likely to push up through sidewalks, roads, or driveways.

- **Black locust** *(Robinia pseudoacacia)*; 30 to 50 feet, Zones 3 to 8

- **Chinese elm** *(Ulmus parvifolia)*; 40 to 50 feet, Zones 5 to 8

- **Dawn redwood** *(Metasequoia glyptostroboides)*; 80 feet, Zones 6 to 8

- **European hornbeam** *(Carpinus betulus)*; to 35 feet, Zones 4 to 9

- **Ginkgo*** *(Ginkgo biloba)*; to 30 feet, Zones 4 to 9

- **Linden** *(Tilia americana)*; 65 feet, Zones 4 to 8

- **Nootka cypress** *(Chamaecyparis nootkatensis)*; 30 to 40 feet, Zones 4 to 9

- **Pin oak** *(Quercus palustris)*; 60 to 70 feet, Zones 4 to 8

- **Red maple** *(Acer rubrum)*; 40 to 60 feet, Zones 3 to 10

- **Trident maple** *(Acer buergerianum)*; 30 feet, Zones 4 to 8

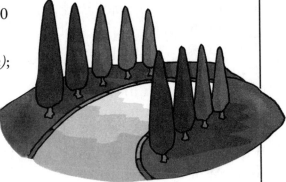

* If you opt for a ginkgo, make sure it's a male. The females produce berries that are some of the messiest, most foul-smelling things in creation!

Sizing Them Up

Trees come in all kinds of shapes and sizes, and you can use them to your best advantage. By choosing ones that work with the size of your house, you can refine what's called a sense of scale — how your house looks in comparison with the trees around it. Here's how it works:

- **If your house is tall and rather imposing,** large trees near it will make it appear less intimidating without taking away from its grandeur.

WATCH IT

Think Ahead

When you're tree shopping, remember this: That cute little tree in its neat little pot may be just the ticket for now, but within a few years, it may grow into a monster that will overshadow your house and garden, send its roots through your driveway, drop its leaves into your gutters, and God knows what else. So always buy a tree that will be the size you want when it reaches maturity — not when you see it at the garden center.

- **If, on the other hand, your house is on the small side,** trees that barely reach the roofline will tend to make it look a little larger, and much more impressive. These tricks work the same in open spaces.

- **Large trees at the back** of your property will seem closer than they really are, which will make a big yard seem a little cozier and more intimate.

- **Small trees viewed from afar** fool the eye into thinking they are quite far away, indeed, which makes a small yard feel much more spacious.

Form and Function

Most of the words used to describe tree form make good sense, but I'll review them here so you'll realize just how many possibilities there are:

- ▲ **Columnar** trees grow straight up. Lombardy poplar and Italian cypress are prime examples.

- ▲ **Weeping** or **pendulous** trees have limbs that curve downward, often sweeping the ground. Everyone knows the weeping willow, but lots of trees, including cherries, hemlocks, and beeches, come in beautiful pendulous versions.

- ▲ **Conical** trees, such as white pines and Douglas firs, feature the classic Christmas tree form.

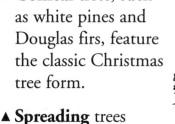

- ▲ **Spreading** trees often show a lateral branching habit, in which the branches form horizontal layers, as in oaks, sycamores, dogwoods, and some Japanese maples. Wherever you put them, they always look elegant.

- ▲ **Round** trees resemble lollipops. Many maples, European hornbeam, and common hackberry fit the bill here.

Trees Set the Stage

As you're thinking of where and how to use trees to solve those problems we discussed earlier, think of your yard as a stage, with trees as actors in a play. You can cast some in group scenes, others as stars. These stars are often called specimen trees, in otherwise open lawn flanked by shrubs or flower beds.

Jerry's TOP TEN

Shade Trees

You may need only one shade tree in your yard, so make it a good one! Keep size in mind, and as your trees grow, prune low limbs to make plenty of room for enjoying life beneath the branches.

- **Beech** *(Fagus grandifolia)*; 50 to 70 feet, Zones 3 to 9
- **Chinese elm** *(Ulmus parvifolia)*; 40 to 50 feet, Zones 5 to 8
- **Ginkgo** *(Ginkgo biloba)*; to 30 feet, Zones 4 to 9
- **Hornbeam** *(Carpinus caroliniana)*; to 30 feet, Zones 2 to 9
- **Red maple** *(Acer rubrum)*; 40 to 60 feet, Zones 3 to 10
- **Red oak** *(Quercus rubra)*; 60 to 90 feet, Zones 4 to 8
- **Sargent cherry** *(Prunus sargentii)*; 30 to 50 feet, Zones 5 to 8
- **Sourwood** *(Oxydendrum arboreum)*; to 25 feet, Zones 4 to 9
- **Sycamore** *(Platanus occidentalis)*; 70 feet, Zones 4 to 9
- **White oak** *(Quercus alba)*; 70 feet, Zones 5 to 9

A Group Act

Specimen trees don't have to play solo. Three of the same species create a grove effect, which can be emphasized with a bed of ground cover plants under them. And believe me, a grove can hide a lot of otherwise ugly scenery! River birches (with dramatic peeling bark) and tall, sinewy hawthorns are great for this use.

Jerry Baker Says . . .

"A grove doesn't have to contain only one species. One of my favorite combos is two Japanese maples keeping company with an ornamental cherry."

Matching Evergreens

There are times when a row of evergreen trees of the same species is just the ticket — for instance, when you want a solid, soldier-straight backdrop for your house or a flowering border. In mild climates, Leyland cypress pulls off this feat like a champ. Up North, look for cold-weather lovers such as arborvitae and Canada hemlock.

Variety Is Nice

If your main reason for wanting evergreens is to watch cardinals flitting through snow-laden branches in winter, or to block an unsightly view, consider using two or three types with varying forms and textures. For example, a stiffly formal blue spruce looks even better beside a gentle white pine. From Zone 7 southward, evergreen magnolias such as the scaled-down 'Little Gem' make great company for evergreens with needled leaves.

Jerry's TOP TEN

Evergreen Trees

You can't beat evergreens for year-round beauty, for blocking unwanted views, and for giving shelter to insect-gobbling birds. Here are my favorites.

- **Arborvitae** *(Thuja occidentalis)*; 20 to 40 feet, Zones 2 to 7
- **Canada hemlock** *(Tsuga canadensis)*; 40 to 70 feet, Zones 3 to 7
- **Japanese black pine** *(Pinus thunbergii)*; to 30 feet, Zones 4 to 8
- **Japanese cedar** *(Cryptomeria japonica* cultivars); 30 to 50 feet, Zones 5 to 8
- **Lacebark pine** *(Pinus bungeana)*; 30 to 50 feet, Zones 4 to 8
- **Red cedar** *(Juniperus virginiana)*; to 30 feet, Zones 2 to 9
- **Spruce** *(Picea* species); 40 to 60 feet, Zones 2 to 7
- **Sweet bay magnolia** *(Magnolia virginiana)*; 30 to 50 feet, Zones 5 to 9
- **White fir** *(Abies concolor)*; 30 to 50 feet, Zones 3 to 7
- **White pine** *(Pinus strobus)*; to 80 feet, Zones 2 to 8

Bustin' Out All Over

Ornamental fruit trees, including cherries, crabapples, pears, and plums, often burst into bloom just as the last freeze passes, announcing the changing of the seasons in grand style. Though newer varieties offer unprecedented levels of disease resistance, ornamental fruits can still be a little tricky to grow, and they need yearly pruning to shape them during their first few years in the ground.

Showers of Flowers

When I go for a walk in spring or early summer and catch a whiff of delightful floral fragrance in the air, I can almost always trace it back to a flowering tree. When one of these babies comes into bloom, the sheer number of flowers creates a cloud of perfume. And a few weeks later, when the blossoms shatter, the petals falling gently to the ground are like autumn in pastel colors.

Jerry Baker Says . . .

"Some of my favorite trees are native species that produce flowers and berries, including wild cherries, dogwoods, hackberries (Celtis), and serviceberries (Amelanchier). Birds love them, and by combining these trees with berry-producing shrubs, you can turn your yard into a wildlife retreat!"

Beyond Fruit Salad

If it's fragrant flowers you're after, there are plenty of trees, including a passel of trouble-tolerant natives, that will give any fruit tree a run for its money. For example, the slow-growing American yellowwood produces fragrant flowers that can pass for wisteria in early summer. Much smaller, but also slow to grow, fringe trees cover themselves with ragged white blossoms in spring, and some go on to set fruit in the fall.

Jerry's TOP TEN

Flowering Trees

These beautiful bloomers will light up your landscape on a grand scale, and many come in dwarf forms that are suitable for growing in flower beds or containers. Choose disease-resistant cultivars that need just the amount of winter chilling that your climate provides.

- **American yellowwood** *(Cladrastis lutea)*; 30 to 50 feet, Zones 4 to 9
- **Bradford pear** *(Pyrus calleryana)*; to 50 feet, Zones 4 to 8
- **Crabapple** *(Malus* cultivars); to 25 feet, Zones 4 to 8
- **Crape myrtle** *(Lagerstroemia* cultivars); 12 to 18 feet, Zones 7 to 9
- **Dogwood** *(Cornus florida*, plus *Cornus* hybrids); to 25 feet, Zones 5 to 9
- **Flowering cherry** *(Prunus* cultivars); 15 to 30 feet, Zones 4 to 9
- **Fringe tree** *(Chionanthus virginicus)*; 15 to 20 feet, Zones 5 to 9
- **Golden-rain tree** *(Koelreuteria paniculata)*; 30 to 40 feet, Zones 5 to 9
- **Redbud** *(Cercis canadensis)*; to 25 feet, Zones 5 to 9
- **Sweet bay magnolia** *(Magnolia virginiana)*; 30 to 50 feet, Zones 5 to 9

SMART TREE SHOPPING

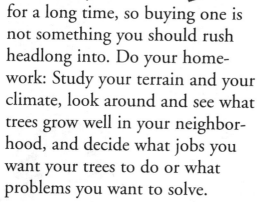

A tree is going to be with you for a long time, so buying one is not something you should rush headlong into. Do your homework: Study your terrain and your climate, look around and see what trees grow well in your neighborhood, and decide what jobs you want your trees to do or what problems you want to solve.

When, Oh When?

Back when most trees were sold with bare roots, early spring was the only good time to buy and plant them. Spring is still the prime season for planting trees with bare roots, or those that have been plucked from nursery fields and sold with their roots wrapped in burlap. Either condition is traumatic for a tree, so the sooner you get them planted, the better off you'll both be.

Potted Up

Nowadays, the majority of young trees are sold in containers, which is good for both you and your trees. Those in containers can be planted anytime except smack dab in the heat of summer or the dead of winter. But it's best to plant in either spring or fall, when the weather won't make heavy demands on them.

WHY TREES CHANGE COLOR

Whether they're wearing their spring and summer greens or their multi-colored autumn coats, trees give our yards some mighty fine color. But do you remember from high school biology why those leaves turn color? Here's a quick refresher course.

The green color comes from chlorophyll, the substance that helps trees convert light, water, and carbon dioxide into food. As trees prepare for winter dormancy, they stop producing chlorophyll, which lets other leaf colors come through. In other words, the bright golds, oranges, and reds of fall were there in the leaves all the time; they were just masked by green!

> ### Jerry Baker Says . . .
>
> "I've always gotten the best results by planting young trees that are less than 8 feet tall. Besides being easier to handle than larger trees, young trees are quick to develop roots and rarely need to be staked to keep them standing upright."

Ten Crucial Questions for Choosing a Tree

As I said earlier, you don't want to plant the wrong trees in the wrong spots. So make a photocopy of this list and take it with you on shopping day to avoid problems later on.

1. How tall will the tree grow?

2. How far will it spread when it reaches maturity?

3. What is its shape and form?

4. Do the roots run deep or stay close to the surface?

5. How much sun does it need?

6. How dense will the shade be five years from now?

7. How fast does it grow?

8. What can you expect in terms of fall color?

9. What will the tree look like in the winter?

10. Is it adapted to your climate and soil?

Jerry's TOP TEN

Small Trees

It's so sad when a tree just reaches maturity and then gets cut down because it's too big for the yard, or it gets in the way of utility lines. So if you're cramped for space, any of the trees on this list will deliver all of the punch of the big guys, but in a smaller package.

- **Bradford pear** *(Pyrus calleryana)*; to 50 feet, Zones 4 to 8

- **Crabapple** *(Malus* cultivars); to 25 feet, Zones 4 to 8

- **Dogwood** *(Cornus florida,* plus *Cornus* hybrids); to 25 feet, Zones 5 to 9

- **Flowering cherry** *(Prunus* cultivars); 15 to 30 feet, Zones 4 to 9

- **Fringe tree** *(Chionanthus virginicus)*; 15 to 20 feet, Zones 5 to 9

- **Ginkgo** *(Ginkgo biloba);* to 30 feet, Zones 4 to 9

- **Golden-rain tree** *(Koelreuteria paniculata)*; 30 to 40 feet, Zones 5 to 9

- **Japanese maple** *(Acer palmatum* cultivars); to 25 feet, Zones 5 to 8

- **Redbud** *(Cercis canadensis)*; to 25 feet, Zones 5 to 9

- **River birch** *(Betula nigra)*; to 30 feet, Zones 4 to 9

TREE PLANTING STEP BY STEP

Tree experts used to recommend planting trees in elaborately prepared holes, but not anymore. Instead, the idea is to choose a variety that's likely to grow well in your climate and soil, and make it stretch its roots in native turf right from the get-go. After all, within a year, your new tree should have roots that reach several feet beyond the hole in which it is planted.

Step 1 Thoroughly water the roots of your new tree.

Step 2 Dig a hole as deep as the root ball and twice as wide. I like to think of it as digging a $10 hole for a $5 tree. Use a spade to make jagged slices into the sides of the planting hole, especially if you have heavy clay soil.

WATCH IT !

No Food for Me, Thanks!

Never overfertilize newly planted trees, because their main task is to develop foraging roots rather than lots of new stems and leaves.

Step 3 Energize the soil with my Tree Planting Booster Mix to help it hold moisture and to encourage good drainage.

Step 4 Lay the container on its side and tap it soundly to help loosen the roots. If the container will not slip off when you pull it from the bottom, use a sharp knife to cut down the side of the container and pry it off. *Do not pull the tree from the container!*

Step 5 Set the tree into the hole at the same depth at which it grew in its container or in the nursery. To make sure, place a board across the hole so that it's level with the lighter part of the bark. Add some soil back into the hole if the tree is sitting too deep.

Step 6 If the tree has been wrapped in burlap, cut away as much of the material as you can after the tree is set into the planting hole.

Step 7 Gently spread out some of the outer roots, but keep your hands off the central taproot; you don't want to disturb it.

Step 8 Refill the planting hole halfway, flood it with water, and then finish refilling the hole. Water again with your hose nozzle turned on at moderately low pressure.

Step 9 Give your tree a nice dose of my Tree Transplanting Tonic. About a quart of this mixture, dribbled onto the roots, will help get that tree off to a stress-free start.

Timely Tonics

Tree Planting Booster Mix

4 lbs. of compost
2 lbs. of gypsum
1 lb. of Epsom salts
1 lb. of dry dog food
1 lb. of dry oatmeal

Mix all of these ingredients together in a bucket. Then work a handful or two into the bottom of the planting hole and sprinkle some over the top after planting.

Tree Transplanting Tonic

⅓ cup of hydrogen peroxide
¼ cup of instant tea granules
¼ cup of whiskey
¼ cup of baby shampoo
2 tbsp. of fish fertilizer

Mix all of these ingredients with 1 gallon of warm water in a bucket, and pour it into the hole when you transplant a tree or a shrub.

Mistaken Stakin'

Most young trees do not need staking to hold them upright. In fact, staking trees can traumatize tender trunks, doing more harm than good. Support your young tree *only* if it is exposed to strong winds or, for reasons of its own, it insists on leaning sideways. Then follow this 3-step routine:

Step 1 At planting time, just after you lower the tree into its hole, insert 3 sturdy wood or metal stakes in a triangular pattern around the tree. They should reach about ⅔ of the way up the trunk.

Step 2 Fasten the tree to the stakes with soft cloth, broad strips of rubber, or lengths of strong panty hose. Make sure the fastenings are loose enough so that the tree can move at least 2 inches in every direction. (The trunk will grow strong and sturdy only if it can move with the wind.)

Step 3 Remove the stakes when the tree can stand firmly on its own, usually within 1 year or so.

To the Rescue!

Here's a tree nightmare for you: You plant a fine young tree, and it flourishes through its first summer. Just after it leafs out the next summer, a drought hits. The soil dries brick hard, and the tree's small root system can't find enough water to satisfy the tree's needs. You jump into action, slowly drip water to the tree all night long from a soaker hose, and save the day.

But . . .

You should have been nursing that tree along the whole time! Young trees need special attention for up to 3 years after planting — and that includes paying close attention to the water supply. That's because it usually takes about 3 years for the roots to stretch out enough to meet the tree's needs for moisture and nutrients.

Chow Time!

Established trees have extensive roots that usually do a fine job of foraging for nutrients. As extra insurance, every spring I feed my trees a batch of my Terrific Tree Chow, followed by my Tree Chow Energizing Tonic. Then a couple of times during the summer, I give my trees a dose of my Timely Tree Tonic.

In early fall, the main thing trees need to be doing is hardening off their new growth in preparation for winter. To give them a little support in this job, supply a nice helping of my Tree Snack Mix. One batch is just right for a mature shade tree or two smaller flowering trees.

Timely Tonics

Terrific Tree Chow

25 lbs. of Garden Food
1 lb. of sugar
½ lb. of Epsom salts

Feed your trees by drilling holes at the weep line (out at the tip of the farthest branches), 8 to 10" deep, 18 to 24" apart in 2' circles. Fill the holes with 2 tablespoons of the above mixture, and sprinkle the remainder over the soil.

Timely Tree Tonic

1 cup of beer
4½ tbsp. of instant tea granules
1 tbsp. of baby shampoo
1 tbsp. of ammonia
1 tbsp. of whiskey
1 tbsp. of hydrogen peroxide
1 tbsp. of gelatin

Mix all of these ingredients in 2 gallons of warm water. Give each tree up to a quart of this Tonic about once a month through the summer for smooth sailing.

Tree Chow Energizing Tonic

1 can of beer
1 cup of liquid lawn food
½ cup of liquid dish soap
½ cup of ammonia

Mix these ingredients in your 20 gallon hose-end sprayer, filling the balance of the jar with regular cola (not diet), and saturate the ground underneath your trees.

Tree Snack Mix

5 lbs. of bonemeal
1 lb. of Epsom salts
1 lb. of gypsum
½ cup of mothballs

Mix all of these ingredients together, and spread in a broad band beneath your trees using a handheld spreader.

TO PRUNE OR NOT TO PRUNE: THAT IS THE QUESTION

Many trees actually grow better if you just let them get on with it. There are times, however, when your young tree will benefit from a haircut. Always feel free to prune when you want to encourage a strong branching pattern or a particular shape. In addition, feel free to cut off any of the following:

• Limbs that have been damaged by wind or disease

• Twiggy "suckers" that grow from the base

• Branches that cross or grow very close together

The Tree Doctor Is In

Before you begin any type of tree surgery, I want you to disinfect all of your tools with denatured alcohol to make sure they're really clean. After you've made your cuts, pour my Tree Wound Sterilizer Tonic into a handheld sprayer bottle, and drench the wounds to the point of run-off. Finally, seal the wounds with my Pruning Wound Bandage Tonic.

Timely Tonics

Tree Wound Sterilizer Tonic

¼ cup of ammonia
¼ cup of liquid dish soap
¼ cup of antiseptic mouthwash

Mix all of these ingredients in 1 gallon of warm water, pour into a handheld sprayer bottle, and drench the spots where you've pruned limbs from trees or shrubs.

Pruning Wound Bandage Tonic

½ cup of interior latex paint
½ cup of antiseptic mouthwash
1 tsp. of Total Pest Control

Mix all of these ingredients in a small bucket, and paint the liquid bandage on pruning wounds to keep bugs and thugs away.

Cover Your Bases

You won't have to worry about bashing into tender trunks with your lawn mower if you mask the bases of your trees with shade-tolerant plants or a broad collar of mulch. As a safeguard against diseases and winter rodent damage, keep the mulch several inches away from the trunk.

WATCH IT !

Respect the Trunk

A tree's main trunk is its lifeline, so don't go hammering nails into it to hang a swing, clothesline, or outdoor ornaments. The holes you make are open doors to pests and diseases. If your kids need an easy way to climb to the lowest limbs, tie a rope ladder in place instead. You can also rope a hammock in place, which is much kinder to a tree than screwing suspension hooks deep into the trunk.

The Geriatric Ward

Old trees are like old people: They are usually pretty set in their ways and are happiest if left alone to live as they want. Don't worry if strong storms leave the ground littered with small twigs and branches. Large trees are what gardeners call "self-pruning," which means they willingly let go of weak or damaged wood.

Leave 'em Be

If your old tree has some dead branches, leave them alone, too, as long as they're not poised to fall on your house or your head. Don't worry that whatever killed the limbs will spread to healthy areas: Trees use miraculous chemical defenses to wall off damaged parts. That's how they're able to live long lives in one place while filling an important niche in nature's food chain. Insects take up residence in deadwood, and in turn, they're gobbled up by bug-eating birds, many of whom also make nesting holes in the soft, dead wood.

TROUBLESHOOTING TREES

Now that you know how trees grow and the many things they can do to enrich your landscape, let's look at some of the problems I often hear about and the best ways to help when your trees are in trouble.

Crazy Caterpillars

Problem: While I was sitting under my oak tree recently, the pages of the book I was reading became littered with little dark "pebbles," which I traced to some hairy brown caterpillars I found eating leaves on a low branch. There seem to be thousands of them. Should I be alarmed? B.G., Zone 4

Solution: I'll bet my bottom dollar that your oak has become a buffet for gypsy moth larvae, those pests of oaks, apples, and, if they're desperate, at least a hundred other plants. The good news is that gypsy moths feed for only about 7 weeks in the summer, and though they may weaken your oak, it's unlikely that they'll kill it. A safe biological pesticide called BTK, a.k.a. Caterpillar Clobber, will kill the rascals quickly. You'll probably have to hire an arborist to do the spraying — oaks are so huge that it's very difficult for a homeowner to spray them thoroughly enough to stop the damage. As an alternative, band all trees with burlap and Tree Tanglefoot or other sticky substance to trap the bugs as they move to the ground each day. Then burn those bothersome bugs.

If I were you, though, I'd enlist some *real* professional help in the form of chickadees and tufted titmice — two small songbirds that gobble up gypsy moth eggs like nobody's business. To place a help-wanted ad, simply stock a feeder with peanut butter, sunflower seeds, or thistle, and station it close to your oak. The winged warriors will beat a path to your buffet and hang around to polish off the pests!

Ropy Roots

Problem: I love the river birches I have in my side yard, but I hate the roots that grow right at the surface. I have a maple in the backyard that's even worse, so that mowing under it is

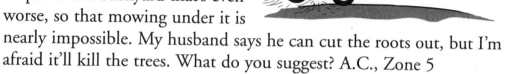

nearly impossible. My husband says he can cut the roots out, but I'm afraid it'll kill the trees. What do you suggest? A.C., Zone 5

Solution: Some trees have more surface roots than others; it's just the way they like to grow. Cutting out a few surface roots won't kill trees that are large and healthy, but I have a better idea — make friends with those surface roots! Bring in some topsoil to raise the soil level around the roots, and then plant the area with an evergreen ground cover like English ivy (see Chapter 7). Another way to take some of the pain out of mowing near surface roots is to mulch around them with finely shredded bark, so that your mower easily rides up and over the roots.

Two-Toned Foliage

Problem: I have a young oak tree that was healthy until last year, when the leaves suddenly turned yellow while the veins in the leaves stayed green. What should I do? R.Z., Zone 4

Solution: It sounds like your tree has an iron deficiency. As soon as you can, I want you to apply Liquid Iron at the rate recommended on the label. Repeat the application after 6 weeks, and in the meantime, treat your tree to my All-Season Green-Up Tonic (recipe on page 27).

Beating Bagworms

Problem: My spruce tree has dozens of little elongated things hanging from its branches that are covered in bits of foliage. At first, I thought they were growths of some kind, but when I squeeze them, they feel hollow inside. What are these things? F.H., Zone 5

Solution: Those "things" you are squeezing are the houses bagworms make for themselves. In addition to harvesting pieces of foliage, the inhabitants venture out to eat their fill of your spruce's needles. The best control is attentive hand-picking of the sacks, but be sure to wear gloves, because the dry needles are sharp and scratchy. If you have cedar or fir trees, be sure to check them for bagworms, too.

Fuzzy Pines

Problem: We planted 12 pines along our fence, and several of them have white fuzz on the branches, right where the needles are attached. What should we do? O.W., Zone 7

Solution: That white fuzz is the sheep's clothing worn by small sucking insects called pine bark adelgids. Since you've noticed them early, I think a few good soakings with my All-Season Clean-Up Tonic will bring them under control. Be sure to soak the trees thoroughly, and repeat after 10 days.

Timely Tonic

All-Season Clean-Up Tonic

1 cup of baby shampoo
1 cup of antiseptic mouthwash
1 cup of Tobacco Tea (recipe on page 61)

Mix these ingredients in a 20 gallon hose-end sprayer, and give everything in your yard a good shower with it every 2 weeks during the growing season.

Yellow Needles

Problem: Two years ago, I planted a white pine, which wasn't growing much but at least looked fine until this year. Now the color has faded to yellow-green, and there is very little new growth. What do you think is wrong? Y.K., Zone 6

Solution: The first thing you need to do is to check your soil's pH. If it's above 6.5, it's too alkaline for white pine, and you'll need to apply sulfur to the soil to increase its acidity. Under alkaline conditions, white pines can't take up nitrogen or iron, so they literally starve to death. So, while you're lowering the soil pH with sulfur, spray your tree with Liquid Iron and spread 5 pounds of all-purpose plant food over the root zone of your tree.

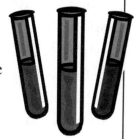

Oozing Trunks

Problem: I have a beautiful flowering cherry that's growing well enough, but there are several places in the trunk where dark, gooey stuff is oozing out. I scraped away some of it and found holes underneath. What should I do? R.M., Zone 6

Solution: Sounds like you've been hit with peach tree borers! These are little wood-eating caterpillars, which are the larvae of two species of fast-flying moths. The moths lay their eggs on the bark, and when they hatch, they start eating. In addition to ornamental cherries, peach tree borers infest flowering plums and all types of peaches.

It's a little gruesome, but what you need to do is bend out a wire paper clip, insert it into each hole and stir it around to kill the borers. Follow up with a good dose of my All-Season Clean-Up Tonic (recipe on page 60) and keep a close eye on your tree to get after any new borers as soon as you see new holes filled with gummy sap. As a preventive measure, I want you to sprinkle mothballs in a 3-foot circle around the tree, which will keep the pests away. If the damage was severe, you may have to replace the tree; wait at least one season to see.

Brown Blossoms

Problem: I've been looking forward to pretty pink crabapple flowers since I planted a young tree in my front yard two years ago. This spring, the tree finally bloomed, but the blossoms turned brown within days. Do you think it has some kind of disease? B.I., Zone 5

Solution: I think your tree is more cold than sick. Many trees that bloom in spring get hit by late frosts, which cause the flowers to wither right away. If your tree is growing in a low spot where cold air accumulates, you can expect this kind of trouble almost every spring. But let's be patient and optimistic. Continue to give your tree good care along with a little more time to settle in. After another year or two, I'll bet that both of you will be much happier.

Winter Worries

Problem: I planted several trees this year, and I'm worried about their surviving the winter. Is there anything special I can do to give them a helping hand? G.B., Zone 4

Solution: There sure is! Just follow this 6-step routine, and your trees will sail through winter with flying colors.

Step 1 In late fall, spray your trees with an all-season horticultural or dormant oil to stop any napping pests dead in their tracks.

Step 2 Before the ground freezes, soak the soil well, and apply an extra layer of mulch to keep moisture in the ground.

Step 3 Coat your trees with an anti-transpirant: It will lock moisture in and seal out the harsh winter elements.

Step 4 Wrap the trunks to prevent splitting, cracking, and sunscald.

Step 5 Stake young trees so they don't get whipped about in heavy winter winds.

Step 6 If your trees are in exposed areas, put up burlap screens to protect against sun, wind, salt, and pollution damage.

Gone with the Wind

Problem: I live near the ocean, and last month, a big storm came through and blew over my favorite, old oak tree. Not only is my tree gone but I'm left with a big, ugly stump. What can I do now? F.O., Zone 7

Solution: When you lose a tree to a windstorm (or by any other means), the first thing to do is to treat the stump with Stump Remover. This will help it rot and soften, so that it can be easily burned out of the ground. Meanwhile, remember that good things can come from bad: Bulbs and wildflowers often spring up like magic after waiting decades for their chance in the sun.

CHAPTER 5

The Rub on Shrubs

I f you think shrubs are boring, think again, my friends. In truth, shrubs are real workhorses in your yard, where they can be used to solve all kinds of problems as well as define space, direct foot traffic, create privacy, or mask the bases of trees and fences. In addition, every well-dressed yard includes foundation shrubs that visually anchor the house to the site. Almost like magic, foundation shrubs form a textural transition zone between the lawn and the house.

SO EXACTLY WHAT IS A SHRUB?

A shrub is a bush, of course, which is a woody plant that has numerous spreading branches. Shrubs may be evergreen or deciduous, and they come in a huge array of shapes and sizes. I'll give you the scoop on the major shrub forms in a minute, but first let me point out what I think is the most important reason to include shrubs in your landscape: Per square foot, well-chosen shrubs provide more ornamental value, season after season, than any other type of plant. And they do all this while requiring the least amount of maintenance. Talk about a bang for your buck!

Shapely Shrubs

The natural shape of a shrub is called its form, and different forms do different things in the landscape. Here are the five main forms, and how to best use them in your yard:

Rounded, upright shrubs create structure the same way that walls separate rooms in a house. Use them to define spaces, create screens or backdrops, or visually anchor the corners of your house. Abelia, burning bush, boxwood, and yew come in this shape.

Cushion or mounding shrubs naturally grow into symmetrical mounds, so they are ideal for foundation plantings, where neatness counts most. Examples include evergreen azaleas, northern bayberry, dwarf boxwood, Japanese holly, and some junipers.

Open, upright shrubs make fine accent plants, because they are usually deciduous plants with showy, colorful blooms. Weave them in with evergreens, or feature them in special beds. I put rhododendrons, roses, and most viburnums into this category.

Spreading shrubs have a low, horizontal branching pattern, so you can use them almost like ground covers. Good candidates include bearberry, cotoneaster, creeping juniper, and spreading shrub roses.

Fountain shaped shrubs provide spectacular fireworks when they are in bloom. Use them to accent corners, anchor large flower beds, or define your yard's boundaries. Forsythia, bridal wreath spirea, and star magnolia are star performers.

Hold That Slope!

Judging from the letters I get, one of the most common yard problems in the country is a steep slope. If one of your woes is a hillside that's the dickens to mow, or just won't stay put, cover it with spreading shrubs. Their branches and foliage will break up hard rainfall that can start a mudslide, and below ground, the shrubs' spreading fibrous roots will hold the soil in place. Your worries will be over!

Recycling Roundup

When you're washing windows outdoors, don't fight with your shrubs. Instead, haul out an old shirt, and tie lengths of rope to the wrists and tail. Then pull the shirt against the shrub and away from the house. Secure the ropes to a stake, and get to washin' those windows!

Fantastic Flowers

The glowing gold of forsythia in bloom always takes my breath away, but it's a good thing that the plants look good the rest of the year, too. Like most other blooming shrubs, forsythias provide very concentrated color, but it doesn't last very long. Most flowering shrubs bloom for only a few weeks, and in a specific season. So vivid color from blooming shrubs is always a come-and-go affair.

The vast majority of flowering shrubs bloom in spring or early summer, so early-season color is easy to come by in shrubs. A precious few shrubs save their show for later in the year. Abelia and butterfly bush (buddleia) are always major players in the summer landscape, and where they are hardy (from Zone 7 southward), compact crape myrtles give off strong sparks of color through the dog days of August.

GRANDMA PUTT'S OLD-TIME TIPS

BRING 'EM INSIDE

Grandma Putt knew that shrubs look just as good inside as they do out in the yard. Her flower arrangements always included branches full of leaves and berries, and even bare twigs in interesting shapes and colors.

Jerry's TOP TEN

Flowering Shrubs

For beautiful color year after year, you gotta have flowering shrubs. This is a small sample of the best and brightest. Explore your local nurseries for more blooming bushes that grow well in your area.

- **Abelia** *(Abelia)*; to 5 feet, Zones 5 to 9; shades of pink or pink-tinged white, often fragrant

- **Azalea** *(Rhododendron)*; to 6 feet, Zones 4 to 9; just name a color and you can have it!

- **Butterfly bush** *(Buddleia)*; to 8 feet, Zones 6 to 9; pink, red, white, yellow, and all shades of purple, blue, lilac, and lavender; usually fragrant

- **Forsythia** *(Forsythia × intermedia)*; to 8 feet, Zones 5 to 8; bright yellow; great for indoor displays

- **Hydrangea** *(Hydrangea)*; to 12 feet, Zones 6 to 9; white and shades of pink, blue, and purple

- **Lilac** *(Syringa)*; to 15 feet, Zones 3 to 8; white, pink, magenta, blue, and (of course) lilac; very fragrant

- **Rhododendron** *(Rhododendron)*; to 12 feet, Zones 4 to 8; just about every color in the rainbow

- **Rose** *(Rosa)*; to 6 feet, Zones 3 to 9; every color imaginable; often they are fragrant

- **Star magnolia** *(Magnolia stellata)*; 15 feet, Zones 5 to 9; star-shaped, fragrant flowers, mostly pure white, sometimes flushed with pink

- **Viburnum** *(Viburnum)*; to 8 feet, Zones 5 to 8; white, cream, or pink; sometimes fragrant

Shrubs for the Birds

If you want your yard to draw songbirds like a magnet, plant shrubs that produce berries, such as Oregon grape, cotoneaster, and viburnum. Besides giving them food, shrubs provide birds with shelter and nesting sites. You benefit, too, because most of the birds who flock to your shrubs will also devour insects that might otherwise feast on your plants, or even on you! The berries don't have to be ones that humans like to eat — birds don't share our sweet tooth!

Jerry Baker Says . . .

"Don't be surprised if birds ignore berries for a long time, and then feast on them in mid to late winter. Berries of holly and juniper, for example, are simply unpalatable to birds until they have been frozen several times, and actually begin to ferment. Some wildlife experts suspect that birds actually enjoy the alcohol that is present in well-weathered berries."

Mix and Match

Shrubs are the real workhorses of the garden. Here are 10 terrific tips for putting them to work solving problems in your yard:

1. Jazz up groupings of uniform, horizontal shrubs with upright shrubs to break up the monotony.

2. Mix evergreen shrubs of one form with deciduous shrubs of another. For example, place rounded boxwoods near a large, fountain-shaped spirea, or pair spiky spreading junipers with a bushy lilac.

3. Plant masses of spreading shrubs in problem spots that are not needed for outdoor activities. On slopes, the branches and foliage of spreading shrubs break up hard rainfall and keep the soil from washing away. Below-ground, the shrubs' spreading fibrous roots hold the soil firmly in place.

4. Place showy shrubs near entryways, walkways, and other places where they are sure to be noticed.

5. Employ large shrubs as green screens. They're less expensive than fences, and fill in much faster than trees.

6. Choose shade-tolerant shrubs where sunlight is limited. Popular choices include aucuba, azalea, rhododendron, and Oregon grape.

7. If you truly want a hedge, keep it short and sweet. A small hedge comprised of fine-textured evergreens often has the visual impact of a large one, but it takes much less time to maintain.

8. Thickets made of wild and woolly shrubs can deter all kinds of unwanted visitors, including burglars and deer, but wild birds love them. A thicket planted just outside your back fence is a fine use for a thorny and prickly unwelcome mat.

9. Avoid planting hollies, shrub roses, and other prickly plants close to walkways and driveways for obvious reasons. Ouch!

10. Soften the appearance of brick walls or wood fences with repetitive plantings of small shrubs. Small ground lights installed between the shrubs will make the scene dreamlike at night.

LANDSCAPE LINGO

Shrubs come in three types. **Deciduous** plants shed their leaves in winter and grow new ones in the spring. **Evergreens** do exactly what their name implies: They keep green leaves on their branches year-round. They do shed leaves, though. Pines, for example, lose about a third of their needles each fall. **Semi-evergreen** plants can go either way. Where winters are very cold, they will be decidedly deciduous, and where winter temperatures are considerably milder, they will be evergreen.

Jerry's TOP TEN

Shrubs for Slopes

These guys have deep roots and spreading form, so they can really cover some ground once they get going. Check plant tags to see how wide a certain cultivar grows before you decide how many plants you need, because many grow three times as wide as their mature height.

- **Bearberry cotoneaster** *(Cotoneaster dammeri)*; to 3 feet, Zones 4 to 8

- **Creeping juniper** *(Juniperus horizontalis)*; less than 1 foot, Zones 5 to 9

- **Creeping Oregon grape** *(Mahonia repens)*; 1 foot, Zones 5 to 8

- **Dwarf pittosporum** *(Pittosporum tobira* culitvars)*; 3 feet tall, Zones 8 to 10

- **Heather** *(Calluna vulgaris)*; to 15 inches, Zones 5 to 9

- **Japanese barberry** *(Berberis thunbergii)*; to 3 feet, Zones 5 to 9

- **Rockspray cotoneaster** *(Cotoneaster horizontalis)*; to 3 feet, Zones 5 to 8

- **Shrubby cinquefoil** *(Potentilla fruticosa)*; 2 to 4 feet, Zones 2 to 7

- **Shrub rose** *(Rosa* hybrids, like 'Scarlet Meidilland')*; to 4 feet, Zones 4 to 9

- **Wintercreeper** *(Euonymus fortunei)*; to 2 feet, Zones 5 to 9

Sizing Up
Foundation Shrubs

You can use foundation shrubs to solve a lot of design problems, and you don't have to be a landscape architect to do it. These simple strategies will keep you on course:

- Put the tallest, fullest plants near the corners of your house. As long as they don't block the views from nearby windows, they can be up to two-thirds the height of the eaves of the house.

- In front of windows, no foundation shrubs should grow taller than the lowest edges.

- Have shrubs gradually become smaller as they get closer to the main entryway. This design "funnels" the eye toward the door.

- For extra entryway emphasis, use an upright shrub, such as a small columnar juniper, near the front door.

- Don't fret about keeping foundation shrubs all the same type or size unless you're a naturally orderly person who simply likes things that way. Changes in height and plant texture make foundation plantings more interesting.

LANDSCAPE LINGO

Dioecious. This tongue-twister is all about sex. Individual plants of dioecious (dy-ee'-shus) shrubs, including holly, yew, and bittersweet, are either male or female. Both sexes produce flowers, but only the females set fruit — if they are fertilized by pollen from a male plant. One male plant is usually sufficient to pollinate three females. Don't worry; nurseries identify the sexes of dioecious plants for you and show the sex of the plant on the label.

Too Big for Their Britches

Instead of making houses look prettier, shrubs that get too big for their britches make houses look small. It's not being prideful to want your house to look at least as large as it really is, and one of the ways of doing this is to control the size of foundation shrubs.

Buyer's Guide to Bushes

Before I go to buy anything, I always make sure my checkbook is ready to cover it. If you're on a tight budget, you can save money by starting with small shrubs and temporarily fill in between them with annuals (page 132), perennials (page 144), or bulbs (page 159). And an old landscaper's trick is to install small but very high-quality shrubs at their proper spacing, and put little, inexpensive shrubs between them. Two to three years later, you can dig up and dispose of the supporting cast, leaving ample room for the star players to strut their stuff.

WATCH IT !

Clear Vision

When planting a shrub at the entrance to your driveway or anywhere near the street, choose one that will never grow more than 30 inches tall. That way, you will always be able to see over it, and oncoming traffic can see you, too.

What exactly is proper spacing? In most situations, you want your shrubs to barely grow together when they reach mature size. So if a shrub is expected to grow 4 feet wide, plant it at least 3½ feet from its nearest neighbor.

Shrub Shopping Checklist

Most of this stuff is common sense, but if you want to cover all your bases, take this checklist with you when you go to select new shrubs:

✔ Are the leaves healthy and free from dark spots or yellow patches?

✔ Is the soil in the container firm and free from weeds?

✔ Are stems and leaves free from insects such as scale, mealybugs, and spider mites?

✔ Have broken twigs been removed, or are they still hanging there?

✔ Is there a readable plant tag attached that accurately identifies the plant?

Jerry's TOP TEN

Shrubs with Colorful Foliage

Sometimes a dash of gold or some leaves with cream margins are just the thing a shrub grouping needs to keep things interesting. Don't get carried away, though, because a little blush of bronze or chartreuse will go a long way in your landscape.

- **Aucuba** *(Aucuba japonica)*; to 6 feet, Zones 7 to 9; green leaves with yellow margins, splashes, or speckles

- **Chinese juniper** *(Juniperus chinensis)*; to 2 feet, Zones 3 to 9; gold, bluish green, gray-green, or light blue foliage; pungent aroma

- **Drooping leucothoe** *(Leucothoe fontanesiana* 'Rainbow'); to 6 feet, Zones 5 to 8; variegated leaves of red, yellow, and cream

- **Golden privet** *(Ligustrum)*; to 12 feet, Zones 5 to 9; leaves can be green with cream margins, gray-green with white margins, or solid golden yellow

- **Japanese barberry** *(Berberis thunbergii)*; to 3 feet, Zones 5 to 9; red-purple or purplish bronze foliage; glossy red fruit in fall

- **Japanese spirea** *(Spiraea japonica)*; 6 feet, Zones 4 to 9; leaves can be gray-green, bronze, bronze-red, or yellow; some are margined in white

- **Redtwig dogwood** *(Cornus alba)*; to 10 feet, Zones 2 to 8; leaves of yellow, gray-green margined with white, or pink-flushed with yellow margins; red or blackish purple shoots in winter

- **Sawara cypress** *(Chamaecyparis pisifera)*; to 10 feet, Zones 3 to 8; blue-green, golden to bronze-yellow, or yellowish gray-green

- **Smokebush** *(Cotinus coggygria)*; to 15 feet, Zones 5 to 9; purple, wine-red, or pinkish bronze leaves

- **Wintercreeper** *(Euonymus fortunei)*; to 2 feet (can be trained as a climber to 20 feet), Zones 5 to 9; leathery green leaves variegated gold or white

Jerry's TOP TEN

Evergreen Shrubs

Think of these shrubs as the constants that will tie your landscape together year-round. Pay close attention to the different shades of green you can get, too. Pair evergreen shrubs with light-colored bulbs and flowers, and you have a combo that can't be beat!

- **Arborvitae** (*Thuja* species and cultivars); to 15 feet, Zones 2 to 9, depending on selection

- **Boxwood** (*Buxus* species); to 5 feet, Zones 5 to 9

- **Drooping leucothoe** *(Leucothoe fontanesiana)*; to 6 feet, Zones 4 to 8

- **Japanese holly** *(Ilex crenata)*; to 4 feet, Zones 5 to 8

- **Juniper** (*Juniperus* species and cultivars); wide range of sizes, Zones 3 to 9

- **Mugo pine** *(Pinus mugo)*; to 10 feet, Zones 2 to 8

- **Oregon grape** *(Mahonia aquifolium)*; to 4 feet, Zones 5 to 8

- **Sawara cypress** (*Chamaecyparis pisifera* cultivars); to 10 feet, Zones 3 to 8

- **Spruce** (*Picea* species and cultivars); to 15 feet, Zones 3 to 8

- **Yew** (*Taxus* species and cultivars); to 12 feet, Zones 4 to 8, depending on selection

START 'EM OUT RIGHT

Ready to get dirty? Planting a number of shrubs is pretty heavy work, but it's also one of those things that you have to do only once if you do them right. Then, with a little luck, you can sit back and enjoy the rewards of your labor for years and years to come.

The Routine

Shrubs really appreciate good soil preparation, so work at least 3 to 4 inches of my Super Shrub Soil Mix (see page 76) into each bed or planting hole. And because roots need to reach far and wide, pronto, make those holes big. Make them three times wider than the container and at least 14 inches deep. Then partially refill the planting holes with my Super Shrub Soil Mix (see page 76), if needed, to make sure your shrubs will be at the same depth at which they grew in their containers.

Before you set the plant into its hole, untangle the outer roots with your hand, or use a sharp knife to make shallow cuts in the bottom third of the root mass. This treatment will encourage new roots to grow outward, which helps the plant establish itself more quickly.

Recycling Roundup

Newly planted shrubs need daily water for the first 3 or 4 days, and the best way to deliver that supply is with a soaker hose. You don't have to buy one, though: Just poke holes in an old hose and lay it out on the ground among the plants.

Never plant shrubs just after a heavy rain, when the soil is very wet. It will form clumps that refuse to crumble, and soil that won't break apart won't be in good contact with the roots. Very dry soil makes for difficult planting, too, because it's so hard to dig. Water dry soil very deeply 2 days before planting shrubs to soften it and make it easier to cultivate.

Feeding Time

Most of the shrubs you buy in containers have been fed regularly to support fast growth while making up for the restricted root situation plants must tolerate in pots. Your new shrubs will breathe a sigh of relief as you set those roots free in well-prepared soil, but don't feed shrubs immediately after planting. Wait at least 4 weeks. Since most shrubs aren't meant to grow more than 10 to 12 feet high, a well-balanced garden food (5-10-10) can be applied in early spring in most parts of the country, and in both fall and spring in the southern regions. You can also feed your shrubs by sprinkling ¼ pound of Epsom salts onto the soil beneath them and then watering it in with my Shrub Stimulator Tonic.

Jerry Baker Says . . .

"Once shrubs reach mature size, they need little care. It's good to feed them once a year, though. You can feed spring-blooming shrubs in late fall, but wait until early spring to fertilize evergreens and shrubs that bloom in summer or fall. Pull back the mulch, scatter the fertilizer over the soil around the plant, and then replace the mulch."

Timely Tonics

Super Shrub Soil Mix

2 bushels of compost
½ cup of Epsom salts
½ cup of bonemeal
1 tbsp. of medicated baby powder

Mix all of these ingredients together in a container, and work about a cup into each hole when you plant your shrubs.

Shrub Stimulator Tonic

4 tbsp. of instant tea granules
4 tbsp. of bourbon, or ½ can of beer
2 tbsp. of liquid dish soap
2 gal. of warm water

Mix all of these ingredients together, and sprinkle the mixture over your shrubs in spring.

Two to Tango

Even though shrubs are sturdy customers, I have found that with the addition of two simple steps, you'll have the healthiest, most robust flower-producing shrubs around.

Step 1 Feed them my Super Shrub Tonic every 3 weeks throughout the growing season.

Step 2 Give them a good root pruning every other year or so.

Root Pruning — Getting Deep

You want to do this only to mature, healthy shrubs that have been in place at least 3 years. This is the equivalent of a pedicure to humans.

To root prune, simply take a flat-back spade with a razor-sharp edge and plunge it into the ground out at the tip of the farthest branch as deep as it will go, in a circle all the way around the shrub. Once that's done, I want you to pour ¼ pound of Epsom salts evenly into the cuts, all the way around the shrub. Then pour a quart of my Root Pruning Tonic into the cuts over the Epsom salts.

Timely Tonics

Super Shrub Tonic

½ can of beer
½ cup of fish fertilizer
½ cup of ammonia
¼ cup of baby shampoo
2 tbsp. of hydrogen peroxide

Mix all of these ingredients in a 20 gallon hose-end sprayer, and spray the plants to the point of run-off.

Root Pruning Tonic

1 can of beer
4 tbsp. of instant tea granules
1 tbsp. of shampoo
1 tbsp. of ammonia
1 tbsp. of hydrogen peroxide
1 tbsp. of whiskey

Mix all of these ingredients in 2 gallons of very warm water. Then pour a quart of the elixir into the soil where you've cut your shrubs' roots.

PRUNING TO PERFECTION

With flowering shrubs, the standard rule of thumb is to prune plants just after they've finished blooming. This gives them nearly an entire year to develop new bud-bearing branches, and woody shrubs often need that long to renew themselves and get prepared for a fine display of flowers.

Prune evergreens only as needed, and resist the impulse to prune junipers that are looking just fine as they are. It's fine to lop or saw off damaged branches or others that stick out in awkward directions, but don't assume that just because a shrub exists, it needs to be pruned.

Jerry Baker Says . . .

"Whatever you do, don't get carried away at pruning time! Over-enthusiastic pruning can do more harm than good, and can create extra work and problems for you in the long run."

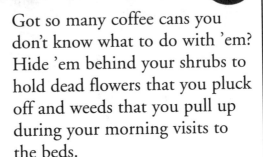
How Pruning Works

Shrubs want to grow, and they are quite determined in their quest. If you cut off the tip of a branch, new branches will quickly begin to grow from just below

where you cut off the tip. After a month or so, you will be tempted to go back and trim the two or three new twigs that have sprouted up. The plant may be happy for you to do this, because supporting the demands of hundreds of new shoots is bound to be pretty darned exhausting.

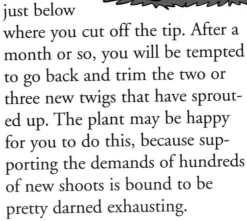

Renewal Pruning

Thinning out old branches and topping off those that have grown long and leggy is called renewal pruning. If you remove about one-third of old growth in this way, the shrub will respond by producing a huge flush of energetic new growth.

There is a definite rhyme and reason to renewal pruning, so here's how to go about it in 5 easy steps:

Step 1 Find any dead stems, which often have gray rather than brown bark, and cut them off as close to the ground as possible. Or cut off deadwood where it joins a healthy stem.

Step 2 Repeat step one with any stems that show evidence of disease — dark cankers, nasty splits in the bark, or leaves that are covered with yellow spots or patches.

Step 3 Take two steps backward, and look for stems that cross each other or stick out in odd directions. Remove the weaker one, which is often the older branch.

Step 4 Trim off very low branches that are spindly because they get so little sunlight.

Step 5 If a tall stem towers above all the others, reach down into the shrub and cut it off where it joins a larger stem.

Go with the Flow

Pruning is more technical than doling out handfuls of organic or timed-release fertilizer, but it doesn't have to be brain-bending or super time-consuming. With pruning, your goal should always be to work with the natural shape of the plant. If you insist on forcing all of your shrubs to grow into big green balls, you're setting yourself up to fight a losing battle!

Jerry Baker Says . . .

"After you've pruned your shrubs, take the same precautions you do when you give your trees a haircut: Treat them with my Tree Wound Sterilizer Tonic and Pruning Wound Bandage Tonic (see page 56)."

Be Kind to the Elderly

If it gives you an uncomfortable feeling to think about cutting a big, overgrown shrub back to the ground, go with your gut. There is a much kinder way to restore the health and shapeliness of elderly shrubs, but it takes a little time and patience. Being a senior citizen myself, of course I think old shrubs deserve this kind of respectful regard.

It's really pretty easy. Every year for 3 years running, cut out one-third of the branches. You will probably need a pruning saw to do this, because you want to cleanly sever old branches deep inside the plants. That's right, whole limbs will come out, but only one-third of the total count. In the second year, you will already see lots of new growth eager for the room you're about to create with your pruning saw. By the third (and final) rejuvenation pruning, you'll be taking out only old wood, which will now be in close proximity to lots of vigorous new branches.

Old Shrubs on the Rebound

Because they have such extensive root systems, established old shrubs often become glorious specimens if you prune them thoughtfully, replace old mulches with new material, and give them a nice pick-me-up that cleans old stems and leaves and washes off little pests that may be hiding in the foliage. My Super Shrub Restorer is just the ticket for perking up old shrubs and getting them started on their way to a robust new life.

Timely Tonic

Super Shrub Restorer

1 can of beer
1 cup of ammonia
½ cup of liquid dish soap
½ cup of molasses or clear corn syrup

Mix all of these ingredients in your 20 gallon hose-end sprayer. Drench shrubs thoroughly, including the undersides of leaves, where little critters often hide. If you have some left over, spray it on your trees and lawn, too.

Shaping Hedges

I have a confession to make. Even though I've been railing on about gardeners' addiction to shrub pruning, and have gotten positively preachy about the laborious demands of hedges, I myself have a modest hedge that I shear at least three times every summer. Maybe it's a nostalgia thing, because I still remember how Grandma Putt sometimes used her hedge to dry clothes when she ran out of space on the clothesline.

But I take pride in doing that shearing right. A healthy hedge needs to be wider at the bottom than at the top, so that sunlight can reach the lowest branches. Otherwise, it will die out around the bottom, and that'll make it look pretty shabby.

A LITTLE JAVA, PLEASE
Like most of us, Grandma Putt always had plenty of leftover coffee grounds. And do you know what she did with them? She sprinkled them on the soil all around her shrubs. Believe you me, she had the healthiest, most vigorous shrubs in the neighborhood — and when those plants bloomed, they bloomed *big time.* Those flowers just about knocked your socks off!

Get It Right the First Time!

Folks waste countless hours and a lot of energy trying to tame shrubs that are too big, or reshape them to fit unnatural contours. But you can avoid that hassle — when you're shopping, check plant tags and catalog descriptions to make sure the shrub you have in mind fits the place where you want to plant it — and will still fit it when the bush grows to its mature size. A little bit of thinking beforehand will save a lot of headaches in the long run!

PROBLEMS & SOLUTIONS

TROUBLESHOOTING SHRUBS

In general, shrubs are just about the most carefree plants I know of. But every once in a while, trouble strikes. Here are some of the most common problems folks have asked me about recently.

Cotoneaster Critters

Problem: There is something wrong with the stems of my cotoneaster. I could tell that the plants were not growing very well this year, but it was not until the leaves fell that I noticed gray bumps all over the stems. What's causing them, and is there anything I can do to help? N.P., Zone 5

Solution: Sounds to me like scale, which are little insects that suck the sap out of the stems. They're covered with a tough shell, so they're hard to reach with sprays. But if you time things right, you should be able to control them by next spring. Begin by spraying your plants with a good horticultural/dormant oil now, which will suffocate some of the scale. If the plants can do with a little pruning, cut out the most badly infested parts. The scale will come to life in spring and start moving around, which is the best time to hit them with my Hot Bug Brew. Once you've got those villains on the run, keep them from coming back by drenching your cotoneaster (and other shrubs as well) with my Shrub Pest Preventer (see page 323) once a month from spring until fall.

Timely Tonic

Hot Bug Brew

3 hot green peppers (canned or fresh)
3 medium cloves of garlic
1 small onion
1 tbsp. of liquid dish soap
3 cups of water

Purée the peppers, garlic, and onion in a blender. Pour the purée into a jar, and add the dish soap and water. Let stand for 24 hours. Then strain out the pulp, and use a handheld sprayer to apply the remaining liquid to bug-infested plants, making sure to thoroughly coat the tops and undersides of all the leaves.

Brown Boxwoods

Problem: Some kind of disaster has struck my boxwoods! One by one, those on the side of my house are turning brown, and I think they're dead. The ones in the front yard look fine, but I'm worried. What has happened? C.F., Zone 7

Solution: Disaster is right! Your plants have been killed by root rot, a disease that's often present in soil, and really takes off when the roots get damaged. Did you dig close to them to plant flowers? You'll want to be very careful digging around your healthy boxwoods, because that's how this disease gets inside the plants. As for your dead boxwoods, there is no hope for them. Dig them out and replace them with another type of evergreen. Japanese hollies might be your best bet.

Hollies in Sick Bay

Problem: My holly bushes look sick. The older leaves are dark green, but most of the newer ones are light green with yellowish spots. What kind of disease causes this problem, and what should I do about it? J.M., Zone 7

Solution: Your hollies aren't diseased; they're just growing in soil that's too sweet for their liking. Either your soil is not naturally acidic or you got a little too close to your bushes with lime. If hollies don't have a pH below 6.5, they can't take up iron from the soil, which makes them look yellow. The same thing sometimes happens with azaleas, hydrangeas, and rhododendrons. As a quick fix, spray your bushes with Liquid Iron (follow the label directions), and dust a little sulfur onto the soil beneath your plants. Top it with chopped leaves or pine straw, and you should start seeing new growth that's deep, holly green. Also, have a look at a related question from L.B. in Zone 9 (see page 86).

Unhappy Hydrangeas

Problem: I thought I had finally figured out how to make my hydrangeas happy — by giving them lots of water — but suddenly, they have started to sulk. Some of the leaves are kind of yellow and droopy, and even water doesn't perk them up. The weather has been hot and dry, so I've made sure they've gotten water at least once a week. Could something else be wrong? S.B., Zone 6

Solution: To figure out this mystery, take a magnifying glass and get a close look at the undersides of those droopy leaves. If there's a faint white webbing there, you've got spider mites, which are tiny sucking insects that drain leaves of juices and nutrients. These pests often get going when the weather is hot, but you should be able to set them back in a big way with biweekly applications of my All-Season Clean-Up Tonic (see page 60). Make sure you hit the undersides of the leaves. Then throw an old sheet or blanket over your plants right after you spray them, and let it stay there for a couple of days. Spider mites hate shade, but your hydrangeas will appreciate a break from the hot sun as they begin their recovery.

Ugly Euonymus

Problem: Our older home has a huge euonymus bush by the front porch. I'd love to keep it, but by the end of the summer, it has mildew so bad that I hate to even look at it. Do you know of a good cure? F.A., Zone 7

Solution: I sure do! Once you get that grand old bush in shape, I want you to start giving it the TLC it deserves, and the mildew will become a distant memory. Begin by getting behind a pair of pruning loppers and cutting out about a third of the branches. Try to follow the natural shape of the plant, and set your sights on improving the air circulation through the branches. Then rake up all the fallen foliage and put it into the garbage.

Don't put down new mulch until spring, after more leaves have been shed and gathered up. As soon as temperatures warm in spring, drench your bush with my Baking Soda Spray. And be sure to include your euonymus with your other shrubs when you fill your hose-end sprayer with my All-Season Green-Up Tonic (recipe on page 27). This procedure also works on lilacs.

Pale Azaleas

Problem: This spring, I fed my azaleas with a special fertilizer for acid-loving plants just after they bloomed. But now the leaves have gotten pale, with tiny yellow specks. What causes this kind of problem? L.U., Zone 8

Solution: Lace bugs, that's what! If you go check your plants again, I bet you'll be able to find a few on the undersides of leaves, because they almost never crawl up top. While they're under cover, lace bugs suck the juices from leaves of all kinds of azaleas, rhododendrons, and mountain laurel. The good news is that they're soft-bodied, so they're pretty easy to control with a spray that contains good old soap. My Amazing Aphid Antidote should cure the problem.

Timely Tonics

Baking Soda Spray

2 tbsp. of baby shampoo
1 tbsp. of baking soda

Mix these ingredients in 1 gallon of warm water, and mist-spray your plants lightly once a week.

Amazing Aphid Antidote

1 small onion, chopped fine
2 medium cloves of garlic, chopped fine
1 tbsp. of baby shampoo or liquid dish soap
2 cups of water

Put all of these ingredients into a blender and blend on high. Let sit overnight, and then strain through a coffee filter. Pour the liquid into a handheld mist sprayer, and apply liberally at the first sign of aphid trouble.

Buggy Viburnums

Problem: When I returned from an early-summer vacation, my beautiful viburnum was almost gray with aphids. I sprayed them right away with a pesticide and I think they're gone now, but there were so many that a lot of the new leaves — and even stems — are twisted. Should I cut off these damaged parts or let them grow? Also, is there a way to prevent this problem next year? I'd really like to take another vacation. B.W., Zone 5

Solution: You don't need to do any special pruning because of the plant parts that were damaged by aphids, unless you can't stand looking at them anymore. Just shape the plants a little as you normally would, and keep a close eye in case those aphids stage a comeback. This winter, after the leaves fall and the plants become dormant, spray your plant thoroughly with dormant oil to kill any eggs that have been left on the stems. That's where this year's aphid extravaganza probably came from. Finally, send me a postcard when you're on the road!

Yellow Leaves

Problem: Help! My beautiful rhododendrons are all turning yellow. What can I do about it? L.B., Zone 9

Solution: Judging from your Sunbelt Zone number, I'd say that your shrubs are suffering from iron-poor sap. In warm weather — which in the South and West means all year long — shrubs need a substantial amount of iron in their diet. If they don't get it, they'll suffer from chlorosis, which is a yellowing of the foliage. So as an immediate fix, I want you to apply Liquid Iron at the recommended rate, making sure that you give the plants a thorough drenching.

Folks in the cooler areas of the country generally don't have to worry about this until just after the forsythias bloom. For you southwesterners, though, early February is the time to spray your shrubs with my Fantastic Flowering Shrub Tonic. It'll give them the exact dose of iron they need to get off and running for their big spring extravaganza.

Timely Tonic

Fantastic Flowering Shrub Tonic

1 tbsp. of baby shampoo
1 tsp. of hydrated lime
1 tsp. of iron sulfate

Mix all of these ingredients in 1 gallon of water. For an extra "kicker," add 1 tablespoon of Liquid Iron to the mixture. Then spray the excellent elixir on your flowering shrubs.

Balcony Blues

Problem: I live in an apartment that has a wonderful balcony that I can see all year long through my big glass doors. Are there any shrubs that will grow well in containers and look good in the fall and winter? K.T., Zone 6

Solution: You bet there are! Boxwood, juniper, cotoneaster, and many other shrubs come in compact varieties that will grow happy as clams in big pots. But one of my very favorite shrubs for container growing is euonymus. It comes in both deciduous and evergreen versions, so make sure you look for one of the latter to use on your balcony. You can't go wrong with *E. fortunei* 'Silver Queen,' which will thrive just about anywhere and is one of the best-looking plants I can think of. It has dark green leaves with silver margins that take on a pink and cream cast in the winter. Plant a pair of these, and you'll have the best-dressed balcony in town!

CHAPTER 6

Coming Up Roses

Lots of folks think a garden isn't complete without a few roses, and I agree! Nowadays, there are fine roses for every climate, including superhardy ones for the North and special ones grafted onto nematode-resistant rootstocks to grow in Zones 8 and 9. What's really exciting is that old roses have staged a big-time comeback over the past 10 years or so. These charmers go back to long before Grandma Putt's day, and most of them are as tough as they are beautiful — and sweet-smelling.

PUTTING ROSES TO WORK

Believe it or not, roses are not just pretty faces! When well grown, they are attractive shrubs. Many perfume the air with lovely scents, so you will want to grow them where they can't be missed. Roses, however, do have thorns, so it's best not to place them close to walkways or play areas. Instead, give them prominent places in flower beds, or let them star in a spacious grouping of shrubs. Train climbers over arbors or fences, and use especially vigorous varieties as specimen shrubs in your front yard.

Bare Root or Container?

In late winter and very early spring, garden centers sell bare-root roses — dormant plants with their roots tightly wrapped in plastic. Although they don't look very lively, good-quality, bare-root roses are excellent buys. They are easy to plant and usually require no pruning — only deep, fertile soil in which to stretch their roots. Be sure to wash and soak your bare-root roses in my Rose Revival Tonics before planting.

Timely Tonics

Rose Revival Tonics

This dynamic duo will get your bare-root roses off and growing like champs. First, wash your newly purchased bare-root rose bushes, roots and all, in a bucket of warm water with the following added.

1 tbsp. of liquid dish soap
¼ tsp. of liquid bleach

Then before planting, soak your bare-root rose bushes in a clean bucket filled with 1 gallon of warm water for about half an hour, with the following added to it.

2 tbsp. of clear corn syrup
1 tsp. of liquid dish soap
1 tsp. of ammonia

As spring gets under way and roses emerge from dormancy, it's better to buy them in containers. Still, I want you to get them into the ground as early as possible. Roses that are not set out until late spring or summer are often slow to develop extensive roots, which puts them at increased risk of damage from diseases and drought.

What's in a Name?

Roses have been culti-vated for 10,000 years, so it's no wonder there are so many kinds. **Hybrid teas** are often challenged by diseases, but they look great and usually bloom continuously when given good care. **Floribundas** develop clusters of flowers, so they make great accents along a picket fence. **Climbers** reach to 10 feet or more, and **miniatures** are pint-size versions of hybrid teas, floribundas, and climbers. My favorites, though, are the **shrub roses** that offer excellent disease tolerance, and the thousands of hardy and great-smelling **old roses** that have been rescued from extinction by rose lovers all over the world.

Soil Is Key

To get the most out of any rose, give it the best possible growing conditions. Roses need at least 6 hours of direct sunlight, preferably in the morning, so that it dries the dew from the leaves first thing in the day. Roses also need deep, fertile soil, so don't cut corners when you get ready to prepare a site to plant them.

Jerry Baker Says . . .

"Call me a purist, but I hate to sniff a rose and find that there's nothing there. At shopping time, check variety descriptions carefully to make sure you're buying roses with fragrance. Many heavy-bloomers are not fragrant, which is fine as long as you're not expecting perfume. If your roses are supposed to deliver fragrance but you're not getting any, plant some parsley around the bushes; it'll heighten the aromatic display."

Begin by digging a roomy planting hole at least 16 inches wide and just as deep. Place about one-third of the excavated soil in a wheelbarrow, and mix with it plenty of composted manure or other organic matter. A 3-inch layer, or about half of a 40-pound bag of composted manure, is about right. Dump half of this mixture into the hole, shape the loose soil into a cone, and set the plant in place with its roots arranged around the cone. Then gently cover the roots with more of your amended soil, and continue filling the hole with alternate spadefuls of soil and the mixture from your wheelbarrow.

Jerry's TOP TEN

Hybrid Tea Roses

Hybrid teas need exacting care, but if you get them growing well, they'll produce beautiful flowers all summer long. Most plants grow to be less than 4 feet tall and are angular and upright in habit.

- **'Dainty Bess'**, fragrant lavender-pink single flowers, disease-tolerant, Zones 4 to 9

- **'Double Delight'**, fragrant yellow flowers edged with pink, Zones 5 to 10

- **'Fragrant Cloud'**, very fragrant coral-red blossoms, Zones 5 to 10

- **'Just Joey'**, fragrant apricot flowers, tolerates humid heat, Zones 5 to 10

- **'McCartney'**, very fragrant deep pink blossoms, Zones 5 to 9

- **'Midas Touch'**, fragrant yellow flowers, long stems, Zones 5 to 9

- **'Mister Lincoln'**, fragrant red flowers, strong rebloomer, Zones 5 to 10

- **'Pascali'**, fragrant creamy white blossoms, rugged and reliable, Zones 5 to 10

- **'Peace'**, fragrant yellow blossoms blushed with pink, Zones 4 to 9

- **'Tropicana'**, fragrant vivid orange-red blossoms, Zones 4 to 9

Seven Super Steps to Superior Roses

Your roses will grow like champs if you follow this simple 7-step routine.

Step 1 Choose a site that gets full morning sun and a total of at least 6 hours of sun each day.

Step 2 Monitor the soil pH closely to keep it between 5.5 and 6.5.

Step 3 Fertilize roses with an organic or timed-release rose fertilizer in early spring. After the first buds form, begin feeding them my Rose Ambrosia every 3 weeks. Stop feeding roses 8 weeks before the first frost is expected.

Step 4 Water as needed so that your roses get the equivalent of 1 inch of water each week during the summer when they are actively growing.

Timely Tonics

Rose Ambrosia

If your roses could talk, they'd have great things to say about this grand elixir, which gives them just what they need to grow strong and bloom like gangbusters.

1 cup of beer
2 tsp. of instant tea granules
1 tsp. of Rose/Flower Food
1 tsp. of fish fertilizer
1 tsp. of hydrogen peroxide
1 tsp. of liquid dish soap

Mix all of these ingredients in 2 gallons of warm water, and give each of your roses 1 pint every 3 weeks. Dribble it onto the soil after you've watered, so it will penetrate deep into the root zone.

Rose Clean-Up Tonic

Fall is the best time to set back the insects and diseases that plague roses. After your plants have shed their leaves and been pruned, but before you mulch or wrap them with winter protection, spray them thoroughly with this Tonic.

1 cup of baby shampoo
1 cup of antiseptic mouthwash
1 cup of Tobacco Tea (recipe on page 61)

Place all of these ingredients in your 20 gallon hose-end sprayer, and spray your plants well from top to bottom.

Step 5 Prune roses *after* they bloom. Prune them back to an outward-facing 5-leaf cluster, keeping your eyes open for pruning patterns that will help sunlight and fresh air reach every leaf on the plant.

Step 6 Mulch roses with 2 inches of organic material such as pine needles, straw, or compost. As a defense against diseases, replace old mulch with fresh material each spring.

Step 7 After the first hard freeze, hill up 8 inches of soil over the base of your roses, toss a handful of mothballs on top, and then add a loose mulch of straw, held in place with burlap or chicken wire. If you live from Zone 7 southward, roses need more modest winter protection — a 4-inch mulch of pine straw will do just fine.

Salty Dogs

When you've almost finished planting a new rose, just before you water it in well with my Rose Start-Up Tonic and add mulch, sprinkle a tablespoon of Epsom salts over the soil's surface. Roses love the stuff, so I always give my established roses a spring feeding of Epsom salts, too. In spring, just before I replace old mulches with fresh material, I sprinkle a tablespoon over the soil around each bush.

EPSOM SALTS

THEY'LL GO BANANAS If you want the best-looking and most trouble-free roses in your neighborhood, do what Grandma Putt did: Work banana skins, or whole rotten bananas, into the soil near the base of your bushes. The potassium in the skins will give them a power-packed boost that'll help the plants fend off pests and diseases, and deliver up boatloads of beautiful blossoms.

GRANDMA PUTT'S OLD-TIME TIPS

Jerry's TOP TEN

Floribunda Roses

These are the best choices to grow as hedges or plant along fences. They bloom very heavily in late spring or early summer, and then can be coaxed to rebloom with careful pruning and a steady diet of my Rose Ambrosia (recipe on page 92).

- **'Angel Face',** lemon-scented lavender blooms in cuttable clusters, Zones 5 to 9

- **'Auguste Renoir',** richly scented ruffly pink blossoms, Zones 5 to 9

- **'Betty Prior',** fragrant single pink flowers, tolerates humid heat, Zones 4 to 9

- **'Europeana',** large clusters of lightly fragrant red flowers, Zones 4 to 9

- **'Guy de Maupassant',** spicy scent in ruffly pink blossoms, Zones 5 to 9

- **'Iceberg',** lightly fragrant white flowers, usually reblooms, Zones 4 to 10

- **'Intrigue',** citrus-scented plum-red blooms, Zones 5 to 9

- **'Playgirl',** lightly fragrant single rich pink flowers, strong rebloomer, Zones 5 to 9

- **'Singin' in the Rain',** lightly fragrant yellow-apricot blooms, Zones 5 to 9

- **'Toulouse-Lautrec',** lemon-scented yellow cupped blossoms, Zones 5 to 9

Climbing Roses

Every climber is different, so get to know your plant and how it likes to be pruned to bring about maximum bloom. Winter hardiness varies, too, so choose varieties carefully.

- **'America'**, scented pink blossoms in spring, often into fall, Zones 4 to 9
- **'Belle of Portugal'**, elegant old pink climber for mild climates, Zones 7 to 10
- **'Blaze Improved'**, lightly fragrant red blooms in clusters, Zones 5 to 9
- **'Climbing Iceberg'**, lightly scented semi-double white blossoms, Zones 4 to 9
- **'Golden Showers'**, lightly fragrant shapely yellow blooms, Zones 5 to 9
- **'Joseph's Coat'**, red blossoms age to rich yellow, Zones 5 to 9
- **'Lady Banks'**, huge, old rose covers itself with yellow blossoms, Zones 7 to 10
- **'Leontine Gervais'**, old rose with copper buds that age to almost white, Zones 4 to 10
- **'Madame Alfred Carrière'**, huge, old rose with blush pink blossoms, Zones 4 to 10
- **'Zéphirine Drouhin'**, richly scented old pink rose, thornless, Zones 6 to 9

Shrub Roses

These plants are bushy and vigorous, and they produce beautiful blooms with lots of lush foliage.

- **'Carefree Wonder'**, medium pink blooms all summer, Zones 5 to 9
- **'F. J. Grootendorst'**, red blossoms in clusters, Zones 4 to 9
- **'Fair Bianca'**, scented white cupped blossoms, Zones 4 to 9
- **'Graham Thomas'**, richly scented yellow blossoms, Zones 5 to 9
- **'Mary Rose'**, scented double pink blossoms, Zones 6 to 9
- **'Mutabilis'**, multicolored single blossoms, reddish foliage, Zones 7 to 10
- **'Othello'**, fragrant dark burgundy blossoms on vigorous plants, Zones 6 to 9
- **'Red Meidiland'**, single red blooms repeat well, Zones 4 to 9
- **'Royal Bonica'**, pink double blooms repeat well, Zones 4 to 9
- **'The Fairy'**, classic pink polyantha shrub rose, Zones 4 to 9

TROUBLESHOOTING ROSES

As you'll see in this section, roses have more than their fair share of problems, so you'll need to watch them closely and spring into action at the first sign of trouble. All summer long, right after I mow my lawn, I head straight for my roses. By checking them once a week, I nip problems in the bud. Rosebud, that is!

Aphid Invasion

Problem: The stems and buds of my roses are covered with tiny insects that hardly move at all. Otherwise, the plants seem healthy. What should I do? T.L., Zone 6

Solution: Get rid of those rose aphids, that's what! They are sucking precious juices out of the plants, which will weak-  en them. Because aphids are food to ladybeetle larvae and several other beneficial insects, don't treat your plants with a pesticide. Instead, reach for my Rose Aphid Antidote.

Gray Leaves

Problem: I thought shrub roses were supposed to be disease-resistant, but some of the leaves on my 2-year-old English rose look grayish and wilted. Is this some kind of unusual blight? N.L., Zone 7

Solution: Even disease-resistant roses sometimes have trouble with powdery mildew, a fungus that reaches deep into the leaves and can spread like wildfire. So the first thing I want you to do is to snip off all of those gray and wilted leaves and put them into the garbage. Next, make up a small batch of my Mildew Relief Tonic, and spray it onto the leaves that were near those that had mildew. Be sure to do this on a cloudy day, and don't forget to keep feeding your plants every 3 weeks with my Rose Ambrosia (recipe on page 92).

Bud-Eating Beetles

Problem: The Japanese beetles that are eating my rose blossoms are pretty, but my roses are prettier. They are really bad this year, and they're back within 2 days after I spray them. Is there something else I can do? O.L., Zone 6

Solution: In the long run, you can reduce Japanese beetle problems by treating your lawn with a safe and effective powder called Milky Spore. That's right, your lawn! That's because Japanese beetle larvae over-winter as grass-root-eating, white grubs, so Milky Spore can help your lawn and your roses, too. Meanwhile, keep spraying your roses as often as you need to with Total Pest Control (the active ingredient, pyrethrin, will knock them down quick). Or, if you want a spray break, go out first thing in the morning and jiggle the beetles into a bowl of soapy water. The good news is that the beetles will stop feeding after about 6 weeks, so there is plenty of time to bring your roses back into bloom in late summer.

Timely Tonics

Rose Aphid Antidote

1 lemon or orange peel, coarsely chopped
1 tbsp. of baby shampoo
2 cups of water

Put these ingredients into a blender and blend on high for 10 to 15 seconds. Use a coffee filter to strain out the pulp. Pour the liquid into a handheld mist sprayer. Before applying the Tonic, get out your hose, attach a high-pressure spray nozzle, and blast your plants with water to dislodge some of the aphids. About 10 minutes later, thoroughly spray buds and young stems with Rose Aphid Antidote. Repeat after 4 days, and your aphids should be history.

Mildew Relief Tonic

1 tbsp. of baby shampoo
1 tbsp. of hydrogen peroxide
1 tsp. of instant tea granules
2 cups of water

Mix all of these ingredients in a handheld mist sprayer and apply to rose leaves. Midafternoon on a cloudy day is the best time to apply it.

Bad Black Spots

Problem: Help! My roses are losing leaves every day. There are black spots on many of them, and they turn yellow before they drop off. Is there any hope? Y.S., Zone 5

Solution: Of course there's hope, but first you need to launch an all-out attack on your problem, which is a very common fungal disease

called rose black spot. Here's what I want you to do:

Step 1 Pick up all of the leaves that have fallen, clip off those that are about to, and put them all into the garbage.

Step 2 Rake up the mulch under your plants, and replace it with fresh straw or pine straw.

Step 3 Prune your plants, if needed, so that sunshine and fresh air reach every leaf.

Step 4 When you water, take care that you don't wet the foliage.

Step 5 Feed your roses with my Rose Ambrosia (page 92) every 3 weeks. If some bushes are free from disease, give them an ounce of prevention in the form of my Fungus Fighter Tonic (see page 152).

Jerry Baker Says . . .

"You can set black spot problems way back by painting every last speckled leaf with my Black Spot Remover Tonic. If you love roses, it's well worth the trouble, even if you have to borrow some tomato leaves from a veggie-growing neighbor to make this brew."

Timely Tonic

Black Spot Remover Tonic

15 tomato leaves
2 small onions
¼ cup of rubbing alcohol

Chop the tomato leaves and onions into finely minced pieces, and steep them in the alcohol overnight. Use a small, sponge-type paintbrush to apply the brew to both tops and bottoms of any infected rose leaves.

Streaked Blossoms

Problem: I have a lovely old rose in my yard that blooms baby pink, but this year, the flowers have lots of brown streaks in them, and some of them look lopsided. A red rose not far away seems just fine. Can you explain this mystery? T.J., Zone 5

Solution: First, do a little detective work for me. Cut one of those marred blossoms, and lay it onto a piece of white paper. After a few minutes, shake it hard. If little black things fall out, they're rose thrips, and they really like white and pastel roses. What they don't like is garlic! So snip off all old blossoms and put them into the garbage. Then spray every new one that opens with my Garlic Tea Tonic. Put up a good fight this year, and you may never see thrip damage in your roses again!

Cookie-Cutter Leaves

Problem: I've been feeding my roses with your Rose Ambrosia and they look better now than they have in years, except for one thing — circles that are disappearing from otherwise healthy leaves. What could it be? G.W., Zone 8

Solution: Leaf-cutter bees, that's what! They move so fast that you'll almost never see them at work, which consists of gathering bits of leaf that they use to build their nests. Don't chase them: Scientists have a hunch that those holes stimulate your plants' immune systems, making them hold up better to other, much worse pests and diseases.

CHAPTER 7

Grasses and Ground Covers

Did you ever wonder why, when a portrait photographer takes a picture of a beautiful woman, he often dresses her in a flowing velvet drape? It's because the plush texture of velvet makes everything near it look elegant and well defined. In your yard, the fine texture of a lush lawn works the same magic. It makes your house look more sophisticated, and it gives trees, shrubs, and flowers a whole lot more definition and punch.

IT'S NO ACCIDENT

A beautiful lawn doesn't just happen. It requires time and attention. It's not hard, though. In this chapter, I'll share my secrets to growing gorgeous green grass, and show you tricks that will bring out the best in your yard's welcome mat. Plus, I've got great ideas for those problem areas where grass just doesn't want to grow.

The Lowdown on Lawns

First, let me tell you the honest truth about lawns: No matter what kind of grass you have, it will not look its best unless it gets plenty of water, regular feedings, and periodic baths with my All-Season Clean-Up Tonic (see page 60) to keep pests and diseases at bay. You also need to mow it in just the right way, and then turn around and mow it again a week or so later. In other words, a fine lawn requires a certain level of commitment.

Five Fine Ways to Shrink Your Lawn

If you don't feel inclined to give your lawn the care it needs, there's a great alternative to having thin, weedy grass: Shrink your lawn down until it's the minimum size you need. The smaller your lawn, the less time you'll have to spend giving it proper care. And don't despair: There are several ways to get small areas of lawn grass to do the work of much larger ones. Here are 5 tried-and-true strategies:

#1. In the front yard, have a section of lawn near the entryway (which makes it feel spacious and open) and another one near the street. In between, fill a large, flowing bed with small trees and shrubs.

#2. Tie shade trees together by planting ground cover at their feet. Grass doesn't grow well in shade, anyway, and you'll again never have to maneuver your mower around tree trunks — or whack them with your weed trimmer.

#3. Install a circular platform lawn right in the middle of your yard, with its edges framed in brick, stone, or bands of dwarf evergreens. The circular shape casts a spell that unifies everything around it, and it looks great, too!

#4. In your backyard, have your lawn adjacent to your patio or deck, so that it works as an extension of your outdoor living areas. Farther away from your house, install ground covers or ornamental grasses where you don't want to mow.

#5. Use wide bands of grass as broad corridors that link the different parts of your yard. Any area where you want to invoke a feeling of spaciousness is a good place for grass.

The Green Stuff

Lawn grasses come in two major types: cool season and warm season. Cool-season grasses are bred to handle the moist and cold climates of the North. They enjoy peak growth spurts in spring and fall, and slow down during the summer. Warm-season grasses, on the other hand, like it hot, hot, hot! They tend to turn brown when the temperature slips consistently below 60°F, and they grow well during the long, hot summer.

The Return of the Buffalo

In recent years, plant breeders have worked wonders with a native of the Great Plains called buffalo grass. New cultivars are propagated by division, so they are sold as plugs or sod. Buffalo grass is warm-season, bunching grass that's ideal for areas that really bake in the summer sun, like the central plains. The special trick with this grass is to let it grow really high between mowings, to 4 inches. The great advantage of buffalo grass is that once it's well established, it needs very little water in times of summer drought.

Beat the Heat!

As a general rule of thumb, the majority of warm-season grasses handle the sun's blazing rays better than their cool-season counterparts, which tend to slow down in growth and even go dormant during hot weather. But among both types, some grasses take the heat better than others. If you live where summers get steamy (even though the map may say you live in cool-season territory), go with one of the heat lovers.

Warm-season grasses
Bermuda grass
Buffalo grass
Centipede grass
St. Augustine grass
Zoysia grass

Cool-season grasses
Fine fescue
Tall fescue
Kentucky bluegrass
Perennial ryegrass

They're Not Seedy Characters

Unlike cool-season grasses, the better warm-season grasses are not grown from seed. Instead, they're planted from sod or plugs, and they're all strong creeping grasses that knit themselves together into a tight turf.

The In-Betweens

Poor Zone 7. In many areas, summer is too hot for cool-season grasses, but winter is too long for warm-season grasses. Sure, you can grow bluegrass or Bermuda, but bluegrass becomes dormant in summer, and Bermuda stays dormant so long in winter that it's easily overtaken by weeds.

Enter the new turf-type tall fescues. Easily grown from seed sown in the fall, they're great problem solvers for many parts of the upper South and Mid-Atlantic regions. Just be sure to go with an updated named variety — not the much cheaper grandpappy of them all, Kentucky 31. Named varieties are more petite, have better texture, and are more tolerant of drought and disease, so they are well worth the extra cost.

Jerry's TOP TEN

When it comes to weather, some grasses like it hot and some like it cool. This lineup features the best of both kinds.

Warm-Season Grasses

Use one of these winners if you live in the South or Southwest.

- **Bermuda grass** prefers fertile soil but adapts to other types. It looks good, handles heavy foot traffic, repels most diseases, and tolerates heat. It spreads aggressively, though, and it needs regular watering and frequent feeding to retain its color.

- **Buffalo grass** is a busy yard-keeper's dream: It needs virtually no feeding and no irrigation, even in places that get little rain. It grows best in heavy soil but can handle finer-textured soils. Unfortunately, it's prone to browning during very hot or cold weather.

- **Centipede grass** performs well in any soil, repels most insects, and needs infrequent mowing. Its flaws: It can't handle heavy foot traffic or low temperatures, and it needs frequent watering.

- **St. Augustine grass** prefers moist, sandy soil, but it tolerates the full gamut of southern soil conditions. It can handle intense heat, but it needs plenty of water and fertilizer, and it's no match for chinch bugs and warm-weather lawn diseases.

- **Zoysia grass** requires less than average mowing and watering, resists drought, and fends off most pests and weeds. On the downside, it's vulnerable to billbugs, can't handle cold temperatures, and tends to thatch easily.

Cool-Season Grasses

In northern regions, go with one of these types.

- **Colonial bent grass** likes ordinary, slightly acidic soil and full sun. To stay disease-free and shipshape, it needs a lot of TLC; but if you're hankering to have your own home putting green, this is *the* grass to go for.

- **Fine fescues** are the best low-maintenance grasses for the Northeast. There are at least a half dozen species to choose from, including Chewings, hard, and slender red. They all perform best where they don't get much foot traffic.

- **Kentucky bluegrass** needs fertile soil; it's the ideal choice for northern lawns that get plenty of sun and water.

- **Perennial ryegrass** grows in a wide range of soils, sprouts quickly, and controls erosion. It's great for areas that get heavy foot traffic (it's a favorite on golf courses). The downside: It doesn't fare well in shade, extreme cold, or heat and drought.

- **Tall fescue** adapts to most soils, stands up to salt, and can handle a lot of wear and tear. It also has deep roots that make it good for erosion-prone slopes. It needs regular watering to prevent summer dormancy, and it can spread aggressively, crowding out other grasses.

CARE AND FEEDING 101

All lawn grasses take off like race-horses in the spring, but your climate will affect what they do the rest of the year. Where summer heat waves are common, cool-season grasses often become semi-dormant in summer, then go through a second growth spurt in early fall. In the Sunbelt, warm-season grasses laugh at hot weather. In fact, the best time to plant most warm-season grasses is late spring, when warm soil temperatures encourage fast growth of new runners and roots.

Wait for Late Risers

Warm-season grasses, like hybrid Bermuda, zoysia and buffalo grass, don't wake up as early as cool-season grasses. If you have Bermuda but your neighbor has fescue, don't worry if your lawn is still buff brown while his is green. As soon as the nighttime temperatures rise or stay above 55°F, your lawn will green up, too, and it will get more lush and beautiful the hotter the weather becomes.

Recycling Roundup

When you install flower beds or mini-groves of trees in your yard, dig a trench about 5 inches deep around each plot to separate it from the lawn. Then roll up newspaper, insert it into the trench, and cover it with mulch. It'll prevent weeds from jumping the gulch, and make it easy to mow right up to the edge of the gardens.

SPRING WAKE-UP CALL

When the early-spring sun warms the soil, grass plants are among the first to green up and start growing. If you want the best-looking turf in town, try my lawn feeding program this year, and your grass will look better than it ever has! But first, rake up all leaves, sticks, and other debris. This allows more sunlight and warmth to get to the emerging grass plants.

Then give your lawn a shot of my Rise-'n'-Shine Clean-Up Tonic. It'll get it up off its grass and growing in the right direction.

Get Crabby with Crabgrass

One of the fastest-growing weeds on the planet, annual crabgrass, is larger and more coarse than any lawn grass, so it can ruin the looks of an otherwise lovely lawn. The best way to control crabgrass is to prevent the seeds from germinating in the spring. You can check with your local Cooperative Extension Service to get the best dates for applying a preemerge crabgrass control, but most folks just wait for forsythias or dogwoods to start blooming — nature's sign that soil temperatures are almost warm enough to promote the germination of crabgrass seeds. Before you apply any preemerge crabgrass control, wash down the turf with my Crabgrass Control Energizer Tonic.

Follow label directions when applying any type of crabgrass control. Many products are combined with fertilizers, so you can give your lawn its spring feeding and prevent crabgrass problems at the same time.

Timely Tonics

Rise-'n'-Shine Clean-Up Tonic

This Tonic will roust your yard out of its slumber in spring, nailing any wayward bugs and thugs that were overwintering in the comfortable confines of your lawn and garden.

1 cup of Murphy's Oil Soap
1 cup of Tobacco Tea (recipe on page 61)
1 cup of antiseptic mouthwash
¼ cup of hot sauce

Mix all of these ingredients in your 20 gallon hose-end sprayer, filling the balance of the sprayer jar with warm water. Apply to everything to the point of run-off.

Crabgrass Control Energizer Tonic

1 cup of baby shampoo
1 cup of hydrogen peroxide
2 tbsp. of instant tea granules

Mix all of these ingredients in your 20 gallon hose-end sprayer and saturate the turf to the point of run-off. The potent potion will jump-start the crabgrass control into action.

Instant Tea

Bust Up Thatch

Thatch is a buildup of decaying grass clippings, leaves, and other organic material that causes a "roof" effect over the soil that separates the crowns of grass plants from their roots. It prevents food, water, oxygen, and tonics from penetrating into the soil, and puts your lawn at risk of damage from pests, diseases, and drought. Use your fingers to see if there is a layer of thatch more than a quarter of an inch thick at the base of your lawn, and then take action. There are a number of things you can do to keep your yard thatch-free:

1. Wear golf shoes or aerating lawn sandals whenever you walk on your lawn. This will punch holes in the surface tension barrier between the soil and the grass blades.

2. Just before fertilizing your lawn in the spring and fall, when the weather is conducive to fast growth of your grass, mechanically remove thatch with a dethatching rake — a special tool with sharp tines that cut into thatch so you can rake it up and dump it into your compost pile. For large areas, you can rent a power rake to do the same job.

3. Apply my Thatch Buster Tonic once a month starting in spring, as soon as temperatures stay above 50°F.

4. Don't overfeed your lawn. Pushing your luck with fertilizers can cause thatch problems that wouldn't otherwise exist if the lawn were allowed to grow at a more reasonable rate.

Timely Tonic

Thatch Buster Tonic

1 cup of beer or regular cola (not diet)
½ cup of liquid dish soap
¼ cup of ammonia

Mix all of these ingredients in your 20 gallon hose-end sprayer. Fill the balance of the jar with water, and spray the entire turf area. Repeat once a month during the summer, when grass is actively growing.

Jerry's Fabulous Fertilizer Formulas

If you want to have the best lawn in the neighborhood, you need to feed it just right. Here's my 5-step, foolproof program for green grass magic:

Step 1 As soon as you catch a whiff of spring in the air, mix up a batch of my Spring Wake-Up Tonic (which is dry rather than wet; see page 110), and spread it over your lawn with your handheld broadcast spreader.

Step 2 As soon as you finish Step 1, give your lawn a soaking with my Get-Up-and-Grow Tonic (see page 110). These two steps get your lawn energized and ready to grow, but they don't really feed it, which brings us to Step 3.

Step 3 A week to 10 days after you've completed Steps 1 and 2, break out a bag of quality dry, controlled-release lawn food. Make sure it's packed with nitrogen, which means its analysis will have a high first number (like 20–5–10 or even 29–3–4). For each bag that's labeled to cover 2500 square feet, mix in 3 pounds of Epsom salts. Do some arithmetic in keeping with the application rate given on the label, and figure out how much you need to feed your lawn at half of the recommended rate. Measure it and spread it evenly, using a drop spreader or broadcast spreader, working in parallel lines that run from north to south across your lawn.

Step 4 Kick the fertilizer into high gear by soaking your lawn with my Lawn Snack Tonic (see page 110) no more than 2 days after you apply the dry fertilizer/Epsom salts mix. After a couple of sunny days, you'll start seeing gorgeous green right before your eyes.

Step 5 One week later, repeat Step 3, only this time work in an east to west direction as you apply the dry fertilizer/Epsom salts mixture. And, unless you're getting lots of late-spring rain at this point, follow up with another dose of Lawn Snack Tonic. Then stand back and prepare to be as impressed as all get-out.

Timely Tonics

Spring Wake-Up Tonic

Springtime is the right time to get your lawn off on the right root, and there's no better way to do it than to apply this mix as early as possible.

50 lbs. of pelletized lime
50 lbs. of pelletized gypsum

5 lbs. of bonemeal
2 lbs. of Epsom salts

Mix all of these ingredients in a wheelbarrow, and apply the mixture with your handheld broadcast spreader no more than 2 weeks before fertilizing. This will help aerate the lawn while giving it something to munch on until you start your regular feeding program.

Get-Up-and-Grow Tonic

To energize my dry Spring Wake-Up Tonic, overspray it with a mixture of the following.

1 cup of shampoo
1 cup of ammonia
1 cup of regular cola (not diet)
4 tbsp. of instant tea granules

Mix all of these ingredients in your 20 gallon hose-end sprayer, and apply to the point of run-off.

Lawn Snack Tonic

1 can of beer
1 cup of baby shampoo
½ cup of ammonia
1 tbsp. of corn syrup

Mix all of these ingredients in your 20 gallon hose-end sprayer. Fill the balance of the jar with water, and overspray your lawn to the point of run-off.

Recycling Roundup

Here's a little trick I learned a long time ago: Always keep an old, white golf ball in your 20 gallon hose-end lawn sprayer. It acts as an agitator while you're spraying, keeping the ingredients thoroughly mixed for an even application. And while you're at it, put an old red or orange golf ball into your weed sprayer; that way, you won't confuse the two.

Give It a Bath

No matter what type of fertilizer you choose to use, I want you to always hose down your lawn with a soap and water solution (1 cup of liquid dish soap in a 20 gallon hose-end sprayer) before *and* after you apply any type of fertilizer. This simple step does a number of things: It removes dust, dirt, and pollution from the grass blades; it helps the fertilizer adhere better, wherever it lands; it slows down soil compaction, improves penetration, and helps prevent burning your grass.

Two more things to remember: Sweep up any spilled fertilizer and dispose of it properly, and never apply dry fertilizer during a hot spell. It will burn your grass faster than you can say Smokey the Bear!

WATCH IT

As a rule of green thumb, always apply lawn fertilizer, either dry or liquid, before noon, preferably early in the morning. This gives your grass time to digest the food before the hot afternoon sun can burn it and give it an upset tummy. Be sure to water the area the day before, and then, after you apply the fertilizer, give the grass a light dousing with a soapy water solution.

Jerry Baker Says . . .

"Did you know that the more you use the right amount of fertilizer, the less you will need to mow your lawn? You'd think that a healthy lawn would grow so fast that you'd be out there all the time mowing. But the truth is that healthy, well-fed lawns need less mowing than uncared-for lawns — and they look a whole lot better!"

SMOOTH SUMMER SAILING

Summer lawn care is mostly maintenance — mowing, watering, and what I think is tremendously important — treating your lawn to a regular light shampoo. Regular applications of soapy tonics reduce the lawn's need for water, and help fertilizer and other controls work better. During the summer, apply my All-Season Green-Up Tonic every 3 weeks to keep your lawn lush and green, and ensure that every drop of water you provide goes deep into the soil, where it's needed most (see page 27). For added protection during hot, dry spells, overspray once a week with my Drought Buster Tonic. Your turf will sail through the heat with flying colors!

Jerry Baker Says . . .

"When it comes to using fertilizer, more is not better. Too much can burn your grass. The trick is to apply just the right amount of fertilizer at the right times to keep your lawn growing its best."

Timely Tonic

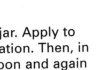

Drought Buster Tonic

1 can of beer
1 cup of Thatch Buster Tonic
½ cup of liquid lawn food
½ cup of baby shampoo

Mix all of these ingredients in a 20 gallon hose-end sprayer jar. Apply to the point of run-off early in the morning to minimize evaporation. Then, in addition to your normal watering, water for 10 minutes at noon and again at 4 P.M. for optimum results.

Mow to Grow

Like all other plants, grass grows mostly at night. So it's best (for you and your lawn) to mow in the late afternoon or early evening. That way, it's cooler for you, and your grass has ample opportunity to recover from the shock of mowing before facing another grueling day in the hot sun.

How often you mow depends on the weather and the grass growth rate — not on any set schedule. Most of the time, weekly mowing is about right, but when it's been very warm and rainy, you may need to mow more, and when it's very dry, you may need to mow less.

WATCH IT ⚠

Look Sharp

Dull mower blades make jagged, unclean cuts that leave grass at risk for developing disease or being damaged by the sun. The unhealthy grass can turn a sickish gray — or brown — and potentially die. So sharpen your blades, and your problems will be over. For best results, sharpen rotary-mower blades every 4 to 6 weeks, if you mow your lawn regularly. If you don't want to tackle the job yourself, have a pro do it.

Change Directions

It's easy to fall into the habit of mowing your lawn in the same pattern over and over again. And no wonder: It's usually easiest to zip straight across in one direction or another. But that kind of mowing can cause your turf to develop unsightly ridges. At least once a month, make it a point to mow in diagonal lines instead. You'll give your lawn a nice, smooth, even appearance.

How High or Low?

During the grass growing season, you should always follow my "one-third mowing rule," which simply means that you should set the height of your mower so that you never cut off more than one-third of the blade of grass at any one time. Set your mower blade to mow bluegrass, cool-season blends, and zoysia about 2 inches above the soil line. Tall fescue can go a little higher, to nearly 3 inches, while hybrid Bermuda grows best when kept clipped back to only 1 inch in height.

With all grasses, it's better to mow just a little high than to cut too low. Longish grass blades shade the soil, which conserves water and discourages weeds. On the other hand, scalping a lawn exposes bare spots, which will sprout up into weeds before you know it.

Timely Tonic

Grass Clipping Dissolving Tonic

If you don't pick up your grass clippings, give your lawn an inexpensive "facial" to help it breathe better. Spray it with this terrific Tonic twice a year.

1 can of beer
1 can of regular cola (not diet)
1 cup of ammonia
1 cup of liquid dish soap

Mix all of these ingredients in a bucket, and pour them into your 20 gallon hose-end sprayer. Apply to your yard to the point of run-off. This'll really speed up the decomposition process for any clippings that are left littering your lawn.

Grass Variety	Best Cutting Height	Mow When
Fine fescue	2"	3"
Kentucky bluegrass	2"	3"
Perennial ryegrass	2"	3"
Tall turf-type fescue	2"	3"
Zoysia	1 to 2"	1½ to 3"

The Ways of Water

When the weather is warm and it hasn't rained for more than a week, I guarantee that your lawn is starting to get thirsty. Clay soil will hold water longer than light-textured sandy loam, but because grass roots are most plentiful in the top 6 inches of soil, they naturally are the first plants to suffer when the dry weather comes. When you water your lawn, do it right by making sure the water goes deep, at least 8 inches below the surface.

You can't beat a sprinkler for watering your lawn, and I suggest buying a really good one that will serve you well for years. Some of the newer ones even move themselves along as they work, so you don't need to shift them from place to place by hand. Of course, if your lawn is one of the loves of your life, you may want to invest in an automatic sprinkler system. They're not that hard to install, and most home supply stores sell user-friendly kits that include everything you need, complete with instructions.

Jerry Baker Says . . .

"If you live in a part of the country that's constantly plagued by water shortages, do yourself (and your neighbors) a favor: Consider shrinking your lawn. See page 101 for easy — and painless — ways to do just that."

Good Morning Watering

Always water your lawn between 5 A.M. and 9 A.M. Watering at night only invites problems with pests and diseases. And watering in the hot afternoon is a waste, because the water evaporates before it has a chance to filter down to the grass roots.

Percolation Calculations

How long should you leave your sprinkler running? A lot of "ifs" are involved in the answer. Soil type, grass variety, and the seriousness of the drought are all parts of the equation. If you've shampooed your lawn recently, the residual soap will help water soak in better, but you're still going to have to get down on your knees and do some snooping around to make sure the water you give your lawn gets where it needs to go. Here are 3 things to check:

✔ **Sprinkler output.** To figure out how much water your sprinkler is putting out, place several low, straight-sided cans (like tuna or cat food cans) on your lawn. Turn your water on, wait 15 minutes, turn off the water, and see how much you've caught. Multiply that figure by 2 to find how much water your grass will get in 30 minutes. If it's a little over an inch, you're right on target.

✔ **Absorption rate.** How long does your sprinkler run before you start seeing water puddle up on the soil's surface? Clay soil needs time to soak up water, so you may need to adjust your watering habits so that you water one spot for 15 minutes, let it have a 15-minute soak-in break, and then turn the water back on again.

✔ **Complete coverage.** As water percolates through the soil, it moves both downward and sideways. Still, it's a good idea to check for big dry spots that your sprinkler may be missing.

Timely Tonic

Lawn Freshener Tonic

A good way to determine whether it's time to water is by walking on the grass. If it doesn't spring back to life, it's definitely thirsty. To help it along, strap on your aerating lawn sandals or golf shoes and take a stroll around your yard. Then follow up with this Tonic.

1 can of beer
1 cup of baby shampoo
½ cup of ammonia
½ cup of weak tea

Mix all of these ingredients in your 20 gallon hose-end sprayer and apply to the point of run-off.

Working with Problem Areas

Serious lawn problems can usually be traced to fundamental flaws, including too much shade, poor drainage, or starvation — in the case of grass that has not been given enough to eat. Sometimes dead patches and spots appear when you least expect them and weather conditions give rise to mysterious diseases. At the first sign of trouble, nip it in the bud by spot-treating suspicious patches with my Lawn Fungus Fighter Tonic.

WINDING DOWN FOR FALL

As another growing season comes to an end, it's time to prepare your lawn for its long winter nap. Fall is a crucial time to fertilize your lawn, but this time around, look for an organic or granular "winterizer" fertilizer that has a balance of nitrogen and phosphorus (a high middle number, at least as high as the first one in the fertilizer analysis). For best results, use that fertilizer as part of my Fall Lawn Food Mix.

Lawn Fungus Fighter Tonic

If your lawn develops brown or yellow patches that eventually die out, fight back with this fix-it formula.

1 tbsp. of baking soda
1 tbsp. of instant tea granules
1 tbsp. of horticultural or dormant oil
1 gal. of warm water

Mix all of these ingredients together in a large bucket, then apply with a handheld sprayer by lightly spraying the turf. Do not drench or apply to the point of run-off. Repeat in 2 to 3 weeks, if necessary.

Fall Lawn Food Mix

1 50 lb. or 2500 sq. ft. bag of lawn food
3 lbs. of Epsom salts
1 cup of dry laundry soap

Mix these ingredients together, and apply at half of the recommended rate with your handheld broadcast spreader or drop spreader. After you apply this mix, I want you to again overspray the turf with my Lawn Snack Tonic (see page 110), which will energize the dry food and give your lawn something to munch on as it heads into the long, cold winter.

The Need to Reseed

When the soil cools down in the fall, it's the ideal time to buck up cool-season lawns with a fresh supply of seed. About 6 weeks before the first frost is expected is the best time to seed or reseed with Kentucky bluegrass, perennial (not annual) ryegrass, tall fescue, or a blend or mixture of different species. Late-summer/early-fall planting gives these grasses time to germinate and mature enough to survive the freezing temperatures of winter. Make sure that you soak the seed in my Grass Seed Starter Tonic before you sow it.

Follow the seeding rates recommended on the bag if you are planting a new lawn area from seed. If your lawn is thin and you want to increase its thickness, you can overseed an existing lawn at half of the recommended rate. Before overseeding, mow your lawn very low, and then rake it vigorously to expose bare soil. Grass seed needs to be in firm contact with soil if it is to germinate properly. After seeding, cover the whole area with a light layer of organic mulch, like straw.

Recycling Roundup

Time to reseed your lawn, and you've got no spreader? No need to fret — just punch holes in the bottom of a coffee can. Then pour your grass seed inside, put on the plastic lid, and walk your yard, shaking as you go. (This method works just as well with fertilizer, or with any of my dry tonic mixes.)

Timely Tonics

Grass Seed Starter Tonic

This nifty Tonic will guarantee almost 100% grass seed germination every time.

¼ cup of baby shampoo
1 tbsp. of Epsom salts
1 gal. of weak tea

Mix these ingredients in a large container. Drop in your grass seed and put the whole shebang into your refrigerator for 2 days. The shampoo softens the seed shells, and the Epsom salts and tea provide nourishment to the emerging plants. The chill makes the seeds think that it's winter, so when they wake (warm) up, they'll be rarin' to grow.

Weed Killer Prep Tonic

To really zing a lot of weeds in a large area, overspray them first with a mix of the following.

1 cup of liquid dish soap
1 cup of ammonia
4 tbsp. of instant tea granules

Mix all of these ingredients in your 20 gallon hose-end sprayer, filling the balance of the sprayer jar with warm water.

Recycling Roundup

Even nice-looking grass is a weed when it's growing where you don't want it. To cut small sections of unwelcome sod out of your yard — like flower beds — use a dull, old, and very sturdy carving knife, slicing as you go.

Worrisome Weeds

I've already explained that the best way to control crabgrass is to keep it from germinating in the first place; but other weeds, including America's No. 1 Least Wanted Weed, the dandelion, often sneak into struggling lawns. If there are only a few of them, go after them by hand by prying them out, roots and all, just before you feed your lawn in the fall. Runaway weed problems call for the use of a broadleaf weed killer labeled for use on your type of grass. Be sure to follow label directions exactly, and prepare your lawn for weed treatment by first wetting it down well with my Weed Killer Prep Tonic.

COPING WITH SHADE

Look around and find the shady "characters" hanging around your yard. I'm referring to the house, garage, shed, trees, fences, and anything else that creates shade. "Made in the shade" sounds good, but when it comes to lawns, inadequate sunlight causes more harm than good. Without a minimum of 4 hours of sunlight a day, the rate of grass growth slows and a lawn thins and weakens. It becomes vulnerable to nasty diseases and insects, and moss may develop.

Let the Sun Shine In

To chase away at least some of your shade, bring out the clippers. Cut off all low-growing foliage and prune tree branches so more sunlight can reach ground level. With a little effort (or a call to a good arborist), you can brighten up the scene considerably.

Shade-Tolerant Grasses

These rugged customers thrive in less light than most other grasses.

Warm-season
Bahia grass
Centipede grass
St. Augustine grass

Cool-season
Fine fescues
Tall fescue

PROBLEM and SOLUTION

Problem: Moss that just won't seem to go away.

Solution: Moss thrives in shady spots with acidic soil, while grass likes neutral to slightly alkaline soil. To grow a good crop of grass in moss-pleasing territory, you need to change the soil's pH; otherwise, not even a shade-tolerant grass will grow. Get rid of your moss by spraying it with a good dose of my Moss Buster Tonic, then go to work on that pH. (See Chapter 1 for tips on making your soil sweeter.)

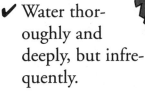

Timely Tonic

Moss Buster Tonic

This powerful stuff will get moss and mold out of your lawn in a hurry.

1 cup of antiseptic mouthwash
1 cup of chamomile tea
1 cup of Murphy's Oil Soap

Mix these ingredients in your 20 gallon hose-end sprayer, and apply to the point of run-off every 2 weeks until the moss is history. For quick results, add 3 ounces of copper sulfate to 5 gallons of water and spray on the moss.

Shade-Fighting Tips

Most turf grasses prefer sunlight to shade. If you're installing a new lawn or renovating an old one on a shady site, use one of the grass types recommended on page 120. Beyond careful seed selection, there are several things you can do to help grass thrive in less-than-ideal light conditions — whether your lawn is old or new:

✔ Mow at higher levels than you do in sunny parts of the yard.

✔ Water only in the morning.

✔ Water thoroughly and deeply, but infrequently.

✔ Make sure that the grass dries out before you water it again.

✔ Go easy on the fertilizer; more is not better!

✔ Discourage foot traffic in shady parts of the lawn.

✔ Take it easy when you rake.

GREAT GROUND COVERS

If you have a place in your yard where grass won't grow or it's difficult to mow, but you still want the ground to be carpeted in green, you need a ground cover. I think of ground covers as any plants that stay low, knit together into a solid mass that crowds out weeds, and come back year after year. Ground covers are the perfect plants for blanketing the ground underneath trees, flanking walkways, or for use as a lawn substitute in areas where a well-groomed look is important.

Ground Covers in Containers

When you need a little something to drip over the edges of large containers or window boxes, consider a few sprigs of periwinkle or ivy. Variegated strains are especially useful, and you can put them to work in cut arrangements, too.

There are two challenges to working with ground covers — finding the right plants for the site, and getting them nicely established. With the first hurdle, it's pretty easy to figure out if the site is mostly sun or shade, but soil quality and drainage are important, too. Some ground covers, like creeping juniper, soapwort, and sedum, are happy in lean, gritty soils, while pachysandra, candytuft, and lamium need fertile, well-worked soil if they are to fill in well. Dig around in the site you're considering for ground covers before you make a final plan. If all you find are isolated pockets for planting, you will do best with a shallow-rooted wanderer like ivy or periwinkle.

Patience Pays Off

If you prepare the soil and set out ground covers with the same care that you give to other perennial plants, you can expect them to form a solid mass in 2 to 3 years. Make sure that you give them a good healthy dose of my Ground Cover Starter Mix when you set them out.

Meanwhile, you will need to keep the open spaces between plants weeded, which can be a thankless, repetitive task. There are now granular herbicides specially made to be used with young ground cover plantings, but be sure to read the label carefully before you buy to make sure the product is labeled for use on the species you are growing.

Mulching between plants when you set them out will make weeding less laborious, and ample moisture and fertilizer will help speed things along so that the plants will cover the open space *before* weeds can get a foothold. Use an organic or controlled-release fertilizer when setting out new ground cover plants, and follow up 6 weeks later with my All-Season Green-Up Tonic (recipe on page 27).

(recipe on page 27).

Jerry Baker Says . . .

"Slugs can be real nuisances in shady spots. But don't let the slimeballs get you down — just sink some cat food cans into the ground and fill 'em with Slugweiser. The neighborhood slugs will belly up to the bar and fall right in. (See Chapter 14 for more tips on keeping these slithery slobs from feasting on your ground cover plants.)"

Timely Tonic

Slugweiser

No matter how bad your slug problems are, this brew will make them a thing of the past.

1 lb. of brown sugar
½ package (1½ tsp.) of dry yeast

Pour these ingredients into a 1 gallon jug, fill it with warm water, and let it sit for 2 days, uncovered. Pour it into slug traps, and watch the culprits drink to their just reward!

Foliage or Flowers?

When choosing ground covers to frame a lawn or entryway, by all means go with an evergreen. It's essential that these front-and-center places look good year-round, and many flowering ground covers disappear completely in the winter.

If you want to blanket a gentle slope with petite bloomers or broad ribbons of color, check out my list of flowering ground covers. When planting in bands, stick with one species, or you can mix several together in larger spaces so that they form a tapestry of color and texture. For example, creeping phlox, which is available in many shades of pink and blue, blends well with white candytuft and yellow sedum to make an excellent trio for sunny banks.

A common use for ground covers is to fill in shady spots — a job that ajuga, ivy, liriope, and periwinkle do very well. To give them a strong start, plant before nearby trees leaf out. In later years, you'll see how these plants wisely make much of their new growth before their sun supply gradually disappears in early summer.

Spring Clean-Up

On one of the first late-winter days when you can smell the coming of spring in the air, take a little time to clean up your ground covers. Just set your mower at its highest cutting height and zip through the planting area. Then rake up trimmings, pulling weeds as you go, and dump it all onto your compost pile. Next, feed your ground cover with an organic or controlled-release fertilizer applied according to label directions. Finally, wash everything down with my All-Season Clean-Up Tonic (see page 60). By the time spring truly arrives, your ground cover should show exuberant new growth, with hardly a weed in sight!

Light Up the Darkness

A dark green ground cover of English ivy need not stand alone. In summer, plug in a few white impatiens for a starry effect. Small clusters of miniature daffodils are easily naturalized in ivy beds, too.

Jerry's TOP TEN

Evergreen Ground Covers

I'm using the word evergreen a little loosely here, because none of these ground covers are at their best in the winter. Ivy, juniper, and periwinkle do a good job of keeping their good looks year-round, but several of the others look pretty ragged once winter starts to rage. Still, they'll hang in with you well into the fall, and make a grand entrance first thing in spring.

- **Creeping juniper** *(Juniperus horizontalis)*; full sun to partial shade, Zones 3 to 9

- **Ferns** (numerous species, both evergreen and deciduous); partial shade, Zones 3 to 9

- **Ivy** *(Hedera* species); partial shade, Zones 3 to 10

- **Lamb's ears** *(Stachys byzantina)*; full sun to partial shade, Zones 4 to 8

- **Liriope** *(Liriope muscari)*; partial shade, Zones 5 to 10

- **Mondo grass** *(Ophiopogon japonicus)*; partial shade, Zones 5 to 10

- **Pachysandra** *(Pachysandra terminalis)*; part to full shade, Zones 5 to 9

- **Periwinkle** *(Vinca minor)*; part to full shade, Zones 4 to 7

- **Soapwort** *(Saponaria ocymoides)*; semi-evergreen, full sun, Zones 3 to 8

- **Wintercreeper** *(Euonymus fortunei)*; partial shade, Zones 6 to 8

Jerry's TOP TEN

Flowering Ground Covers

What's not to love about a rippling carpet of ankle-deep color? Most of these ground covers bloom in the spring, but their foliage will stay with you much longer, usually well into the fall. They are ideal for steep banks and tight corners where you don't want to mow.

- **Ajuga** *(Ajuga reptans)*; partial shade, Zones 3 to 9*

- **Candytuft** *(Iberis sempervirens)*; full sun, Zones 4 to 8*

- **Cranesbill** *(Geranium* species and cultivars)*; partial shade, Zones 3 to 8

- **Creeping thyme** *(Thymus praecox)*; full sun, Zones 3 to 8

- **Creeping phlox** *(Phlox subulata)*; partial shade, Zones 2 to 8*

- **Dianthus** *(Dianthus gratianopolitanus* 'Bath's Pink')*; full sun, Zones 4 to 9*

- **Epimedium** *(Epimedium grandiflorum)*; partial shade, Zones 3 to 8*

- **Golden star** *(Chrysogonum virginiannum)*; partial shade, Zones 5 to 9*

- **Lamium** *(Lamium maculatum)*; partial shade, Zones 3 to 8

- **Sedum** *(Sedum acre)*; full sun, Zones 4 to 9*

*Evergreen in most parts of Zones 7 and higher

TROUBLESHOOTING LAWNS AND GROUND COVERS

Grass Root Robbers

Problem: Since May, I've been finding brown patches in my lawn. They have no predictable shape, and when I pull on the grass, it comes right up, as if the roots are just about gone. Things seem to be getting better, but could there be some kind of disease waiting to make a comeback? H.C., Zone 5

Solution: I want you to carefully dig out a few 3-inch-wide plugs, crumble the soil in your hands, and see if little white grubs fall out. These are larvae of beetles, such as June beetles and Japanese beetles, and they eat the roots off your grass! As soon as you can, inoculate your lawn with Milky Spore, a safe and natural blend of bacteria that will gradually kill future generations of grubs. Meanwhile, you can zap the grubs you have with any soil insecticide that includes Merit (imidacloprid), a soil pesticide that is harmless to birds and other wildlife but lethal to grubs. Be sure to follow label directions exactly.

Gray Grass

Problem: My bluegrass lawn looks great in the summer, but in early spring, I see a lot of gray patches that I think are caused by snow mold. Can this be prevented, or is there a quick cure? D.L., Zone 4

Solution: Don't leave your grass too high in the fall, and rake up the moldy patches as soon as you can in the spring. Given good care and feeding, those spots should fill in nicely by early summer. Because the fungus that causes snow mold becomes inactive in warm weather, there's not much point in treating your lawn with a fungicide. If you ever decide to overseed the damaged areas, look for one of the newer bluegrass varieties, such as 'Park', that are resistant to snow mold.

Mountains of Molehills

Problem: The moles in my yard are so bad that I'm even seeing them in my dreams. What can I do to keep them from tunneling through my lawn and garden? N.L., Zone 7

Solution: First, I want you to take away the buffet of grubs your moles are enjoying. Once you control those grubs (see page 127), you can get after those moles. The remedy I like to try first is a castor oil tonic (see Move On, Moles

Timely Tonic

Move On, Moles Tonic

Mix up a batch of this timely Tonic to rid your lawn of moles.

1 cup of liquid dish soap
1 cup of castor oil
2 tbsp. of alum (dissolved in hot water)

Mix these ingredients in your 20 gallon hose-end sprayer, and saturate any problem areas.

Recycling Roundup

Here's a fun way to keep pesky moles away from your lawn: Push plastic toy pinwheels into the ground at regular intervals. The whooshing sound they make will send the moles packing — and the neighborhood kids'll get a kick out of watching the pinwheels spin around.

Tonic above). But let me tell you, mixing castor oil and liquid soap is so messy that I think you'll prefer using my prepackaged Liquid Mole Repellent as your first defense against moles in your lawn. When moles show up elsewhere, sabotage their runs by lacing them with all sorts of smelly things, including squirts of pine cleaner, slightly smashed garlic cloves, mothballs, and half pieces of Juicy Fruit gum. Last, but not least, are Moley Smoke Bombs, which'll stink 'em out. In any event, keep pressing down the runs that get used over and over.

Dandelion Despair

Problem: Every time I think I've got my lawn just right, new dandelion seedlings show up. I know the seeds are coming from my neighbors' lawns, but they don't seem to get the hints I drop that it would be nice to have fewer dandelions in the neighborhood. E.H., Zone 5

Solution: Congratulations on your lawn, and condolences for your neighbors! Since you have but a few dandelions, I suggest that you get a good weed puller and go after them by hand. (Catalogs and garden centers sell tools made especially for routing out dandelions.) Be especially attentive in the fall, because a lot of seedlings get started then, even though they don't flower until the next year. Now, if more than 20 percent of your lawn is contaminated with dandelions, you'll need chemical help to get them under control. In late spring, when they are up and growing but not yet fully mature, apply a good broadleaf weed killer according to label directions. To increase its effectiveness, first overspray your lawn with my Weed Killer Prep Tonic (see page 119).

Jerry Baker Says . . .

"Young dandelion leaves are some of the tastiest greens you can find. So do what Grandma Putt did: Dig 'em up by the roots, clip off the leaves, and turn your lawn headache into a delicious, fresh garden salad! And here's a bonus: My herbalist friends tell me that the ingredients in dandelion leaves actually help you digest food better. (Be sure to use only dandelions from unsprayed lawns.)"

Browned-Out Ivy

Problem: Last winter, the utility company had to replace the meter by the side of my house, which required extensive digging in my flower bed. The English ivy that grew there seems to be dying now, though some of the stems are still green. Should I pull it all down, or just prune out the dead parts? F.O., Zone 7

Solution: By all means, prune out the dead stems, which besides looking bad may host diseases. And to stimulate new growth on the ivy left behind, snip off the growing tips on the most robust stems. This will push the plants to branch a little more energetically, so you should have plenty of lush, green ivy before you know it!

Fairy Rings

Problem: I always get a lot of mushrooms in my lawn, even when I cut back on watering. Often they are in arches and circles, and a few days after a rain, they seem to appear like magic. Where do they come from, and what can I do? G.T., Zone 6

Solution: Like all mushrooms, the ones that form circular fairy rings grow from threadlike mycelium, which is often anchored to buried, rotten roots and other tree parts a foot or so below the surface. I want you to start collecting your mushrooms by hand rather than running over them with your mower, because the mature mushrooms produce spores that start off your next generation. Each time you gather up a flush of mushrooms and put them into the garbage, set the next crop back with my Fairy Ring Fighter Tonic.

Spring Cleaning

Problem: I live up North, where winters get pretty tough. I must admit that the snow is awfully pretty when it's fresh and sparkling white. But come spring, when the snow melts away, my lawn looks so gray and dirty and gritty that I just want to cry! Is there any way to perk it up? I.R., Zone 5

Solution: There sure is! Dust, dirt, and pollution accumulate like crazy over the winter, causing your lawn to look like a heck of a wreck. But don't worry, relief is at hand: As early as possible in the spring, get out your handheld broadcast spreader and give your lawn a big helping of my Pollution Solution Tonic. Follow this up with my 5-step lawn care program (see page 109), and soon you and your lawn will be rollin' in the green.

Timely Tonics

Fairy Ring Fighter Tonic

1 cup of baby shampoo
1 cup of antiseptic mouthwash
1 cup of ammonia

First, sprinkle dry laundry soap over the problem area. Then mix all of these ingredients in your 20 gallon hose-end sprayer, and overspray the area to the point of run-off.

Pollution Solution Tonic

50 lbs. of pelletized lime
50 lbs. of pelletized gypsum
5 lbs. of Epsom salts

Using a handheld broadcast spreader, apply this mix over 2500 square feet of lawn area. Then wait at least 2 weeks before applying any fertilizer to give the mix a chance to go to work.

CHAPTER 8

Amazing Annuals

A nnuals are my all-time favorite fun flowers in any yard. Give them a decent home, and these fast-growing, single-season wonders will bloom their heads off. You can feature them in a front yard bed, grow them around your mailbox, or use them to edge your shrub beds. And I always grow some annuals in containers so that I can move them around wherever I want a splash of bright color. You can let annuals linger in window boxes, too, and even mix them in with your vegetables and herbs, where they help attract buzzing bees and other beneficial insects. Talk about *amazing!*

ANNUALS IN SEASON

Most of us think of annuals as summer flowers, but a few, like pansies and annual dianthus, are so tolerant of cold weather that they can be planted in fall for bloom the next spring in many areas. Others, like snapdragons and larkspur, really like cool weather, so you can get them out and growing first thing in spring. There are also annuals built to withstand scorching weather. You can use portulaca, zinnias, and other warm-natured annuals to replace cool-season annuals that often wear themselves out just as summer gets into full swing.

Six Ways to Play It Safe with Color

Because annuals make such a strong color statement, you may feel shy about using them in your yard. But guess what? Even imperfect matches often look great, and there are so many combinations to try that you'll never run short of second chances! Here are half a dozen color-savvy tips.

1. Pair bright reds or oranges with white or soft blue flowers, such as red zinnias with blue ageratum, or orange cosmos with white nierembergia. When you give a vivid flower a quiet companion, the result is an eye-popping burst of blooms that also looks clean and well defined.

2. Accent soft pinks or other light colors in places with dark backgrounds, such as near evergreen shrubs or a dark wall or a fence. The contrast will make every blossom light up like magic.

3. Go bold in places that are seen from a distance. Rich red salvias, orange marigolds, or deep pink petunias always attract attention.

4. In big beds where you want to set out lots of plants of a single species, use a mixture of colors. For example, a flowing bed of yellow, white, orange, and red portulaca would look great in sun, or you could use a multicolored mixture of impatiens in a shadier spot.

5. Celebrate small differences in hue by planting different flowers that bloom in slightly different colors. Pinks and blues usually work well together, and yellows and oranges make a natural partnership.

6. Neutral colors, including white, soft yellow, and gray (as in dusty miller), help tie unlike colors together and cool down potential clashes. If you're not sure that a combination will work, plant insurance in the form of neutrals.

Jerry Baker Says . . .

"If you work all day and get to enjoy your yard mostly at night, plant plenty of white flowers — unlike other colors, they hold their star power well into the evening."

Planting Annuals the No-Fail Way

All annuals are fast-growing plants that are eager to get going, whether you plant them from seed or set out bedding plants. Thumb back to Chapter 2 for the basics of seed starting and handling transplants, and do a good job of preparing a fertile, well-drained bed for any annual flower. Whatever you do, don't let bedding plants dry out while they are waiting to be planted.

WATCH IT !

Don't Overfeed

Annual flowers need a balanced diet, but lots of nitrogen (like in lawn foods) can make them superleafy with a sparse show of flowers. Use my Flower Soil Prep Mix when planting, and stick with light liquid feedings of my Flower Power Tonic through the growing season.

Clip Away

Whenever I get ready to set out annual transplants, I tuck a small pair of scissors into my pocket. Then, after I put each plant into its hole, I clip off any blossoms it has. This lightens the burden for the little plants and gives them no choice but to get busy growing new stems and buds. Still, be patient with newly planted annuals, and don't expect overnight results. It usually takes them 3 weeks or so to adjust to life in your garden and start churning out new growth. Once annual plants get nicely rooted, though, there'll be no holding them back when it comes to exuberant blooming!

Timely Tonics

Flower Soil Prep Mix

Here is a great flower planting mixture that'll really energize the soil and produce big, bright, beautiful blooms.

4 cups of bonemeal
2 cups of gypsum
2 cups of Epsom salts
1 cup of wood ashes
1 cup of lime
4 tbsp. of medicated baby powder
1 tbsp. of baking powder

Combine all of these ingredients in a bucket and work the mixture into the soil at planting time.

Flower Power Tonic

1 cup of beer
2 tbsp. of fish fertilizer
2 tbsp. of liquid dish soap
2 tbsp. of ammonia
2 tbsp. of whiskey
1 tbsp. of corn syrup
1 tbsp. of instant tea granules

Mix all of these ingredients with 2 gallons of warm water in a watering can. Drench your annuals every 3 weeks during the growing season to keep them blooming all summer long.

Welcome Volunteers

Some of my favorite annuals shed lots of seeds, which get moved around by the wind, birds, and bugs. Memorize how these seedlings look, and you'll probably find plenty of volunteers that are willing to be dug and moved to where you want them to grow. Here are the most dependable reseeders, and when you can expect them to appear.

- **Bachelor button** — late winter to early spring
- **Celosia** — late spring to early summer
- **Cleome** — early spring to early summer
- **Cosmos** — early spring to early summer
- **Impatiens** — early summer
- **Melampodium** — early summer
- **Portulaca** — late spring to early summer
- **Sunflower** — mid to late spring
- **Zinnia** — late spring to early summer

Beat the Heat

Keep your container plants happy through the long, hot summer by setting up this simple automatic watering system. Here's all you need to do: Before you pot up each plant, run one end of a piece of cord or rope through the drainage hole and into the pot, leaving a long piece outside. Then fill a milk jug with water and set the other end of the cord into it. After that, all you need to do is keep the jug filled with water. This is an especially great trouble-saver if you're planning a summer vacation and won't be around to tend your plants!

After the Frost

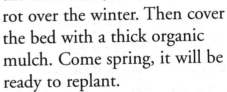

When cold weather turns your summer annuals to mush, pull them up and throw them onto your compost pile. Then dig and turn the bed, working in the old mulch; it will rot over the winter. Then cover the bed with a thick organic mulch. Come spring, it will be ready to replant.

Also pull plants out of containers. Toss the potting soil onto an outdoor bed, and move the pots to a dry place; if they get wet, they may freeze and crack.

Jerry's TOP TEN

Annuals for Edging

Want to trim a bed with a collar of colorful lace? Annuals that stay naturally neat and low do a great job, and they're not hard to grow.

- **Ageratum** *(Ageratum houstonianum)*; bedding plants, full sun to partial shade
- **Annual phlox** *(Phlox drummondii)*; bedding plants, full sun to partial shade
- **Annual verbena** (*Verbena* hybrids); bedding plants or seed, full sun
- **Dusty miller** *(Senecio cineraria)*; bedding plants, full sun to partial shade
- **Impatiens** *(Impatiens walleriana)*; bedding plants, partial shade
- **Lobelia** *(Lobelia erinus)*; bedding plants, full sun to partial shade
- **Nasturtium** *(Tropaeolum majus)*; easy from seed, full sun
- **Nierembergia** *(Nierembergia hippomanica)*; bedding plants, full sun
- **Sweet alyssum** *(Lobularia maritima)*; bedding plants or seed, full sun to partial shade
- **Wax begonia** *(Begonia semperflorens)*; bedding plants, full sun to partial shade

Drought-Tolerant Annuals

You'll need to supply water at first to get even drought-tolerant annuals established, but once they are well rooted, these flowers are naturals at water conservation.

- **Angelonia** *(Angelonia angustifolia)*; bedding plants, full sun
- **Cosmos** *(Cosmos bipinnatus, C. sulfureus)*; easy from seed, full sun
- **French marigold** *(Tagetes patula)*; easy from seed, full sun
- **Gomphrena** *(Gomphrena globosa, G. haageana)*; bedding plants or seed, full sun
- **Lantana** *(Lantana camara)*; bedding plants, full sun
- **Melampodium** *(Melampodium paludosum)*; easy from seed, full sun
- **Portulaca** *(Portulaca grandiflora)*; bedding plants or seed, full sun
- **Snow-on-the-mountain** *(Euphorbia marginata)*; easy from seed, full sun
- **Vinca** *(Catharanthus roseus)*; bedding plants, full sun
- **Zinnia** (*Zinnia* species and hybrids); bedding plants or seed, full sun

Jerry's TOP TEN

Easy Annuals

These annuals are so easy because you can buy most of them as bedding plants. Given just a little attention, they're as close as flowers come to being indestructible.

- **Coleus** *(Solenostemon scutellarioides)*; bedding plants, partial shade
- **Geranium** *(Pelargonium* hybrids*)*; bedding plants, full sun to partial shade
- **Impatiens** *(Impatiens walleriana)*; bedding plants, partial shade
- **Marigold** *(Tagetes* species and hybrids*)*; bedding plants or seed, full sun
- **Pansy** *(Viola* hybrids*)*; bedding plants, full sun to partial shade
- **Petunia** *(Petunia* hybrids*)*; bedding plants, full sun to partial shade
- **Salvia** *(Salvia splendens, S. coccinea)*; bedding plants, full sun to partial shade
- **Sunflower** *(Helianthus annuus)*; easy from seed, full sun
- **Wax begonia** *(Begonia semperflorens)*; bedding plants, full sun to partial shade
- **Zinnia** *(Zinnia* species and hybrids*)*; bedding plants or seed, full sun

Annuals for Containers

These newcomers have been specially developed to grow in pots and baskets. And they look lovely!

- **Angelonia** *(Angelonia angustifolia)*; bedding plants, full sun
- **Fan flower** *(Scaevola aemula)*; bedding plants, full sun to partial shade
- **Fuchsia** *(Fuchsia* hybrids*)*; bedding plants, shade
- **Geranium** *(Pelargonium* hybrids*)*; bedding plants, full sun to partial shade
- **Impatiens** *(Impatiens walleriana)*; bedding plants, partial shade
- **Lobelia** *(Lobelia erinus)*; bedding plants, full sun to partial shade
- **Petunia** *(Petunia* hybrids*)*; bedding plants, full sun to partial shade
- **Sanvitalia** *(Sanvitalia procumbens)*; bedding plants or seed, full sun to partial shade
- **Sweet alyssum** *(Lobularia maritima)*; bedding plants or seed, full sun to partial shade
- **Tuberous begonia** *(Begonia tuberhybrida)*; grown from corms, shade

Make Mine Chilly

Pansies top the list of cold-resistant annuals. They're hardy and available in early spring in much of the country — even ready for late-fall planting in the mildest climates. If you haven't grown pansies for several years, take a look at the newest hybrids. They have larger flowers and more of them in clear pastels or rich, dark colors. Pansies come in single colors, with blotched and even tri-colored faces.

They'll Make an Entrance

Impress your guests with brightly colored posies planted in pots around your front door. No need to spend money on containers — just look around your garage, attic, and kitchen, and you'll find some great ones. (Whatever containers you use, though, be sure to poke drainage holes in the bottom before you tuck in your plants.) Here are some of my favorite home, sweet homes for annuals:

✔ Buckets

✔ Big cans — labels and all

✔ Sprinkling cans

✔ Wheelbarrows

✔ Wagons

✔ Soup kettles

LANDSCAPE LINGO

Cold-resistant is a term used to describe the first annuals you can plant in the spring and those that will survive the nippy days of autumn. These annuals are also used for winter plantings along the Pacific Coast and in the Gulf states. For example, sweet peas, canary creeper, nicotiana, and cleome all come into their own when temperatures dip.

TROUBLESHOOTING ANNUALS

Annual flowers that get fed and watered regularly usually don't have many problems, but sometimes unexpected things happen and you'll have to take action. Do I need to remind you that annuals don't last forever? Sometimes they bloom so long and so hard that they melt away from exhaustion — which is your opportunity to mobilize and plant more annuals!

Mildewed Sunflowers

Problem: A few days ago, I noticed some white spots on the lowest leaves of my sunflowers, and now there are similar patches on my zinnias, too. What is this problem, and how serious is it? B.C., Zone 7

Solution: When powdery mildew shows up on annuals, it's mostly a problem affecting only the plants' appearance. It's usually a sign of old age, too, because annual flowers don't usually get mildew until they are worn out from blooming. Your sunflowers should bloom beautifully anyway, but you might want to go ahead and replace your zinnias with pansies or another cool-season flower that will carry you into fall. Meanwhile, there are several other annuals that might start having mildew problems, including ageratum, petunia, and verbena. Before problems have a chance to start, give your plants a good drench with my Baking Soda Spray (see page 85).

Gloomy Geraniums

Problem: What are the little wedge-shaped bugs that I'm finding on the stems and buds of my geraniums, and, more important, how do I get rid of them? C.I., Zone 4

Solution: Your flowers probably have aphids, and when you have one, you have a whole bunch! A soap spray laced with garlic or orange peels runs them off, but it will work best if you first wash down the plants with a strong spray of water. Since you probably don't want your geraniums to smell like garlic, I recommend using the Rose Aphid Antidote recipe on page 97. If you have nasturtiums or verbena in your flower beds, check them for aphids, too.

Sluggish Petunias

Problem: I thought begonias and petunias were bombproof, but mine are having trouble with slugs. Every night, there are new holes chewed in the leaves. What's the best way to get rid of them? K.N., Zone 6

Solution: It all depends on the size of the slugs! If they are big ones, you can capture most of them in traps baited with my Slugweiser (see page 123). The simplest traps to make are shallow margarine tubs, half buried in soil and mulch, so that only about ½ inch of the rim is above the surface. Slugs dive in for a drink and drown. You will need to dump out the traps and refill them every few days. Tiny slugs that aren't so easy to trap can be brought under control by spraying the affected plants on a weekly basis with my Super Slug Spray.

Timely Tonic

Super Slug Spray

1½ cups of ammonia
1 tbsp. of Murphy's Oil Soap
1½ cups of water

Mix these ingredients in a handheld mist sprayer bottle, and overspray any areas where you see signs of slug activity.

Lazy Alyssum

Problem: Earlier this summer, the sweet alyssum I planted alongside my front walkway looked great. When it started looking raggedy, I cut it back a little and fertilized it, but that was three weeks ago and it's still not blooming. I thought maybe I had overfed them, but I have some French marigolds that aren't blooming, either, and I haven't fertilized them since I planted them. Any suggestions? M.A., Zone 8

Solution: Your plants are a little smarter than you think! Instead of blooming themselves silly in the heat of summer, they're saving themselves for early fall, when nights are cooler. This process is called heat check, and lobelia sometimes does it, too. The solution is to just be patient. You'll be knee-deep in flowers again in no time.

Suffering Salvias

Problem: Until a few weeks ago, I was having fantastic luck with a bed of red salvia I planted around my birdbath. The plants still look nice, but every time I touch them, numerous little white gnats come flying out. What are these creatures? Will they kill my salvia? R.G., Zone 6

Solution: You have whiteflies, which just love salvia. Here's the sure cure: Spray your plants with my Plant Shampoo. About an hour later, when the leaves are dry, give them a good drench with my Whitefly Wipeout Tonic. Repeat the application after a week to control any new whiteflies that hatch from hidden eggs.

Timely Tonic

Whitefly Wipeout Tonic

1 cup of sour milk (let it stand out for 2 days)
2 tbsp. of flour
1 qt. of warm water

Mix all of these ingredients in a bowl and spray the mixture over any plants that are troubled by whiteflies.

Impatiens Impasse

Problem: A few weeks ago, I planted a dozen impatiens in a shady bed in my front yard. Two of the plants appear to be on the verge of dying. Even when I water them, they look droopy and the stems look blackish near the base. I'm afraid the problem will spread to the other plants. What should I do? L.S., Zone 8

Solution: It sounds like your plants are suffering from stem rot, which is what happens when plants get bruised before or during transplanting. Fungi from the soil enter the plants through breaks in the stems and roots, causing them to rot. Plants grown in shade or poorly drained soil are at high risk, but dusty miller and pansies can fall victim to this problem even when grown in sun. Pull out the affected impatiens, and stir some good compost into the soil before plugging in replacement plants.

Confounded Celosias

Problem: Several of my annual flowers have leaves that look yellowish and parched. They're getting plenty of water and fertilizer, but the problem is getting worse instead of better, especially on my celosias and impatiens. Help! G.Y., Zone 6

Solution: I'll bet a nickel that you've got spider mites, which are really tiny insects that make themselves at home on the undersides of leaves. The leaves lose color as the mites suck out the juices. In addition to celosias and impatiens, spider mites sometimes set up shop in ageratum, begonia, and even marigold beds. But they can't stand soap, so you should be able to get them under control with my All-Season Clean-Up Tonic (see page 60). To get good coverage, use a handheld pump spray bottle to get the underside of every leaf dripping wet. Repeat after a week. If you have spider mite problems in shrubs, use the crowd-sized recipe on page 188.

CHAPTER 9

Perfect Perennials

I just can't seem to get enough of perennials, which are becoming increasingly popular with folks who are, shall we say, time impaired. These plants die back to their roots in the winter, and then reappear, rarin' to grow, in the spring. This makes them especially valuable in cool regions, where annuals take their own sweet time getting mature enough to flower. You can use numerous perennials to fill the color gap between spring-flowering shrubs, bulbs (which I'll get to in the next chapter), and summer annuals.

KEEP 'EM COMIN' BACK

The key to growing perennials that come back like champs year after year is to give them a foundation of excellent soil that is fertile (see my Flower Soil Prep Mix on page 135), well drained, and nicely mulched through the winter. Winter soil is naturally soggy, anyway, so growing perennials in beds that are slightly raised above the ground is always a good idea.

Start 'em Out Right

Your plants will get off to a booming start if you prepare the bed a couple of weeks before you actually set out your plants. After you've cultivated to a depth of at least 14 inches and mixed in a 4-inch blanket of organic matter, saturate the prepared soil with my Soil Soother Tonic. Then cover it with mulch to help it mellow.

Planning a Parade of Color

When perennial flowers come into bloom, they do it in a very big way. A group of foxgloves in their prime will stop you dead in your tracks, and the color and fragrance of catmint in full flower makes me want to stay with them all day.

The point I want to make is that you will appreciate your perennials most if you select a few to start with, locate them in groups of 3 or 5 plants, and let them work as seasonal sensations in your yard. For example, you might let peonies paint your garden in spring, followed by black-eyed Susans in summer, with asters, chrysanthemums, or goldenrod as feature flowers for fall.

Mixing and Matching Perennials

Because most perennials are in leaf for much longer than they are in flower, I also like to consider their foliage texture along with the more obvious things, like flower color and form. Plant form is important, too, so let's take a look at different special effects you can expect from perennials in your yard.

A perennial border is an English planting tradition that's spread to this side of the Atlantic big time in the past 20 years. It's basically a long, deep bed in which perennials are layered according to height and form.

A backdrop like a fence, wall, or evergreen shrubs completes the picture, and you can include flowering shrubs, roses, ornamental grasses, and some annuals, too. The main point is to keep it teeming with flowers that are coming in and out of bloom, one after another.

WATCH IT

Perennials on the Run

We all like perennials that mature into robust clumps, but some get carried away and get downright grabby about space. Keep an eye on rampant spreaders like obedient plant, loosestrife, and some artemisias. Or plant them in a place surrounded by lawn that is regularly mowed, and they'll never have the chance to grow out of control.

Fans, Spikes, and Mounds

Just like shrubs, perennials enrich your garden with their natural architecture and texture. Mound-forming perennials such as baby's breath and catmint take on an almost cloudlike look when they are in bloom. Perennials that grow very upright and then go on to produce blossoms on pointed spikes create fireworks in the garden. So you can't go wrong placing clumps of delphinium or foxglove behind or alongside perennials with a rounded, foamy form such as artemisia or threadleaf coreopsis.

Painting with Perennials

Most perennials need 2 to 3 years to reach their full glory, but that doesn't mean that you can't shift them around if you decide you've planted them in the wrong place. If your coneflowers need more sun or your Russian sage needs more elbow room, carefully dig the plants up, keeping as much soil packed around the roots as possible. Place the root mass on a tarp or old blanket, and drag it to its new home. If you can manage to move perennials without disturbing their roots too much, they usually keep right on growing as if nothing at all has happened!

Well-Fed Perennials

"Steady as she grows" is a good way to approach feeding perennials. Lots

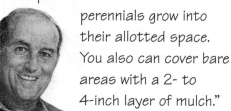

of nutrients all at once can promote soft, floppy growth, while too little food can leave plants on the brink of starvation. I think it's best to begin modestly, by spreading a 2-inch-thick blanket of good compost over the crowns and root zones of plants just as they wake up in spring, followed by a half ration of organic all-purpose plant food in early summer. After that, give plants a drench with my All-Season Green-Up Tonic (see page 27) once a month until the growing season starts winding down about 6 weeks before your first fall frost.

Jerry Baker Says . . .

"A newly planted bed can look pretty bare if plants are spaced at recommended distances for mature specimens. To avoid this bare look, initially space plants closer together, and then transplant a few out of the bed when they become crowded. This will also help control weeds. Or use annual plants in bare areas until the perennials grow into their allotted space. You also can cover bare areas with a 2- to 4-inch layer of mulch."

Jerry's TOP TEN

Perennials for Sun

Plenty of bright light helps these robust bloomers become all-stars in the garden.

- **Black-eyed Susan** (*Rudbeckia* species and cultivars); Zones 3 to 9
- **Blanket flower** *(Gaillardia grandiflora)*; Zones 2 to 9
- **Catmint** *(Nepeta × faassenii)*; Zones 3 to 8
- **Coreopsis** (*Coreopsis* species and cultivars); Zones 4 to 9
- **Daylily** (*Hemerocallis* hybrids); Zones 3 to 9
- **Heliopsis** (*Heliopsis* cultivars); Zones 3 to 9
- **Purple coneflower** *(Echinacea purpurea)*; Zones 3 to 8
- **Shasta daisy** *(Leucanthemum × superbum)*; Zones 5 to 9
- **Stonecrop** *(Sedum spectabile)*; Zones 3 to 8
- **Yarrow** (*Achillea* species and cultivars); Zones 3 to 9

Perennials for Partial Shade

These bloom best if they get a few hours of full sun or a half day of filtered sun.

- **Astilbe** (*Astilbe* cultivars); Zones 4 to 8
- **Bee balm** *(Monarda didyma)*; Zones 3 to 8
- **Bleeding heart** *(Dicentra spectabilis)*; Zones 2 to 8
- **Cardinal flower** *(Lobelia cardinalis)*; Zones 2 to 9
- **Columbine** (*Aquilegia* species and cultivars); Zones 3 to 9
- **Foxglove** *(Digitalis purpurea)*; Zones 4 to 8
- **Heuchera** (*Heuchera* hybrids); Zones 3 to 8
- **Hosta** (*Hosta* species and cultivars); Zones 3 to 8
- **Lenten rose** *(Helleborus orientalis)*; Zones 4 to 9
- **Lungwort** (*Pulmonaria* cultivars); Zones 3 to 7

The Perennial Fountain of Youth

As most perennial plants age, the centers of the clumps become woody and brittle. Happily, these sections are usually surrounded by younger, more vigorous crowns. So every 3 to 5 years, you need to dig and divide them. In the process, you'll get rid of the old dying parts and replant healthy, rooted crowns into fresh, fertile soil.

Divide and Conquer

In most climates, late winter to late spring is prime time for dividing clump-forming perennials to keep them growing happily. (It's also one of my favorite times for getting out in the yard and working off all those calories I've consumed during the winter!) Most years I have more divisions than I can possibly use in my own yard, so I share the extras with friends, neighbors, and the folks who have flower beds in my town's community garden. Here's my simple 6-step division process:

Step 1 With a digging fork, loosen the soil around the outside of the clump and try to lift it out so that it's intact.

Step 2 Drop the clump soundly onto the ground so that it loosens up, or even breaks apart.

Step 3 Pull or cut away the healthiest-looking pieces.

Step 4 Spade a 3-inch layer of peat moss into the soil.

Step 5 Set the divisions into their new homes.

Step 6 Saturate the area with my Perennial Perk-Me-Up Tonic.

Timely Tonic

Perennial Perk-Me-Up Tonic

This excellent elixir will get your newly divided perennials back on their feet in no time at all.

1 can of beer
1 cup of ammonia
½ cup of dish soap
½ cup of liquid fertilizer
½ cup of corn syrup

Mix all of these ingredients in a 20 gallon hose-end sprayer and saturate the ground around the perennials to the point of run-off.

Jerry's TOP TEN

Perennials for Cold Climates

Frozen soil doesn't bother these cold-natured flowers. After the soil freezes in fall, mulch over them to help the soil stay frozen until spring. That way, the plants won't emerge from dormancy until the time is right.

- **Black-eyed Susan** (*Rudbeckia* species and cultivars); Zones 3 to 8
- **Blanket flower** (*Gaillardia grandiflora*); Zones 2 to 9
- **Bleeding heart** (*Dicentra spectabilis*); Zones 2 to 8
- **Campanula** (*Campanula* species and cultivars); Zones 3 to 7
- **Catmint** (*Nepeta × faassenii*); Zones 3 to 8
- **Daylily** (*Hemerocallis* hybrids); Zones 3 to 9
- **Delphinium** (*Delphinium* hybrids); Zones 2 to 7
- **Lady's mantle** (*Alchemilla mollis*); Zones 4 to 7
- **Oriental poppy** (*Papaver orientale*); Zones 2 to 7
- **Peony** (*Paeonia* hybrids); Zones 3 to 8

Perennials for Warm Climates

Warm, humid weather can cause some perennials to rot away, but not these heat-hardy flowers. They also do well with relatively short periods of winter dormancy.

- **Black-eyed Susan** (*Rudbeckia* species and cultivars); Zones 3 to 8
- **Blanket flower** (*Gaillardia grandiflora*); Zones 2 to 9
- **Blazing star** (*Liatris spicata*); Zones 3 to 9
- **Boltonia** (*Boltonia asteroides*); Zones 4 to 8

- **Daylily** (*Hemerocallis* hybrids); Zones 3 to 9

- **Gaura** (*Gaura lindheimeri*); Zones 5 to 9

- **Hosta** (*Hosta* species and cultivars); Zones 3 to 8

- **Stoke's aster** (*Stokesia laevis*); Zones 5 to 9

- **Stonecrop** (*Sedum spectabile*); Zones 3 to 8

- **Verbena** (*Verbena* species and cultivars); Zones 6 to 9

Perennials for Late-Season Bloom

Most perennials emerge from dormancy with blooming on their minds, so much so that by the time summer has reached its halfway point, they're plumb tuckered out. Fortunately, that's when some plants are just getting in the mood to bloom. To have plenty of color in your yard until Jack Frost draws the final curtain, include a few of these autumn wonders in your planting plan.

- **Aster** (*Aster* species and cultivars); Zones 4 to 9

- **Boltonia** (*Boltonia asteroides*); Zones 4 to 8

- **Chrysanthemum** (*Dendranthema* cultivars); Zones 5 to 9

- **Goldenrod** (*Solidago* species and cultivars); Zones 4 to 9

- **Helen's flower** (*Helenium autumnale*); Zones 3 to 7

- **Helianthus** (*Helianthus* species); Zones 4 to 8

- **Heliopsis** (*Heliopsis* cultivars); Zones 3 to 9

- **Joe-pye weed** (*Eupatorium purpureum*); Zones 3 to 8

- **Obedient plant** (*Physostegia virginiana*); Zones 2 to 9

- **Stonecrop** (*Sedum spectabile*); Zones 3 to 8

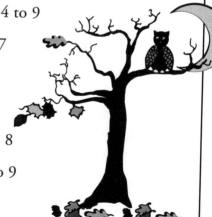

PROBLEMS & SOLUTIONS

TROUBLESHOOTING PERENNIALS

Just like other plants, perennials sometimes have problems with pests and diseases. The most common ones are covered here, but let me remind you that perennials can be a little bit quirky about accepting certain sites. So if you think you've done everything right and a perennial still isn't happy, try it in another place before you give up. Even when I've worked with perennials that are supposed to be easy and adaptable, like yarrow, I've found that I've had to experiment a little to find the sweet spot that brings out the best they have to offer.

Spotted Coneflowers

Problem: This has been a rainy year, and for the first time, I'm seeing dark spots on the leaves of my purple coneflowers. The spots are most numerous on the lowest leaves. How should I handle this problem? S.R., Zone 6

Solution: When leaf spots develop on purple coneflower, foxglove, heuchera, and other perennials, it's usually because fungi have flourished in wet weather and infected the leaves. Clip off spotted leaves to stop the fungi from spreading to healthy ones. On dry days between rains, I want you to start spraying your coneflowers and other perennials with my Fungus Fighter Tonic, and repeat it every 2 weeks as long as the rainy weather lasts.

Timely Tonic

Fungus Fighter Tonic

½ cup of molasses
½ cup of powdered milk
1 tsp. of baking soda
1 gal. of warm water

Mix the molasses, powdered milk, and baking soda into a paste. Put the mixture into the toe of an old nylon stocking, and let it steep in a gallon of warm water for several hours. Then strain, and use as a fungus-fighting spray for your perennials.

Cursed Columbines

Problem: Something is drawing funny circles in the leaves of my columbines. It almost looks as though my little grandson has been doodling on the leaves with a pen. Is this slug damage or what? N.G., Zone 7

Solution: The unusual artistry in your columbines' leaves is being done by leaf miners, which are fly larvae that feed inside the leaves. They rarely cause serious damage, but the leaves do look funny. I think the best thing to do is to simply pinch off affected leaves, which means you won't have to look at them and the leaf miners won't mature into next season's problem.

Crowded Daylilies

Problem: My daylilies didn't bloom well this year, so I think it's time to dig and divide them. I've never done this before, so please give me any tips that will help me do the job right. N.J., Zone 4

Solution: Because daylilies have such thick, resilient roots, you can expect great success from lifting them, pulling the crowns apart, and replanting them as quickly as possible. Follow the procedure I've described on page 149, and make sure you have a well-prepared place to set out the divisions before you dig up the plants. To help the divisions make a smooth transition into their new home, give them a good gulp of my Daylily Transplant Tonic.

Timely Tonic

Daylily Transplant Tonic

½ can of beer
2 tbsp. of liquid dish soap
2 tbsp. of ammonia
2 tbsp. of fish fertilizer
1 tbsp. of hydrogen peroxide
¼ tsp. of instant tea granules
2 gal. of warm water

Mix all of these ingredients together in a large bucket. Just before setting divided daylilies into their new planting holes, dip out 2 cups of the mixture and pour it into each hole.

Angry Astilbe

Problem: Several years ago, I planted a bed of astilbe in what I thought was an ideal spot in partial shade. The plants did beautifully until last year, when they hardly bloomed at all. Have I done something wrong? D.K., Zone 4

Solution: To really bloom well, astilbes need rich soil, regular fertilizer, and dividing every 4 years. Yours have probably become crowded below ground and used up most of the trace nutrients that were in the soil when you made the bed. So get yourself a good supply of compost and a bag of organic all-purpose plant food, and start digging. For good measure, I want you to mix ½ cup of Epsom salts and ½ cup of gypsum into each square yard of your new bed. Dividing does set astilbes back a bit, but after a season in their renovated home, you should expect plenty of blooms next summer.

Mum Marauders

Problem: Earlier this summer, when aphids covered the stems of my chrysanthemums, I pinched off the stems, which makes them bloom better anyway. But now that late summer is here, I don't want to pinch anymore, and the aphids are back in a big way. Do you have a magic potion for this problem? M.C., Zone 5

Solution: Try my Rose Aphid Antidote (see page 97), but I won't guarantee that it will work like magic on these guys. Chrysanthemum aphids are a tough little breed, and at this point, they are poised to do some serious damage to the pretty fall flowers you've been waiting for all summer. So use Total Pest Control (a pyrethrin-based insecticide), which will knock out the aphids but won't persist so long that it will also knock out aphid-eating predators such as ladybeetle and lacewing larvae.

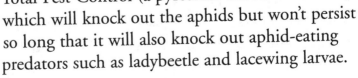

Powdered Phlox

Problem: My mother always grew beautiful garden phlox, but apparently, I did not inherit her talent. My plants bloom well enough, but the leaves turn almost gray with mildew before the summer is half over. Is there something I can do to prevent this problem? M.T., Zone 7

Solution: Garden phlox are at such high risk for powdery mildew that they almost always show a few white patches. Perhaps your mother had a strain that was naturally mildew-resistant — several are, though none are truly immune. With phlox, bee balm, and other susceptible perennials (such as aster, astilbe, black-eyed Susan, and coreopsis), make a habit of drenching the oldest leaves with this tonic every 2 weeks, starting as soon as the weather warms in late spring.

Timely Tonic

Powdery Mildew Control Tonic

4 tbsp. of baking soda
2 tbsp. of Murphy's Oil Soap
1 gal. of warm water

Mix all of these ingredients together. Pour into a handheld mist sprayer, and apply liberally when you see the telltale white spots on your plants, or even before!

Dead Delphiniums

Problem: Last year, when I planted delphiniums, I thought they would bloom this year. Not only have they not bloomed, they have disappeared. Do you think something ate them over the winter? E.T., Zone 4

Solution: Delphiniums are poisonous to mammals, so I don't think a critter ate them. Most likely they fell victim to crown rot, which is caused by soilborne fungi and bacteria. This year, why not try again in a new place? Amend the soil with a little sand and plenty of compost to ensure good drainage, and be careful not to plant your new delphiniums too deep: A low crown can easily turn into a dead one.

Shady Slugs

Problem: My shade garden is so overrun with slugs that I'm ready to scream! I know they hide in the mulch during the day, but water is in such short supply around here that I'm afraid I'll lose my plants to drought if I don't keep them mulched. I catch some of the big ones in traps, but I think the little ones are getting away. Help, please! B.L., Zone 7

Solution: I want you to turn that beautiful mulch of yours into a mine field for slugs by sprinkling diatomaceous earth over every square inch of it. This is a mineral substance that's made of shell particles with such sharp edges that it cuts into slugs when they move across it. For best results, apply the diatomaceous earth when rain is not expected for several days, because water will wash it down into the mulch, reducing its effectiveness.

Once that happens, move in with my Super Slug Spray — your best defense against little slugs (see page 141). Meanwhile, keep those traps baited for the big boys.

Plagued Peonies

Problem: Several of the flowers in my perennial bed are showing tiny silvery streaks in their leaves, but I can't find the pest that's causing the problem. Also, some of my peony blossoms have unusual brown streaks in them. And to make matters worse, half of my shasta daisies have folded or missing petals. Is this a coincidence, or is there a logical explanation? R.A., Zone 6

Solution: The logical explanation is flower thrips, which are so small that you'll need a magnifying glass to see them. Look in leaf and stem crevices or, better yet, take a suspicious blossom indoors and tap it soundly over a piece of black paper. Most flower thrips are light in color, almost translucent, so the black paper helps make them visible. Because you have so many thrips, you'll want to make a triple batch of my Garlic Tea Tonic and spray it on every affected plant. You'll find the recipe on page 99.

Leaping Leafhoppers

Problem: Two of my favorite flowers, asters and baby's breath, are being bothered by an insect I've never seen before. They move so fast that I can't even tell you exactly what they look like — only that they are less than ¼ inch long and that they jump around like crazy when I swish my hand through the leaves. Am I right to blame these critters for the pale color of the leaves and the fact that the plants aren't growing well? H.W., Zone 6

Solution: Yes, and the pests you describe can only be leafhoppers, which Grandma Putt used to call flower fleas. Boy, can they move fast in the heat of the day! That's why I want you to make a move on them in the cool of the morning, when you'll have a fair chance of hitting them hard with Grandma Putt's Flower Flea Fluid. It should take care of them in no time at all!

Timely Tonic

Flower Flea Fluid

Flower fleas was Grandma Putt's name for leafhoppers. When she spotted any of these feisty little guys bugging her veggie garden or her prize asters and dahlias, she'd let the culprits have it with this powerful stuff.

- 1 cup of Tobacco Tea (recipe on page 61)
- 1 tbsp. of baby shampoo or liquid dish soap
- 1 qt. of water

Mix all of these ingredients together in a handheld mist sprayer, and apply to leaves until they're dripping wet on both sides.

Harassed Hollyhocks

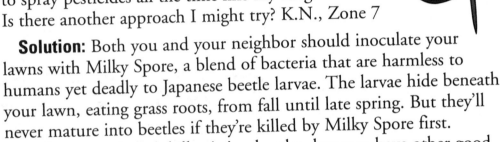

Problem: My neighbor grows roses, and after hearing his complaints about Japanese beetles, I filled my new garden with flowers other than roses. Most of the plants are doing fine, but the Japanese beetles are crazy for my hollyhocks, and they like the asters and peonies, too. I have young children, so I don't want to spray pesticides all the time like my neighbor does. Is there another approach I might try? K.N., Zone 7

Solution: Both you and your neighbor should inoculate your lawns with Milky Spore, a blend of bacteria that are harmless to humans yet deadly to Japanese beetle larvae. The larvae hide beneath your lawn, eating grass roots, from fall until late spring. But they'll never mature into beetles if they're killed by Milky Spore first.

Milky Spore doesn't kill existing beetles, but you have other good options for sending them packing:

- Handpick the culprits. The easiest collection method I've found is to spread sheets on the ground, then shake the plants. When the beetles come tumbling down, gather up the sheets and shake them over a tub of steaming hot, soapy water.

- Plant garlic or tansy among your hollyhocks — both herbs repel Japanese beetles.

- Call out the enemy. Two types of parasitic wasps, the spring tiphia and the fall tiphia, attack the larvae; and two tachinid flies go after the adults. (Your Cooperative Extension Service or a large garden center can give you detailed information about these good-guy bugs.)

- Let the no-goodniks have it with a big dose of my Beetle Juice (see page 201).

- Finally, eliminate plants the beetles zero in on (such as hollyhocks) in favor of species they just can't stomach.

CHAPTER 10

Beautiful Bulbs

Flowers that bloom from bulbs are a low-maintenance gardener's dream. They come equipped with their own stored food supply, and they know exactly what to do to replenish it each year. Best of all, bulbs produce incredibly showy flowers that are great for cutting, and many of them are easy to grow in containers, too!

TO EVERY BULB, THERE IS A SEASON

There are bulbs that bloom at every time of the year, but most fall into one of two man-made categories:

- **Spring-flowering bulbs**, like tulips, daffodils, and hyacinths, which are typically planted in the fall, when they're dormant, and bloom the following spring.

- **Summer bulbs**, such as lilies, gladiolus, and dahlias, which are planted in the spring and bloom in the summer and fall.

It Takes All Kinds

Bulbs have come to American gardens from all over the globe, so they vary tremendously in cold-hardiness as well as the seasons in which they make their active growth. A few, such as grape hyacinths and spider lilies, produce leaves in the fall and flowers months later. But for the most part, bulbs can't wait to flower as soon as they break dormancy. After that, they need time to be green, because that's when they store up energy for next season's flowers.

But I don't want to confuse you too much by going into the crazy ways that some bulbs grow. Instead, I want you to try any bulb that strikes your fancy, because bulbs have a knack for breaking human-made rules.

Some Like It Cold

Without a single exception that I can think of, spring-flowering bulbs are very cold-hardy. All through the winter, they're hard at work growing roots, so by the time they bloom in spring and early summer, they've really hunkered in. Then they hold their green leaves for several months.

In comparison, many summer bulbs aren't hardy at all, because they come from tropical climates. Even the hardiest of the hardies, like lilies, become dormant in winter. And because summer bulbs are not planted until spring, they bloom later than spring-flowering types. Gardeners in very warm climates can grow some of these bulbs as perennials, but where winters are cold, tender bulbs, like dahlias and gladiolus, need to be dug up and stored in a cool place indoors through the winter.

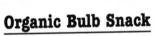

Timely Tonic

Organic Bulb Snack

When planting daffodils and other spring-flowering bulbs, drop 1 tablespoon of this mixture into the bottom of each planting hole.

10 lbs. of compost
5 lbs. of bonemeal
1 lb. of Epsom salts

Store any leftover Bulb Snack in an airtight container to keep it nice and dry.

Putting Bulbs to Work in Your Yard

Most summer bulbs have strappy, pointed leaves, so they are great texture plants for the garden. For example, the swordlike leaves of bearded iris combine beautifully with more billowy flowers, such as artemisia and baby's breath, or you can use them as a backdrop to annual flowers.

The formality of tulips makes them top choices for front-yard display beds, and daffodils are so persistent and long-lived that you can plant them almost anywhere and expect them to bloom for decades.

Starting Off Right

Because bulbs grow roots from their bottoms, I recommend that you work a high-phosphorus fertilizer into the soil under them. Special bulb fertilizers have a high middle number (for phosphorus), because this is the main nutrient bulbs need to maintain their huge and talented roots. Or, mix up your own bulb food following the recipe for my Organic Bulb Snack.

Timely Tonic

Beauty Bath for Bulbs

An hour or two before you plant your bulbs, soak 'em in this mixture to get 'em clean and ready to grow. Just don't peel off the papery skins! The bulbs use them as a defense against pests.

2 tsp. of baby shampoo
1 tsp. of antiseptic mouthwash
¼ tsp. of instant tea granules

Mix all of these ingredients together in 2 gallons of warm water. After your bulbs are planted, dribble any leftover Beauty Bath on the soil around your evergreen trees and shrubs.

WATCH IT

No Drain, No Gain

Above all else, bulbs crave great drainage. So always keep your soil chock-full of organic matter like compost or leaf mold.

Bulbs in Your Landscape

If one of your garden-variety woes is simply that your yard looks, well, boring, look no further. Bulbs can put pizzazz into the scene faster than you can say "Look at that!" Here are my top 10 tips for putting bulbs to work around the old homestead:

1. Plant little hardy bulbs in an informal section of lawn, like along an edge that's bordered in trees. Crocus, grape hyacinth, squill, snowdrops, and snowflakes usually bloom very early, before the mowing season gets into full swing.

Recycling Roundup

Here's a neat trick to keep squirrels away from your bulbs: After planting new areas, lay old window screens in frames on the ground, and cover them with the newly worked soil. The screen weighs just enough to foil the squirrel, but allows for air circulation and rainfall. Once the ground has settled, remove the screens and store for future use.

2. Naturalize early daffodils in a wooded area that gets winter sun and summer shade. The foliage often emerges before the last snow is gone, and the flowers bloom before the trees leaf out in late spring.

3. Plant tulips and hyacinths in fertile, sunny beds surrounded by perennials such as daylilies or peonies that will hide their fading foliage in early summer.

4. Plan ahead for lilies to take center stage in the summer garden. Give them excellent drainage and full sun, and add a nearby stepping-stone if you are growing fragrant Oriental lilies, which *demand* frequent sniffing.

5. Color-coordinate crocus with spring-flowering shrubs. For example, plant purple crocus beneath yellow forsythia, or yellow ones near pink azaleas.

6. Instead of planting tulips, daffodils, or other large-flowered bulbs in straight lines, plant them in groups of 5 or more. They'll give a much better show, and won't ever look lonely.

7. Surround spring-flowering bulbs with hardy pansies or hybrid violas, which are widely available for fall planting wherever they are hardy. In spring, the bulbs push up through the flowers, forming a symphony of color.

8. Create special beds for bulbs that must be dug and stored for winter, such as dahlias, so you won't disturb nearby plants each fall.

Many bulbs come back year after year; others diminish in blooming strength over time. To get more bang for your buck, and to lessen your planting chores, look for bulbs labeled "Good for Naturalizing" or "Good for Perennializing." **Naturalizing** means that the bulbs will multiply and their flowers become permanent seasonal features. This type includes daffodils and other narcissi, crocuses, and grape hyacinths. **Perennializing** means that the bulbs (such as many tulips and Dutch hyacinths) will come back strong for 3 years or so, then taper off.

Think Three

A bulb should be planted at a depth that's three times its size. That means that tulip bulbs, which are usually about 2 inches in diameter, go 6 inches into the soil. About 3 inches is just the ticket for miniature daffodils (small 1-inch bulbs, perfect for planting close to small trees and shrubs).

9. Where winters are cold, grow dramatic cannas in large containers, and move the containers to a half-heated garage through the winter. Then all you have to do in spring is move them back to the great outdoors.

10. Starting in mid-spring, set out gladiolus corms in groups, planting a new group every 2 to 3 weeks. Infinitely cuttable, inexpensive glads bloom 10 to 12 weeks after planting, so staggering planting dates gives you a long parade of flowers.

Jerry's TOP TEN

Bulbs for Spring

Bulbs that burst out of the ground and bloom almost before the last snow is gone deserve a spot in every yard. These beauties are always planted in the fall so they'll have a long time to develop roots before they get ready to bloom.

- **Bluebells** (*Scilla campanulata*); Zones 3 to 9

- **Crocus** (*Crocus* species and hybrids); Zones 4 to 7

- **Daffodils** (*Narcissus* species and cultivars); Zones 3 to 9

- **Dutch iris** (*Iris hollandica*); Zones 6 to 8

- **Grape hyacinth** (*Muscari* species); Zones 5 to 8

- **Hyacinth** (*Hyacinthus* hybrids); Zones 4 to 9

- **Ornamental onions** (*Allium* species and cultivars); Zones 3 to 8

- **Siberian squill** (*Scilla siberica*); Zones 2 to 9

- **Snowdrop** (*Galanthus elwesii*); Zones 2 to 9

- **Tulips** (*Tulipa* species and hybrids); Zones 3 to 8

Bulbs for Summer

Cold-hardiness varies with these summer bloomers. The ones that can't handle winter temperatures in your Zone will need to be lifted and stored indoors until spring. But I've found that it's well worth the trouble.

- **Amaryllis** (*Hippeastrum* hybrids); Zones 8 to 10

- **Anemone** (*Anemone blanda*); Zones 6 to 8

- **Bearded iris** (*Iris* × *germanica*); Zones 3 to 9

- **Caladium** (*Caladium* × *hortulanum*); Zones 9 to 10

- **Canna** (*Canna* × *generalis*); Zones 7 to 10

- **Crocosmia** (*Crocosmia* hybrids); Zones 5 to 8

- **Dahlia** (*Dahlia* hybrids); Zones 7 to 10

- **Gladiolus** (*Gladiolus* hybrids); Zones 7 to 10

- **Lilies** (*Lilium* hybrids); Zones 4 to 8

- **Tuberous begonia** (*Begonia* species and hybrids); Zones 9 to 10

Pull It Out and Plop It In

One garden gadget I'd never be without is a bulb planter. It's a hand tool that you shove into the ground to the right depth for your bulb, and it pulls out a plug of soil. Then you just toss in a little of my Organic Bulb Snack (see page 160), set in your bulb, root side down, and fill in the soil. It's easy as pie!

Amazing Multipliers

Many bulbs reproduce with great enthusiasm, so much so that plantings become so crowded that they no longer bloom well. If there's a noticeable decline in flowering, that's your huge hint that it's time to dig, divide, and replant those bulbs.

Timely Tonic

Bulb Cleaning Tonic

When you remove your summer bulbs, tubers, and corms from the ground in the fall, wash them in this Tonic.

2 tbsp. of baby shampoo
1 tsp. of hydrogen peroxide

Mix these ingredients in a quart of warm water and give your bulbs a bath. Just be sure to let them dry thoroughly before you put them away for the winter — otherwise, they'll rot.

Because bulbs often disappear completely when they become dormant, use a Popsicle stick or other marker to remind you of where crowded daffodils or other bulbs are sleeping. Then, whenever you can, during the dormant period, dig up the clumps and replant the bulbs in more spacious quarters. You don't need to hurry, because crocus, daffodils, grape hyacinth, and most other spring bloomers can be stored in a cool place indoors through late summer, and then you can replant them in the fall.

Other Seasons

There are exceptions to the fall-division rule. Bearded iris are best dug, divided, and replanted in one fell swoop in summer. Lilies rarely need dividing, but if you want to turn one big clump of vigorous Asiatic hybrid lilies into several, it's best to dig, divide, and replant them first thing in the spring.

Sear the Stems

When you cut them to put into a vase, the stems of many bulbs bleed a milky sap, and the more they bleed, the less energy they have to keep them looking good in arrangements. To stop the bleeding, sear the cut ends of bulb stems in a candle flame for a few seconds as soon as you can. This will seal in the sap, making the flowers last much longer.

WATCH IT ⚠

Bruisers, Beware

Although bulbs and other storage roots look tough, they are easily bruised by rough handling. Bruised spots can quickly become rot spots, so handle all bulbs with a gentle touch.

Jerry's TOP TEN

Bulbs for Naturalizing

Plant these bulbs once, and they will usually flower for many years to come. You won't need to do much beyond feeding them once a year. If they stop blooming well, dig, divide, and replant them.

- **Bluebells** (*Scilla campanulata*); Zones 3 to 9
- **Crocosmia** (*Crocosmia* hybrids); Zones 5 to 8
- **Crocus** (*Crocus* species and hybrids); Zones 4 to 7
- **Daffodils** (*Narcissus* species and cultivars); Zones 3 to 9
- **Dutch iris** (*Iris hollandica*); Zones 6 to 8
- **Grape hyacinth** (*Muscari* species); Zones 5 to 8
- **Ornamental onions** (*Allium* species and cultivars); Zones 3 to 8
- **Siberian squill** (*Scilla siberica*); Zones 2 to 9
- **Snowdrop** (*Galanthus elwesii*); Zones 2 to 9
- **Snowflake** (*Leucojum aestivum*); Zones 3 to 8

TROUBLESHOOTING BULBS

Because bulbs never come to the garden as babies but as strapping, ready-to-bloom adults, they are seldom bothered by the kinds of problems that plague juvenile plants. In fact, you may work with bulbs for years before you encounter any difficulties, which says a lot about the character of these fun-to-grow plants. If you do have problems, then you'll probably find the answers below.

Irritated Iris

Problem: Two years ago, I planted a bed of bearded iris that have been just beautiful. They bloomed well this year, too, but now the leaves have begun to yellow and die back. Some of them look chewed along the edges, and others have little pinholes in them. Some plants look worse than others. I know something's wrong, but what could it be? O.C., Zone 6

Solution: Most likely, you have been hit by iris borers, a widespread pest that eats holes in iris rhizomes and leaves. Oh, well, it's high time you dug and divided your iris, anyway, and if you do it now, you can throw out the roots that have borers in them. Replant any small healthy ones, and you'll still have pretty flowers next spring! Examine each root, and get rid of those that have several holes in them. If you find that some roots look good but they have a single hole in them, bend out a paper clip and stick it into the hole to skewer the pink caterpillar that's probably hiding inside. Then sprinkle a handful of mothballs in and around the plants to deter further infestations.

Sad Glads

Problem: Every year, I grow a long row of gladiolus, which I cut and use as arrangements for my church. This year, I'm worried because many of the plants have light streaks in their leaves, and they're not growing as fast or as tall as they should. The corms looked fine when I planted them, but now I'm wondering if they have developed some kind of disease. Should I just wait and see? H.N., Zone 7

Solution: Don't wait, because you don't have a moment to lose! I think your glads are being gobbled by thrips, which are tiny insects too small to see. They rasp away at the leaves, draining them of sap, so of course your plants are losing precious energy with each passing moment. Right now, today, I want you to get out there and drench every plant with my Double Punch Garlic Tea — a souped-up version of an old favorite that's custom-made for emergencies like this one. Hit the thrips with it again after a week, and then be sure to follow up with a nice drench of my All-Season Green-Up Tonic (recipe on page 27). Save those glads or they'll surely be missed in church!

Lily Lice

Problem: I take a lot of pride in my collection of lilies, especially the fragrant Oriental ones that I've had for years. I have some herbs planted near the lilies that I plan to eat, so I'm looking for an aphid cure that's not poisonous to people. Please share a good tonic recipe if you have one. M.B., Zone 6

Solution: Boy, do I, and you might get good results by simply giving your lilies a nice washdown with liquid dish soap, because aphids hate soap. In fact, Grandma Putt used to use a little lye soap in water for what she called lily lice. But if you need something stronger that won't interfere with the lovely scents from your lilies, try the Rose Aphid Antidote (see page 97). By the way, if you have any tiger lilies in your collection, I suggest giving them away. They host a virus that doesn't hurt them but could really wreak havoc with your Orientals if the aphids spread it from plant to plant.

Tulip Thieves

Problem: I thought I had won my war with squirrels by covering my tulip bed with chicken wire, but now that the plants are up and growing, those varmints are stealing the unopened buds! How can I keep them from nibbling the stems? R.G., Zone 6

Solution: Apply my Hot Bite Spray, but it's strong medicine, so I want you to wear rubber gloves while you're handling it. Like most other mammals, squirrels get quite a jolt from capsaicin, the hot stuff in hot peppers. So make this spray as hot as you dare, and spritz your tulips with it every few days. Let some drip around the plants, too, so that squirrels quickly learn the lesson you're trying to teach them, which is to stay away from your tulips!

Timely Tonics

Double Punch Garlic Tea

Use this brew to thwart thrips and other bugs.

5 unpeeled cloves of garlic, coarsely chopped
2 cups of boiling water
½ cup of Tobacco Tea (recipe on page 61)
1 tsp. of instant tea granules
1 tsp. of baby shampoo

Place the chopped garlic in a heat-proof bowl, and pour boiling water over it. Let it steep overnight. Strain through a coffee filter, and then mix it with the other ingredients in a mist sprayer bottle, and thoroughly drench your plants.

Hot Bite Spray

3 tbsp. of cayenne pepper
2 cups of hot water
1 tbsp. of hot sauce
1 tbsp. of ammonia
1 tbsp. of baby shampoo

Mix the cayenne pepper with the hot water in a bottle, and shake well. Let the mixture sit overnight, then pour off the liquid without disturbing the sediment at the bottom. Mix the liquid with the other ingredients in a handheld sprayer bottle. Keep a batch on hand as long as new tulip buds are forming, and spritz the flower stems as often as you can to keep them hot, hot, hot!

CHAPTER 11

Low-Care Ornamental Grasses

In the past few years, ornamental grasses have become the rage, and for good reason. They are easy to grow in any sunny spot, where they create a nice textural frame for other landscape features that looks good almost year-round. Most ornamental grasses grow into clumps, which makes them ideal for mixing with daffodils and other spring-flowering bulbs. The tallest ones make great backdrops for perennials, while smaller ones are perfect for edging driveways or mass planting on gentle slopes.

WHERE, OH WHERE?

Height is the main thing to keep in mind when deciding where to plant ornamental grasses. The biggest ones, which grow to 6 feet tall and 3 feet wide, can be used as screens or hedges, while smaller ones, that grow no more than 2 feet tall, mix well with perennials and shrubs.

Because ornamental grasses tolerate drought so well, clumps of midsize species such as maiden grass are great to plant near driveway entries, which can be difficult to water. Where it is hardy, tall pampas grass makes a great accent for distant property lines or empty corners in small yards. Wherever you plant them, you will find that 3 or more clumps placed close together look better than scattered loners.

Getting into Grasses

Plant ornamental grasses just like you would any other long-lived perennial, by setting out container grown plants in early spring, in well-prepared planting holes. Good drainage is more important than soil fertility, so be sure to choose a site that doesn't stay damp for long periods of time. When digging planting holes, mix in a good helping of my Ornamental Grass Chow, but don't worry about fertilizer.

WATCH IT !

Don't Bowl 'em Over!

When you're dragging a garden hose around, it's easy to demolish a stand of ornamental grass and not know it until it's too late. Protect your grasses, and all the other plants in your beds, by installing hose guards near them. Just bury bricks on end at the corners of each bed and at strategic intervals along the edges. You'll keep all your plants on the up-and-up!

Easy Keepers

The first season after planting, the main task of any grass is to develop extensive roots rather than lots of top growth. Do provide water during droughts for the first summer after planting. After that, your ornamental grasses should do just fine with minimum care.

No Bad Side

Ornamental grasses form circular clumps, so they have no bad side. Take advantage of this trait by planting them where they will be seen from different vantage points — for instance, in a circular bed surrounded by lower-growing perennials.

A Grass by Any Other Name

There's no doubt about it: Ornamental grasses can solve a lot of problems in your yard. If they have one drawback, it's the fact that most of them need full sun to do their best work. So what do you do if your yard is on the shady side? You reach for one of grass's kissin' cousins, that's what! Sedges and rushes are grass look-alikes and work-alikes that flourish in moist shade, where most grasses (ornamental and otherwise) grow poorly. Some of these versatile plants, like wood rushes and blue sedge, even hold up to light foot traffic, so you can use them as substitutes for lawn grass in low-sun areas.

Just one word of warning: Many sedges spread like crazy, so choose their homes carefully!

Recycling Roundup

When you're pruning your grasses, protect your knees by making a kneeling pad. Just stuff an old hot-water bottle with rags, handkerchiefs, or panty hose, then — *voilà* — no more sore knees!

Jerry's TOP TEN

Ornamental Grasses

Give them sun and good drainage, and these grasses will enliven your landscape year-round. Be patient and you will enjoy big, robust clumps 2 to 3 seasons after you first set out new plants.

- **Blue fescue** (*Festuca glauca*); 1 foot tall, Zones 4 to 8
- **Blue oat grass** (*Helictotrichon sempervirens*); 2 feet tall, Zones 4 to 8
- **Feather reed grass** (*Calamagrostis* cultivars); to 6 feet tall, Zones 5 to 9
- **Fountain grass** (*Pennisetum alopecuroides*); 4 to 5 feet tall, Zones 6 to 9
- **Japanese sedge** (*Carex morrowii*); 1 to 2 feet tall, Zones 5 to 9
- **Maiden grass** (*Miscanthus sinensis*); 4 to 6 feet tall, Zones 5 to 9
- **Oat grass** (*Chasmanthium latifolium*); 3 to 4 feet tall, tolerates shade, Zones 3 to 8
- **Pampas grass** (*Cortaderia selloana*); 4 to 7 feet tall, Zones 7 to 9
- **Silver spike grass** (*Spodiopogon sibiricus*); 5 feet tall, Zones 4 to 8
- **Switch grass** (*Panicum virgatum*); 3 to 4 feet tall, Zones 3 to 9

Cut Back with Care

Unless you see evidence of disease, it's fine to leave the dried leaves of ornamental grasses intact through the winter. Then, first thing in the spring, use sharp pruning loppers to trim the plants back to about 1 inch above the crowns — the places where new leaves will emerge. The height of the crown varies with species, but it is usually at least 4 to 6 inches above the ground with grasses that grow more than 3 feet tall.

After cutting them back, feed ornamental grasses with an organic or timed-release fertilizer spread around the clump in a close circle. Because ornamental grasses shade the area right around them, it is not usually necessary to mulch them, unless you simply like the way mulch looks.

WATCH IT

Learn Not to Burn

Even if you see other people doing it, never set fire to ornamental grasses instead of pruning them. Burning can seriously injure the new growth, which is present before you can see it, and may kill roots as well.

Recycling Roundup

Some grasses and grasslike plants, such as bamboo, are rampant spreaders. Keep 'em under control by planting them inside a large garbage can with the bottom cut out. Leave a 2-inch rim above the soil to keep their runners from jumping the curb.

Renovating Old Clumps

Every 6 to 10 years, most ornamental grasses begin to die out in the middle, a sign that it's time to dig up and divide them. This is a heavy job for which I like to get help. Basically, you dig up the clump in early spring, use a sharp spade or ax to chop the root mass into 6-inch-square pieces, and replant them. If the clump is so huge that you can't get it up whole, dig out chunks from the outside of the clump, replant them, then discard the middle.

TROUBLESHOOTING ORNAMENTAL GRASSES

Because ornamental grasses normally stay in the pink of health no matter what, you will quickly notice when things go wrong. On the rare occasions when it's wise to prune back actively growing grasses, be sure to wear gloves and a long-sleeved shirt to protect your skin from cuts and scratches. They don't call them grass *blades* for nothin'!

Fountain Grass Fungus

Problem: Just as my fountain grass begins to produce tops in late summer, a lot of the leaves turn brown. The other day, when I went to gather some tops for a flower arrangement, my shirt had traces of orange powder on it. Is this normal? Z.W., Zone 7

Solution: It is, if your plants are infected with rust, a fungal disease that gets into fountain grass (and corn, too) and has a heyday producing masses of rusty, orange, powdery deposits on the leaves. This takes place at the expense of the fountain grass, which becomes weakened the longer the rust runs rampant. The rust spores spread and germinate when the foliage is wet, so wait for a very dry day to get in there and clean up your clump. Use pruning shears to cut out as many infected leaves as you can, and then drench the plants well with my Fungus Fighter Tonic. There will still be plenty of spores left behind, so instead of letting the remaining foliage stand through

Timely Tonic

Fungus Fighter Tonic

½ cup of molasses
½ cup of powdered milk
1 tsp. of baking soda
1 gal. of warm water

Mix the molasses, powdered milk, and baking soda into a paste. Put the mixture into the toe of an old nylon stocking, and let it steep in a gallon of warm water for several hours. Then strain, and use the liquid as a fungus-fighting spray for your perennials.

winter, go ahead and cut it back as soon as the first frost causes it to turn brown. Next spring, as soon as new green leaves begin to show, I want you to start spraying your clump with my All-Around Disease Defense Tonic (see recipe on page 177) — once in May and once in June. You should have the healthiest fountain grass ever!

Dead Centers

Problem: One of the reasons my wife and I decided to purchase our present house was the big clumps of pampas grass that grow against the back fence. When the sun sets behind them, they absolutely glow. But with each passing year, it looks like the clumps are developing dead centers. Is there anything I can do about this, short of digging and dividing the clumps? They're so big that it might take a bulldozer to do the job. As it is, I have to use a chain saw to cut them back in the spring. V.G., Zone 8

Solution: A lot of readers are going to wish that they had your problem! And a problem it is, though I wouldn't call it an emergency. Elderly pampas grass will hang in there for many years, so I'm going to suggest a multiseason propagation program. Every spring, use a sharp spade and ax to take up healthy 1-foot-wide clumps from the back of your grass, and move them right in front of where your current hedge stands. You'll be planting a new hedge in front of your old one, and once it gets growing well, you can use an herbicide, like glyphosate, to eliminate the old one. Five years from now, you'll have a healthy new hedge that should illuminate your sunsets for a long time to come.

Lazy Maiden Grass

Problem: In the back of my perennial bed, I planted a clump of maiden grass that seems to be miserable. The tops stand up reasonably straight, but the leaves tend to flop over. Are they supposed to do this? The clump gets plenty of water, and I feed it regularly, along with my other flowers. N.J., Zone 6

Solution: Sounds like you need to give your grass some tough love! Maiden grass likes soil on the dry side, and fertilizing it once (or, at the most, twice) each summer is plenty. When it gets too much water or fertilizer, maiden grass tends to lie down on the job. Also, check to make sure your clump is getting at least 5 hours of full sun each day. Maiden grass will tolerate a little shade, but more than half a day in the shadows will make it stretch toward the sun.

Failing Fescue

Problem: We are trying to establish blue fescue as a ground cover on a slope in the front of our house, but many of the plants are refusing to grow. Most of the blades turn brown as soon as warm weather arrives, so that the pretty, blue-green ones hardly show at all. We're getting frustrated. Do you think there's hope? C.H., Zone 4

Solution: It's hard to get blue fescue to grow well on a steep slope, because the soil dries out very quickly, and each rain carries away nutrients that the grass needs to grow. So you will need either to straighten out your bank a little by terracing it with stone or landscaping timbers, or switch to a vining ground cover that does a better job of controlling erosion. But don't give up on using pretty blue fescue in your yard. It should make a fine addition to mixed flower beds, and it looks wonderful planted at the feet of junipers and other dark evergreen shrubs.

Spotted Blades

Problem: I'm just getting started with ornamental grasses, and I'm afraid that I like them better than they like me. Several of my young maiden grass plants have dark streaks in the leaves, and they are hardly growing at all. What's gone wrong? K.S., Zone 5

Solution: Oh, dear! I'm afraid that your streaky plants are infected with leaf spot fungus, which can be a serious problem. I know it's hard to do, but I want you to remove the infected plants from your garden. It's the only way to keep the fungus from spreading to your healthy maidens. Giving them extra-wide spacing may improve air circulation, too, which also will help stop the leaf spot fungus from spreading. As an extra defensive strategy, spray the survivors with a copper-based fungicide labeled for use on miscanthus. Assuming the rest of this season goes well, first thing next spring, begin spraying your plants with my All-Around Disease Defense Tonic. Finally, don't take this problem personally. There's a good chance that your plants were carrying the starter spores when you bought them, which means you're the best thing that ever happened to those struggling grasses.

Timely Tonic

All-Around Disease Defense Tonic

1 cup of chamomile tea
1 tsp. of liquid dish soap
½ tsp. of vegetable oil
½ tsp. of peppermint oil
1 gal. of warm water

Mix all of these ingredients together in a bucket. Mist-spray your plants monthly before the really hot weather (75°F or higher) sets in. This elixir is strong stuff, so test it on a few leaves before spraying the whole plant. Stop spraying when summer really heats up in your area.

CHAPTER 12

Divine Vines

Avine is any plant that likes to grow up some kind of support, and I tell you, I love 'em all. They are easy to grow, and work miracles when grown on boring fences and outbuildings, or when planted strictly for the magical beauty that happens when a vine twines its way over a pretty arbor or arch. As a matter of fact, from a landscaping point of view, there is simply no better way to accent the entry to a garden than to celebrate it with an arbor adorned with a flowering vine!

IT TAKES ALL KINDS

Vines come in all shapes and sizes, so it's not hard to find the right vine for any site. I've divided them into annual and perennial vines for a very good reason. If you're a little afraid to plunge in with a big perennial vine in a certain area, experiment first with a single-season annual. For example, in a sunny site in a warm climate, you might try growing hyacinth bean this summer before installing a wisteria later on. In cooler regions, you could see how asarina looks on a section of your chain-link fence before investing in more costly clematis.

Four of a Kind

All vines, whether they're annual or perennial, grow in one of four ways. So if you want to head off problems, you need to give each kind a slightly different support system:

- **Twining vines,** such as morning glory, clematis, and wisteria, twist themselves around their supports as they grow. They grow happily on any arbor, trellis, or openwork fence.

- **Clinging vines,** including climbing hydrangea and Boston ivy, send out rootlets or "holdfasts" that cling to any surface they encounter. Just plant them at the base of any wall or fence, then stand back — they'll be off and scrambling before you can say "Cover that shed!"

- **Tendril vines,** like sweet peas and grapes, wrap themselves around their supports using little shoots that grow out from the main stem. The important thing to remember with these guys is to match the strength of the support to the weight of the mature vine. Sweet peas, for instance, are happy with a nylon mesh trellis, or even lengths of string fastened to a wall. A grapevine, on the other hand, needs the sturdiest arbor you can give it.

- **Procumbent, a.k.a. scrambling, vines,** such as honeysuckle and some jasmines, have no way to support themselves. You need to treat them as you would climbing roses, securing the stems to a fence or trellis.

Jerry Baker Says . . .

"When it comes to choosing sites for vines, there's an easy rule of thumb that will serve you well. Almost all vines like to have their roots in the shade and their heads in the sun. So look for spots where shrubs or porches will shelter your vine's root zone, but where they can rise up into the light with ease. It's as easy as that!"

Gentle on Their Stems

Even self-supporting vines benefit from a little guidance in their early days. When the first shoots emerge, steer them in the direction you want them to grow, and secure them loosely to their supports using coated wire twist ties, old panty hose, or strips of fabric torn from an old shirt, sheet, or cotton kerchief.

ANNUAL VINES

Annual vines grow for only one season, and most of them grow really fast! If you have a porch that gets too much hot sun, a vigorous annual vine is a perfect solution. Simply install a trellis, train a morning glory or scarlet

Let 'em Scramble

Vines are most dramatic when they're grown to rise up high, but many can do double duty as ground covers on slopes. Akebia and silver-lace vine are good perennials for this job, or you can try sweet potato vine as a summer ground cover.

runner up the support, and you have a cool place to relax after you've cut your grass.

Let's Put On a Show

The flowers of annual vines can be very showy, indeed! Canary creeper is an old favorite that I love to see on a white picket fence, and I've never understood why more northerners don't cloak chain-link fences with asarina. In the South, black-eyed Susan vine grows so thick that it will completely hide a chain-link fence, and it reseeds so well that it usually comes back year after year. But don't let me limit your choices! Until you've tried every one of the annual vines on my list on page 182, you're missing out on some major summer fun.

An Old-Time Favorite

Everybody loves the old-fashioned fragrance and charm of sweet peas, me included. It's a good idea to move them around to different places in your garden, because growing them in the same spot year after year invites problems with soilborne diseases that don't kill them but make them grow puny. I soak the seeds overnight in my Seed Starter Tonic before I plant them (see page 15). In most areas, plant sweet peas about 3 weeks before your last spring frost is expected. But in Zones 7 to 9, sow them 2 weeks earlier, so they'll have time to bloom before hot weather comes.

Be a Big Wheel

Got an old bicycle wheel in the garage? Turn it into a trellis. Here's how: First, get a wooden stake about 8 feet high and just wide enough to fit tightly inside the hole in the middle of the wheel. Sink the stake into the ground, slide the wheel over the top, and put some screws into the stake — just under the wheel — to make sure it stays put. Next, pound short stakes into the soil around the perimeter of the wheel. Finally, run strings or lengths of nylon fishing line from the spokes to the ground, and tie each one to a stake. Bingo! You've got a trellis that's perfect for annual vines, such as morning glories, or for a vining vegetable crop, like beans or peas. Just plant a couple of seeds beside each stake, and they'll grow right up the strings and over the wheel.

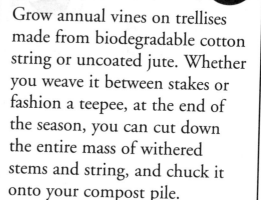

Recycling Roundup

Grow annual vines on trellises made from biodegradable cotton string or uncoated jute. Whether you weave it between stakes or fashion a teepee, at the end of the season, you can cut down the entire mass of withered stems and string, and chuck it onto your compost pile.

Jerry's TOP TEN

Annual Vines

Like other annuals, annual vines usually have a penchant for either cool or warm weather. Grow cool-season vines in early spring, or all summer long if you live in a mild climate. Warm-season vines get bigger and better as summer heats up, reaching their peak in late summer, when many other flowers are on the wane.

- **Asarina, chickabiddy vine** *(Asarina barclayana)*; full sun, cool season, procumbent

- **Black-eyed Susan vine, clock flower** *(Thunbergia alata)*; full sun, warm season, twining

- **Climbing nasturtium, canary creeper** *(Tropaeolum peregrinum)*; full sun, cool season, twining

- **Cup-and-saucer vine, cathedral bells** *(Cobaea scandens)*; full sun, warm season, tendril

- **Hyacinth bean, ornamental butterbean** *(Dolichos lablab)*; full sun, warm season, twining

- **Moonflower** *(Ipomoea alba)*; full sun, warm season, twining

- **Morning glory** *(Ipomoea purpurea* and hybrids*)*; full sun, warm season, twining

- **Scarlet runner bean** *(Phaseolus coccineus)*; full sun, cool season, tendril

- **Sweet pea** *(Lathyrus odoratus)*; full sun, cool season, tendril

- **Sweet potato vine** *(Ipomoea batatas)*; full sun, warm season, twining

Taming the Perennial Giants

Big perennial vines need discipline, or they can take over your whole yard. Pruning improves flowering, and encourages vigorous new growth on vines grown mostly for their foliage. Decide when and how to prune based on how the vine grows:

✔ **On any kind of vine,** prune away dead, diseased, or damaged wood at any time during the year.

WATCH IT ⚠️

Save Your Woodwork

Always keep vines pruned away from the woodwork of your house, because they can cause wood to rot. I like to keep my vines on a lattice trellis that's stationed about 6 inches away from the exterior wall of my house. This does double duty: The wall stays clean and dry, and the vines benefit from good air circulation.

✔ **Vines that flower on old wood** should be pruned in summer, just after the flowers fade, so that they will have the rest of the season to grow new bud-bearing stems.

✔ **Those that bloom best on new wood** can be cut back in late winter, just before new growth begins. Late winter is also the best time to prune vines that have simply gotten too big.

✔ **Prune vines grown mainly for foliage**, such as Virginia creeper and Boston ivy, in late winter or early spring.

Support Your Local Vines

The sound of creaking wood is not something you want to hear just as your climbing hydrangea or wisteria is blooming! I've heard it, and it's really spooky to worry about a weak trellis crashing down from the weight of a massive perennial vine. I'm not trying to scare you — only to emphasize the importance of providing super sturdy support for big perennial vines.

Of course, not all perennial vines are monsters. Still, because they are so long-lived — wisteria can carry on for 50 years or more — I think it's a good idea to include some wire or metal in any support scheme you dream up for a perennial vine. These vines really do get bigger and better over time, so they deserve an arbor befitting their permanent natures.

Some Clematis Comments

Clematis is often called "queen of the climbers," because it's such a royally fine vine. Different cultivars need different kinds of pruning, so take a season or two to get to know a new one and how it likes to bloom. Grandma Putt grew truly magnificent purple clematis, and she developed a special Clematis Chow. You may need to lighten up on the lime if your soil is naturally alkaline. The idea is to keep clematis roots moist, well fed, and luxuriating in soil that always has a near-neutral pH.

Jerry's TOP TEN

Perennial Vines

Many perennial vines produce showy flowers, while a few are grown mostly for their foliage. All of these are deciduous vines that shed their leaves in winter, except in very mild climates.

- **Akebia** *(Akebia quinata)*; full sun, Zones 4 to 9, tendril

- **Boston ivy, woodbine** *(Parthenocissus tricuspidata)*; partial to full sun, Zones 4 to 8, clinging

- **Clematis** *(Clematis* species and hybrids); partial to full sun, Zones 3 to 8, tendril or twining

- **Climbing hydrangea** *(Hydrangea petiolaris)*; partial sun, Zones 5 to 7, clinging

- **Confederate jasmine** *(Trachelospermum jasminoides)*; Zones 7 to 10, procumbent

- **Dutchman's pipe** *(Aristolochia durior)*; partial sun, Zones 4 to 8, twining

- **Everblooming honeysuckle** *(Lonicera × heckrottii)*; partial to full sun, Zones 4 to 8, twining

- **Silver lace vine** *(Polygonum aubertii)*; partial to full sun, Zones 4 to 8, twining

- **Trumpet creeper** *(Campsis radicans)*; partial to full sun, Zones 4 to 9, clinging

- **Wisteria** *(Wisteria floribunda)*; partial to full sun, Zones 4 to 9, twining

TROUBLESHOOTING VINES

Not much can stop a healthy vine from twining its way through life, but there are a few pitfalls to watch for. Keep in mind that most vines like to be airborne, where the breezes blow freely, so poor air circulation can lead to minor problems with leaf spot diseases. It's also a good idea to mark the places where young vines have been planted, because they sometimes die back to the ground their first winter. But don't worry, and wait as patiently as you can, because new stems will probably arise as soon as the soil warms in the spring.

Moody Moonflower

Problem: I thought I'd give my dog some shade by planting annual vines on the south side of her chain-link dog run, but I'm having trouble getting the seeds to sprout. I still have partial packets of moonflower, morning glory, and cup-and-saucer vine seeds left. Should I soak them or something to get them to germinate? P.N., Zone 7

Solution: Soaking alone won't do it with hard-shelled moonflower seeds. You have to scarify them first. That means nicking them with a sharp knife, or filing them with a metal file, to make small openings in the hard seed coat so moisture can get inside. Morning glory and cup-and-saucer vine seeds are hard nuts to crack, too, so I like to rough up their surfaces before I plant them. Do soak your seeds overnight before planting, but scarifying them first will make a world of difference.

Mealybugs on a Dutchman's Pipe

Problem: The new growing tips on my dutchman's pipe are badly infested with mealybugs. I recognize them because I sometimes see them on my houseplants, but I can always get rid of a few with rubbing alcohol on a cotton swab. This is a much bigger problem! Is there a less time-consuming way to control them? O.D., Zone 6

Solution: I'm going to suggest two methods and let you decide which one to use. If your plant is in the shade, you may get good results by simply making up a half-and-half mixture of rubbing alcohol and water and spraying it on your mealybugs. However, the alcohol may cause leaf damage if your plant is in the sun. If it is, then you'll want to play it safe by mist-spraying your bugs with a mixture of 1 teaspoon of baby shampoo and liquid Sevin (carbaryl) or Total Pest Control at the rate recommended on the label per quart of water. The baby shampoo will help the insecticide coat those mealybugs, and they will be gone within a day.

Unhappy Honeysuckle

Problem: Help! Instead of new buds, the tips of my honeysuckle vine look like a different plant entirely! They look like little drooping mops of string. Is this some kind of virus? I really don't want to lose this plant. I.C., Zone 5

Solution: That crazy growth is what Grandma Putt used to call witch's broom, and believe it or not, it's caused by sap-sucking aphids. Adult aphids laid their eggs in the growing tips last fall, and when they hatched, the little critters turned those tips into tassels. I want you to prune them off and put them into the garbage, and then follow up with a good drench of my Rose Aphid Antidote (recipe on page 97). This winter, after your honeysuckle sheds its leaves, spray it with a horticultural dormant oil to smother any eggs that are waiting to stage a repeat performance next spring.

Gritty Silver Lace Leaves

Problem: When my silver lace vine blooms, it's always the star of the neighborhood, so I think it's worth the heavy pruning I have to do every winter. But I think something is wrong this year, because I've noticed that the leaves are yellowish and dull, and they feel gritty when I rub them between my fingers. What could be bothering this giant of a vine? T.W., Zone 6

Solution: Spider mites have no respect for beauty, and they have no qualms about hiding on leaf undersides to quench their thirst by sucking out plant juices. These spider relatives are too small to see without a magnifying glass, and even then, you might see just their faint webbing, but not the mites themselves. A big silver lace vine will give those mites plenty of room to hide, so I want you to follow a 2-step program to get them under control. First, I'm going to have you white out those mites with my Super Spider Mite Mix. It will leave quite a bit of white residue on the leaves, so a week later, I want you to clean up your vine (and zap any escapees) with a big batch of my All-Season Clean-Up Tonic (recipe on page 60). Put it into your 20 gallon hose-end sprayer, and blast both sides of the leaves as thoroughly as you can. By the time your silver lace vine blooms later in the summer, it should be just as beautiful as it's ever been.

Timely Tonic

Super Spider Mite Mix

4 cups of wheat flour
½ cup of buttermilk (not fat-free)
5 gal. of water

In a big bucket, make a slurry of the flour, buttermilk, and 2 cups of the water. Then add the rest of the water. Apply to both sides of mite-infested leaves with a hand-held mist sprayer.

CHAPTER 13

Excellent Edibles

Every time I turn around nowadays, I run into a brand-new vegetable gardener. It seems everybody wants to find a place in the yard for at least a few favorite veggies and herbs. And no wonder: As Grandma Putt used to say, if you want to taste the best there is, you'll have to grow it yourself!

HOMEGROWN FAVORITES

My best advice on family food gardening is simple: Grow what you like to eat! Keep track of the produce you buy in the supermarket week after week, and you won't have to wonder which veggies and herbs will bring you the most satisfaction when you grow them in your own backyard. Then, to make the adventure even more fun, get yourself a few books and seed catalogs, and find some special varieties that the supermarkets don't sell. You'll get more bang for your buck in terms of flavor and nutrition — and often even disease resistance and suitability for your climate.

Bring Out the Flavor

In order to taste their best, almost all vegetables need plenty of sun and deep, rich soil to go with it. Veggies (and most herbs) are fast-growing annuals, so it's important to give them what they need to zip right along in your garden, without suffering setbacks that can make their productivity plunge. You won't have to worry about this if you put your back behind a shovel or garden fork in the spring and give your soil a good going-over. Get it so that it's fluffed up at least 14 inches below the surface. And as long as you're digging, work in a 2-inch blanket of organic matter (like compost or bagged humus). It'll help make your soil light and porous, just the way vegetables like it. (See Chapter 1 for the full lowdown on getting your soil rarin' to grow.)

Timely Tonics

Veggie Tonic #1

Even vegetable plants appreciate a little variety in their diet. My All-Season Green-Up Tonic is great stuff (see page 27), but every so often, use this Tonic as a change of pace, alternating it with my Veggie Tonic #2.

1 can of beer
1 cup of ammonia
4 tbsp. of instant tea granules
2 tbsp. of baby shampoo

Mix all of these ingredients in your 20 gallon hose-end sprayer. Then spray everything in the garden to the point of run-off.

Veggie Tonic #2

Alternate this potion with Veggie Tonic #1.

½ cup of fish fertilizer
2 tbsp. of whiskey
2 tbsp. of Epsom salts
2 tbsp. of instant tea granules
1 tbsp. of baby shampoo

Mix all of these ingredients in your 20 gallon hose-end sprayer. Then spray everything in the garden to the point of run-off.

Gimme That Old-Time Nutrition

Back in Grandma Putt's day, folks didn't have all the fancy chemical fertilizers we have now. They had to use whatever was on hand that suited the purpose. For my money, you still can't beat this good old-fashioned, stick-to-your-roots kind of food.

Eggshells. Crush them, soak them in water for 24 hours, then use the water for your plants. All that calcium is especially good for peppers and tomatoes.

Hair. Whether it comes from a human or any other kind of animal, hair is full of iron, manganese, and sulfur. Work it into the soil or toss it onto the compost pile, and watch your plants eat it up.

Seaweed. This is still a valuable fertilizer. Before you dig it into the soil, rinse it in fresh water and dry it out to get rid of most of the salt.

Fish. Any fish parts will make your plants take off like a buffalo stampede. Just make sure you bury the stuff deep in the garden. Tossed onto the compost pile or dug in too close to the soil surface, it'll create quite an odor and attract unwanted wildlife besides.

Sawdust. Mixed into the compost pile, it's a great source of carbon, which all plants need. But don't use sawdust from pressure-treated lumber. It contains toxic chemicals that you don't want in your vegetable garden.

WATCH IT ⚠️

Beware of a Nitrogen Overload

Leaf crops like lettuce and spinach need plenty of nitrogen, but for other veggies, go easy on the Big N. If they get too much, they'll lose interest in setting fruit (like squash or melons) or producing big, plump, tasty roots and tubers (like potatoes, turnips, and carrots).

Feeding Your Food

You'll keep your vegetables happiest and healthiest if you give them a steady diet that's packed with balanced nutrition. You want to feed food plants so that they never run short of anything. I think the vegetable garden is the best place to use organic fertilizers, which are a little bulkier than synthetic plant foods, but a lot more wholesome in the long run.

Make 'em Feel at Home

I think of my Vegetable Power Powder as comfort food for your vegetable garden — kind of like mashed potatoes or macaroni and cheese, only for your soil and the plants that grow there. Work it into your soil in early spring, and then overspray the prepared beds and rows with Spring Soil Energizer Tonic. By the time your seeds and seedlings are ready to plant a couple of weeks later, your soil will be rich and mellow, and begging to be filled with great things to eat!

Timely Tonics

Vegetable Power Powder

25 lbs. of organic garden food
5 lbs. of gypsum
2 lbs. of diatomaceous earth
1 lb. of sugar

Mix all of these ingredients and put them into a handheld broadcast spreader. Set the spreader on medium and apply the mixture over the top of your garden. Follow up immediately by overspraying the area with my Spring Soil Energizer Tonic.

Spring Soil Energizer Tonic

If you already have an established garden that you replant each spring, wake it up by applying this fantastic formula 2 weeks before you start planting.

1 can of beer
1 cup of liquid dish soap
1 cup of antiseptic mouthwash
1 cup of regular cola (not diet)
¼ tsp. of instant tea granules

Mix all of these ingredients in a bucket, and fill your 20 gallon hose-end sprayer. Overspray the soil to the point of run-off. This recipe makes enough to cover 100 square feet of garden area.

Some Like it Hot

I've already mentioned that most vegetables are fast growers, and some will really surprise you with their speed. Radishes are ready in less than a month, and snap beans rush their way to harvest about 6 weeks after the seeds hit the ground. But here's the tricky part. Vegetables can grow fast and strong only if they get the kind of weather they like, which can be cool, warm, or downright hot. So, depending on your climate and tastes, you'll need to shuffle planting times to make sure your vegetables get just the kind of weather they prefer. Check out my Top Ten lists to keep your timing on track.

Jerry Baker Says . . .

"When you're shopping for seeds and transplants, always look for varieties that have been bred to thrive in your climate. They'll grow up stronger and be better able to fend off pests and diseases."

Think Small

You say you'd love to have a vegetable garden, but you don't have room for one? Sure you do! Why, I know plenty of folks who grow bumper harvests on apartment building balconies. Here's a trio of space-saving ideas:

1. Grow up. Grow vining crops like tomatoes, squash, melons, and kiwi fruits on fences, walls, or trellises. They taste great, look terrific, and perform the same problem-solving work as ornamental vines (see Chapter 12 for more on these upstanding plants).

2. Spread out. Plenty of vegetable and fruit plants are as good-looking as any just-for-show orna-mentals. Fill up all the sunny nooks and crannies around your yard. Grow pole beans up the lamppost, or peppers and eggplants in the flower border.

3. Use containers. You can grow a great crop of lettuce, radishes, or baby beets in a window box. And with the right variety, almost any vegetable will thrive in a big pot or a wooden barrel.

Help from the Hearth

When you're through roasting chestnuts this year, don't throw those fireplace ashes out! Use them to solve a whole passel of problems in your vegetable garden. Instead, try one of the following:

1. Control cucumber beetles by mixing ½ cup of wood ashes with ½ cup of hydrated lime in 2 gallons of warm water. Spray this mix on both the upper and the lower sides of the leaves.

2. Protect your plants from snail and slug damage by sprinkling a 2-inch-wide band of wood ashes around them. Replenish the supply every time it rains, and those slinky slimers will keep their distance!

3. Raise the pH of acidic soil by working some wood ashes in at a rate of 1 pound per 25 square feet.

4. Energize your garden soil in the spring by mixing 5 pounds of gypsum, 5 pounds of bonemeal, and 5 pounds of wood ashes per 100 square feet of soil area.

5. Protect and feed your prize rhubarb through the winter. Simply mix a heaping shovelful of wood ashes with some ground-up leaves, and heap the health-giving mulch around the plants.

6. Say "so long" to maggots, club root, and all sorts of good-for-nothing lowlifes by sprinkling wood ashes liberally around the base of your plants.

7. Keep rascally rabbits and roaming rodents at bay by sifting wood ashes onto all of the plants in your garden.

WATCH IT ⚠

Just Say No

Wood ashes are real miracle workers for your plants, but they're not good for everybody. In fact, they're highly toxic to toads, so don't use the stuff anywhere if you have one of these princely predators on garden guard duty.

Summertime

Come summertime, the livin' gets pretty easy around my place — so easy that I sometimes forget that, if I want to head off trouble in the vegetable garden, I need to keep on top of a few chores. So I always keep this checklist taped to the fridge. That way, I don't overlook anything when I get an attack of the midsummer lazies:

✔ Make sure the garden is getting enough water.

✔ Check for sagging stems, and tie 'em up before they break.

✔ Keep an eagle eye out for pesky pests.

✔ Pick all vegetables as soon as they're ripe.

✔ Inspect the mulch now and then, and add more if needed.

✔ Wash down the whole garden every 2 weeks with my All-Season Clean-up Tonic (see page 60).

✔ Along about midsummer, overspray the mulch around your veggie plants with my Mulch Moisturizer Tonic (see page 30).

My, How Time Flies!

Sometimes, I get so busy having fun in my yard that I don't notice that the days start getting shorter after the Fourth of July, but, by golly, my vegetables do! By August, they've begun to gear down a little, in keeping with the lengthening nights. To make sure those crops get their ripening done before Jack Frost strikes, I like to give my plants a little kick in the you-know-where with my Hurry-Up-the-Harvest Tonic.

Timely Tonic

Hurry-Up-the-Harvest Tonic

When I know Old Man Winter is waiting in the wings and my plants are still chock-full of unripe veggies, I give my garden a big drink of this Tonic.

1 cup of apple juice
½ cup of ammonia
½ cup of baby shampoo

Mix all of these ingredients in your 20 gallon hose-end sprayer jar, filling the balance of the jar with warm water. Then spray the Tonic on your garden to the point of run-off.

Jerry's TOP TEN

Cool-Season Vegetables

These vegetables and herbs grow best in cool weather, and often have trouble when temperatures rise above 80°F or so. If summer really heats up in your area, get them into the ground as early as you can, even if the last frost hasn't yet passed. In many regions, these cool-season wonders grow well in the fall, too.

- **Broccoli.** Set out seedlings in well-drained soil, in a place that gets good air circulation. Great in the fall!

- **Brussels sprouts.** Set out seedlings. Sprouts need a long, cool-weather season; in fact, their flavor actually improves after a few frosts.

- **Cabbage.** Set out seedlings in soil with a pH between 7.2 and 7.5 (this stuff is fussy about pH).

- **Carrots.** Direct seed in loose soil, and avoid high-nitrogen fertilizers. Best in the spring.

- **Kale.** Direct seed, preferably in the fall. Thrives in cold weather, and lives through the winter.

- **Lettuce.** Direct seed or set out seedlings; make repeat sowings to ensure a steady crop.

- **Peas.** Direct seed as early as 5 weeks before the last frost in the North. Down South, plant in December.

- **Potatoes.** Plant cut-up seed potatoes first thing in spring in highly acid soil (pH below 5.5).

- **Radishes.** Direct seed in small batches; *very* easy to grow — and great for repelling spider mites from tomato plants.

- **Spinach.** Direct seed; great in the fall, extremely cold-hardy.

Warm-Season Vegetables

These vegetables can't stand the barest hint of frost, so hold off planting until warm weather has arrived to stay. To avoid having too much of a great thing all at once, make small sowings of beans, cucumbers, and squash 2 to 3 weeks apart. In mild climates, choose varieties that tolerate cooler temperatures.

- **Beans.** Direct seed, and for pole beans, erect trellises or other supports at planting time.

- **Corn.** Direct seed; give it plenty of space and goodness in triple time: good light, good drainage, and good, rich soil.

- **Cucumbers.** Direct seed when both air and soil temperatures have reached 70°F.

- **Eggplant.** Set out seedlings in 70°F soil; for best results, grow in raised beds.

- **Melons.** Direct seed in full sun and 70°F soil that has a pH between 6.0 and 7.0.

- **Okra.** Direct seed in the South; up North, choose a fast-maturing variety and start seeds indoors.

- **Peppers.** Set out seedlings, and expect to wait at least 70 days before you can eat the first fruits — sweet or hot.

- **Squash.** Direct seed, and don't plant too many, unless you're planning to feed the Seventh Infantry Battalion.

- **Sweet potatoes.** Set out rooted stems (slips), and up North, be very sure to choose a variety bred for a short growing season.

- **Tomatoes.** Set out seedlings, and train vining types on stakes or trellises.

Unforgettable, Edible Herbs

Each year, more and more people discover the fun of growing herbs. And it's no wonder: These are mostly tough plants that are easy to grow, are seldom plagued by diseases, and have very few enemies in the insect world. Plus, they're always ready to lend a hand with all kinds of jobs, whether you want to spice up your food, make your house smell nice, or cure a sore throat.

Scram!

Not only are herbs first-class helpers around the house, but many of them are also real workhorses in the garden. That's because the fragrant oils that make them taste and smell so great to us have the opposite effect on plenty of pesky pests. Here's a rundown of some herbs that can send your problems packing:

Plant	To say "scram" to
Basil	Flies and mosquitoes
Borage	Tomato worms
Garlic	Groundhogs
Hyssop	Cabbage moths
Mint	Ants, white cabbage moths
Rosemary	Bean beetles, cabbage moths, carrot flies
Rue	Japanese beetles
Sage	Cabbage moths, carrot flies
Summer savory	Bean beetles
Tansy	Ants, flying insects, Japanese beetles, squash bugs, striped cucumber beetles
Thyme	Cabbage worms
Wormwood	Black flea beetles, carrot flies, white cabbage butterflies

Jerry's TOP TEN

Herbs

For my money, these are some of the easiest, most useful, and best-looking herbs you could ask for.

- **Basil** *(Ocimum basilicum)*. Fragrant, flavorful leaves are natural partners for tomatoes, and the key ingredient in pesto. Annual.

- **Dill** *(Anethum graveolens)*. Ferny foliage is flavorful, the flowers are pretty enough to cut, and the seeds are a must for pickle-making. Annual.

- **English lavender** *(Lavandula angustifolia)*. An evergreen shrub, and an all-time favorite of Grandma Putt's, with fragrant gray-green leaves and flowers in white or shades of — what else? — lavender. Zones 5 to 9.

- **Garlic** *(Allium sativum)*. A perennial bulb that's a snap to grow, an essential ingredient in many of my tonics, and a great repellent for all kinds of pests from bunny rabbits to vampires. Zones 5 to 10.

- **Mint** *(Mentha* species). A must for iced tea and mint juleps — but keep an eye on it. This stuff spreads like crazy! Perennial, Zones 3 to 9.

- **Oregano** *(Origanum vulgare)*. Easy to grow, spicily fragrant, and an absolute must for marinara sauce. Perennial, Zones 3 to 9.

- **Parsley** *(Petroselinum crispum)*. Easy to grow from seed, rich in vitamins, and a great breath freshener. Perennial, Zones 2 to 10.

- **Rosemary** *(Rosmarinus officinalis)*. A tender shrub that can reach 6 feet high in Zones 8 to 10. Elsewhere, grow it in pots to take indoors for the winter. Use it to flavor chicken, meat, and vegetable dishes.

- **Sage** *(Salvia officinalis)*. A hardy plant with leathery gray-green leaves and spikes of blue-purple or white flowers. For my money, no turkey stuffing would be complete without sage. Perennial, Zones 3 to 8.

- **Thyme** *(Thymus vulgaris)*. Compact plants with small, glossy green leaves, woody stems, and clusters of pink or white flowers. Use these savory sprigs daily in the kitchen. Perennial, Zones 4 to 9.

TROUBLESHOOTING EDIBLES

Many of the general pest problems we discuss in Part III cause minor disasters in the vegetable garden, but many plants have specific enemies that I hear about from gardeners all over the country. Good detective work in the vegetable garden pays off, so make a habit of patrolling your garden regularly. That way, you can get after the pests before they have *your* dinner for dinner.

Slow Tomatoes

Problem: Maybe I'm impatient, but it seems to take my tomatoes forever to produce ripe fruits. I'm afraid to overfeed them, which I did once and got huge plants but very little fruit. Is there some little trick to growing fast tomatoes? D.P., Zone 5

Solution: First, I want you to make sure that you are growing some early varieties, such as 'Early Girl' or 'Quick Pick', which often ripen 3 weeks before other kinds. With later-maturing tomatoes, prune out some of the stems as you stake your plants, so that they will concentrate their energy on nurturing the first fruits that set. But I think the biggest favor you can do for your tomatoes is to treat them to my Tomato Booster Tonic in early summer, just as they show a bunch of yellow flowers. It will help them set more fruits, and help the plants take up all the nutrients they need to grow fast and strong.

Timely Tonic

Tomato Booster Tonic

2 tbsp. of Epsom salts
1 tsp. of baby shampoo
1 gal. of water

Mix all of these ingredients together, and liberally soak the soil around tomato plants as they flower to stimulate their growth.

Sabotaged Spuds

Problem: My family loves the little, new potatoes I grow in my garden, but each year, I'm having worse problems with reddish bugs that eat the plants' leaves until there is nothing left but bare stems. I still get nice potatoes, but I think I'd get more of them if I didn't have to compete with these nasty bugs. Got any suggestions? R.B., Zone 6

Solution: It sounds like your garden has become home to a resident population of Colorado potato beetles, a native insect that just loves potatoes. It's the larvae that do the damage, but adult beetles (which you'll know by the yellow stripes on their backs) hide out in weeds and woods through the winter and show up to lay eggs on young potato plants' in late spring. The first thing I want you to do is to start checking the plants' lowest leaves at least once a week, looking for masses of bright yellow eggs. Pinch off eggy leaves and dispose of them. Also, pick off potato bugs as soon as you see them. When there are so many of them that you're ready to scream, collect them in a jar and use them to whip up a batch of my Beetle Juice. It'll stop 'em dead in their tracks.

Timely Tonic

Beetle Juice

½ cup of potato bugs (both larvae and adult beetles)
2 cups of water
1 tsp. of liquid dish soap

Collect ½ cup of beetles and whirl 'em up in an old blender with 2 cups of water. Strain the liquid through cheesecloth and mix in the soap. Pour about ¼ cup into a 1 gallon handheld sprayer and fill the rest of the jar with water. Drench the soil around new plants to keep the beetles from getting started. If they're already on the scene, spray your plants from top to bottom, and make sure you coat both sides of the leaves. Wear gloves when handling this mixture, and be sure to promptly clean your blender with hot soapy water.

Slimed Lettuce

Problem: I am at my wit's end over the little slugs that hide in my lettuce! They refuse to go into the traps I set out, perhaps because they're so darned happy in my lettuce. What else can I do? M.C., Zone 7

Solution: Those little guys are often called milk slugs, and I know how much you want to slug 'em back! I want you to read my round-up of slug cures (see page 222) in case there's something there you haven't tried, because it'll take an all-out effort to reclaim your lettuce patch. But here's a trick that's tailor-made for your problem. In the evening, lay pieces of burlap over the ground around your lettuce, and dampen them slightly. The next morning, you'll find a bunch of those little guys hiding under the cloths. Rinse them out in a bucket of warm soapy water, put the burlap back in place, and repeat this procedure for 5 days in a row. This should deal your slugs a serious blow!

Grim Greens

Problem: I just love greens, and I always plant all kinds of them. Well, this year, they're all full of little squiggly lines. Everything has them — even Swiss chard, which has never given me any trouble before! What could the matter be, and what can I do about it? G.S., Zone 5

Solution: Your crops have been attacked by leaf miners, my friend. And those squiggly lines are actually little tunnels dug by the maggots (see Chapter 14 for the full rundown). In the meantime, blast 'em with my Rhubarb Bug Repellent Tonic.

Timely Tonic

Rhubarb Bug Repellent Tonic

3 medium-size rhubarb leaves
1 gal. of water
¼ cup of liquid dish soap

Chop up the rhubarb leaves, put the pieces into the water, and bring it to a boil. Let the mixture cool, then strain it through cheesecloth. Then mix in the dish soap. Apply the Tonic to your plants with a hand-held sprayer. This Tonic also helps reduce blight on tomatoes.

Part III
JERRY'S BACKYARD TROUBLESHOOTER

Before you can solve problems that rear their ugly little heads in your backyard, you need to understand a little bit about what they are. Insects, animals, diseases, and even good ol' Mother Nature can cause things to go crazy at times, and that's what this part is all about. Knowledge is power, and power over problems is essential to having fun in your yard!

Now, a lot of folks actually enjoy solving problems with pests and such, and I happen to be one of them. There's nothing wrong with a little brain exercise, which is what it takes to keep your yard and garden in the pink of health. Besides, solving most of the yard problems that come up isn't difficult, and as I've found over the years, the rewards are always great!

CHAPTER 14

Insect Invaders

To a new gardener, all bugs look pretty much alike. But the more you're out there in your yard with your plants, the easier it is to see that insects come in all sorts of packages. Most are harmless to both you and your plants, and many are among the best garden helpers you'll ever find. Unfortunately, though, some do get up to no good — at least from a gardener's point of view. In this Chapter, I'm going to explain how different insects tick, and share dozens of easy ways to beat the bad ones at their own game.

THE GOOD, THE BAD, AND THE UGLY

Grandma Putt taught me that God had a reason for putting every last creature on this great green earth, but He also gave us the brains to manage the ones that get out of hand, including enlisting the help of birds, bats, and good-guy bugs — and, of course, applying my terrific tonics at just the right time!

Hospitality, Bug Style

Imagine for a moment what it might be like if you could eat only one food or drink only one drink. This is the fix that many insects are in, because their mouth parts and tummies are custom-built to chomp into and digest a very narrow range of plants. For example, Mexican bean beetle larvae must have beans or they starve to death. They can't eat broccoli or roses, only beans and their close relatives.

I think this is a pretty neat set-up, and it's the main thing you need to understand before you wage an all-out war on every bug in your yard. Except in a few special cases, like cutworms and Japanese beetles, most of the bugs that pester your garden can't spread from one type of plant to another. They gotta have very specific host plants; it's as simple as that.

Jerry Baker Says . . .

"One of the best ways I know of to keep bugs from bugging your yard is to grow many different kinds of plants. That way, most pesky pests will take one look and decide there's not enough of their favorite chow to hang around for."

The Bad News

The other side of the coin is this fact of garden life: When insects do have plenty of host plants, they become eating, egg-laying machines, and celebrate their good fortune by reproducing as fast as they can. Natural predators can't keep up with their exploding populations, so you end up with a problem. What you do about it depends on the type of bug that's bugging you, so I'm going to divide the most common pesky insects into easy-to-identify groups and tell you how to control them. But first let's look at 5 ways to have a nice yard that's naturally low in pest problems.

Beating Bugs at Their Own Game

Here's a handful of the best ways I've found to outsmart the culprits.

1. Keep your eyes open. If you snatch up the bad bugs early — before they produce the next generation — you'll have far fewer problems later on.

2. Move things around. Several common pests of vegetables and annual flowers wait patiently in the soil in hopes that you will again provide them with the same host plant they enjoyed the year before. Moving your annual plants around each year forces pests to venture farther afield to find the plants they need — and often they don't even move. They just lie there and starve to death!

3. Pull out buggy plants. Sometimes a single plant will be seriously infested, while its neighbors are nearly clean. Throw an old sheet over the infested plant, pull it up, and destroy it as fast as you can.

4. Wipe out weeds. Several common pests, including beetles and aphids, make themselves at home among wild relatives of cultivated plants. So get rid of them!

5. Make friends with natural predators. Birds, bats, toads, and dozens of good-guy bugs are just waiting for the chance to chow down on your plants' enemies. The simple act of planting a very mixed-up garden that includes a number of different kinds of plants invites good guys to stay while frustrating the villains. Going a step father and providing a home sweet home can help even more. For more about how to do that, see page 223.

THE BRAINS OF THE OUTFIT

Grandma Putt used to say that the most important thing to remember about bad-guy bugs is this: Even on your worst day, you're smarter than they are. They may have you outnumbered, but you can always outsmart 'em!

Fewer Is Better

Very cold winter weather often strikes a big blow against bad bugs that plague your garden, but my All-Purpose Bug & Thug Spray delivers a knockout punch that'll take care of any malingerer in two ways.

First, it protects your plants from diseases, so that they can defend themselves better against insect invasions.

Second, it suffocates lots of little bitty bugs that lurk in stem crevices through the winter. If you had serious insect problems on a certain plant last summer, use this tonic to prevent a repeat performance.

Timely Tonic

All-Purpose Bug & Thug Spray

This is the way to clobber bugs and thugs in early spring, just when the lowlifes are waking up from their long winter's nap.

3 tbsp. of baking soda
2 tbsp. of Murphy's Oil Soap
2 tbsp. of canola oil
2 tbsp. of vinegar
2 gal. of warm water

Mix all of these ingredients together in a handheld sprayer and mist-spray your plants until they are dripping wet. Apply in early spring, just when bugs and thugs are waking up.

THE BAD BOYS OF SUMMER

You don't have to be a biologist to tell one type of insect from another — just use your head! Insects that are closely related have similar life cycles, which I think is both interesting and important to know. And because understanding a problem is the first step toward solving it, I know you'll feel a lot more confident about the things you do to manage pest problems if you know the reasons behind your actions. So here are some of the most irritating pests you'll ever encounter, and what to do when they turn your yard into a war zone.

Meet the Beetles

Beetles begin life as eggs, deposited in the soil or on the leaves of plants. When the eggs hatch, the larvae start feeding. Below-ground feeders munch on plant roots, while those that feed above-ground eat leaves or, in some cases, other bugs. When they've fed long enough, the larvae enter a pupal stage, then emerge as adult beetles, to start a new generation. Here are 4 of the peskiest pests.

Cucumber Beetles

Conveniently for them, cucumber beetles are the bright yellow color of cucumber blossoms with either black stripes or black dots. Both types eat the roots of cuke family crops when they are larvae; adults chew into stems and fruits, spreading several diseases in the process. Spotted types of beetles also eat flowers, including cosmos, impatiens, and petunias.

1/3"

Control: Handpick the ones you can, and drown them in a bucket of soapy water. If you think your yard has become cucumber beetle heaven, plant a small plot of cucumbers, and just as the plants reach full flower, go out early in the morning and let 'em have it with a dose of my Beetle Juice (see page 201).

Flea Beetles

These tiny guys can be either black or brown, and boy, can they eat! If your leaves are so full of holes that they look like lace, these guys are the likely culprits. They particularly like to snack on eggplant, nasturtiums, potatoes, tomatoes, and sweet potatoes.

1/10"

Control: In the cool of the morning, hit 'em with my Knock 'em Dead Insect Spray (see page 211). Then, for long-term protection, make yellow sticky traps: Just paint 1 x 6-inch boards yellow, tack them to sticks, and coat the surfaces with a sticky substance such as honey or Tangletrap. Then poke the sticks into the soil among troubled plants. For instant traps, coat yellow plastic dish soap bottles with a sticky substance, and catch hordes of the tiny troublemakers.

Japanese Beetles

These beautiful but sinister beetles are the worst pests to hit the eastern United States in the past century. You can't miss them: They're copper colored with iridescent green markings, and they attack roses, grapes, hollyhocks, and dozens

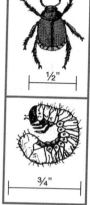

of other beloved garden plants. The larvae, a.k.a. grubs, eat grass roots, sometimes causing brown dead patches in the lawn. The adults cause trouble for about 6 weeks in summer. Then they lay eggs that hatch into larvae in fall and pig out until the cold weather comes. They sleep in the soil through the winter and, come spring, wake up and start eating again. What a life!

Control: Shake adults off leaves and flowers into soapy water. As a long-term control, inoculate your lawn with Milky Spore, a blend of bacteria that are lethal to the larvae but harmless to other soil-dwelling creatures, and to birds and other wildlife that eat them. As a last resort, in mid to late spring, treat your lawn with Merit, a soil pesticide that's less toxic than most.

Mexican Bean Beetles

These south-of-the-border bandits have built-in anti-freeze that

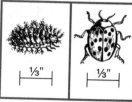

enables them to survive winter as adults hidden away in leaves and mulch. About ⅓ inch long and brown, with 3 rows of black spots on their backs, these beetles want nothing but beans. The adults lay clusters of yellow eggs on the undersides of bean leaves, which hatch into spiny yellow larvae that rasp away at leaves. After eating for about 5 weeks, the larvae pupate into adults, and a new generation is born.

Control: Handpick adult beetles as soon as you see them in late spring, and check the undersides of bean leaves often for eggs. You can squash both eggs and larvae with your fingers. If your beans are covered with the buggers, zap them with my Beetle Juice (see page 201). Unfortunately, sprays don't wipe out eggs, so about a week later, start checking for them and for newly hatched larvae.

We tend to call any creature with 6 legs a bug, but true bugs are a special group of insects that grow a certain way. The babies that hatch from eggs look like miniature adults, and as they feed, they get bigger and bigger, molting their way to maturity. True bugs have sharp, beak-like mouth parts that they use to chew into leaves and suck out plant juices. In the process, they often inject a toxin that causes small dead patches to develop around each bite. Here are some of the worst of the holy terrors.

Four-Lined Plant Bugs

General feeders, these guys enjoy snacking on numerous plants, though I find that they tend to zero in on one or two types in any given season. These critters are ⅓ inch long, yellowish green, with 4 black stripes on each wing. They damage numerous flowers, herbs, and vegetables by sucking juices from plant leaves, leaving behind small brown spots.

Control: Whenever I try to handpick four-lined plant bugs, I get frustrated because they see me coming and drop down to low leaves or mulch, where I can't find them. So as soon as I see a few on my mint, poppies, or whatever, I move in with a thorough drench of my Bug Away Spray. This works so well that I usually have to spray only once, though I always go back after a week to make sure that new four-liners haven't hatched and taken up the work left unfinished by the dead ones. By the way, this is one pest that you can outsmart simply by cleaning up your yard in the fall, removing weeds and old mulches that they are likely to use as winter hiding places.

Timely Tonic

Bug Away Spray

1 cup of Murphy's Oil Soap
1 cup of antiseptic mouthwash
1 cup of Tobacco Tea (recipe on page 61)

Mix these ingredients together in a 20 gallon hose-end sprayer and soak your plants to the point of run-off.

Tarnished Plant Bugs

Either green or brown in color, these little ¼-inch-long bugs always have small yellow triangles on each side near their tail

ends. As they feed on stem tips and flowers, they inject a toxin that makes black spots develop. They can be serious pests when they get going on numerous vegetables (including asparagus, potatoes, chard, and beans), and they also attack dahlias, impatiens, and a few other flowers. Tarnished plant bugs overwinter as adults, and they are much worse in warm climates than in places where winter freezes them out.

Control: Handpick the ones you can and drown them in a bucket of warm soapy water. Then drench plants well with my Bug Away Spray, and your tarnished plant bugs should be history! In case a few escape and look for cozy places to spend the winter in your yard, be sure to clean it up nicely in the fall by removing weeds around your vegetable garden and raking up old mulches and dumping them onto your compost pile.

Squash Bugs

Anyone who's ever grown squash or melons knows these culprits. Adults are dark brown to black, oval in shape, and tiny. When threatened, they give off an unpleasant odor (which is why they're also called stinkbugs). They winter in weeds, wood piles, or tree bark. Come spring, they zero in on young squash crops, lay eggs on the undersides of leaves, and start munching.

Control: Spray plants with water. The bugs will run to the undersides of leaves or drop to the ground, where they become sitting ducks for you and your spray bottle full of Knock 'em Dead Insect Spray. So take aim, and let 'em have it! Then rub off the eggs with your fingers.

Timely Tonic

Knock 'em Dead Insect Spray

6 cloves of garlic, chopped fine
1 small onion, chopped fine
1 tbsp. of cayenne pepper
1 tbsp. of liquid dish soap

Mix these ingredients in 1 quart of warm water and let sit overnight. Strain, pour the liquid into a sprayer bottle, and let 'em have it!

Clashing with Caterpillars

Caterpillars are the larvae of a number of different moths and butterflies. Most of the ones that are yard and garden pests are moth larvae, though parsleyworms hatch into beautiful black swallowtail butterflies. Here's a roster of the major nuisances.

Cabbage Worms

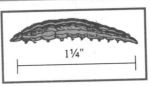

1¼"

These creeps won't catch you by surprise if you keep a sharp eye out for their mamas, which are little white butterflies that appear first thing in spring, flitting here and there in search of any plant remotely related to cabbage. Though they head for the veggies first, they also zero in on flowers now and then. The butterflies lay scattered eggs on the undersides of leaves. The eggs hatch into tiny green caterpillars, and once they start feeding, they grow fast and often reach over an inch in length. If you grow broccoli and other cabbage crops in the fall, you can expect to see cabbage worms then, too, because no matter how well you control them in the spring, a few find wild mustard or other acceptable weeds that carry them through the summer.

Control: There's a certain art to handpicking cabbage worms, because they are exactly the same color as cabbage, broccoli, and cauliflower leaves, and they hide from predators by stretching out along leaf veins, where their cam-

Recycling Roundup

Whenever you need to sprinkle Cabbage Worm Wipeout or any other nonpoisonous powder over your plants, place the powdery mixture in a small paper bag with about 5 small holes punched in the bottom. Blow up the bag with air, twist the neck tightly, and shake away.

Harness Bird Power

Sparrows and other little birds will help you out by pecking up cabbage worms, so I like to push 4-foot-long branches into the soil in my cabbage patch to give birds a place to perch. I figure if the birds pause there for a second, they might spy a cabbage worm or two that will make a tasty snack.

Timely Tonic

Cabbage Worm Wipeout

This terrific mixture will keep cabbage worms where they belong: far away from your plants.

1 cup of flour
2 tbsp. of cayenne pepper

Mix the ingredients together, and sprinkle over your cabbage heads and all over your broccoli and cauliflower to give them a good coating. The flour swells up inside the worms and bursts their insides, while the hot pepper keeps other critters away.

Cutworms

Every seed sower has to beware of these pests. They

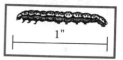

come out at night and chop down any flower and vegetable seedling they come across. Cutworms also can damage tomato seedlings set out in spring, and young bedding plants, from dianthus to pansies, are not immune to damage. These dastardly critters are the larvae of several types of dull-colored moths. They are most active in late spring and early summer, just as night temperatures rise into the 60°F range. During the day, cutworms hide in the soil, and they always do their dirty work under cover of darkness. A real heartbreaker of a pest, cutworms damage plants by curling their bodies around the main stem, eating through it, and then leaving it to die.

Control: Because the adult moths lay their eggs around the bases of weeds and grasses,

ouflage is nothing short of amazing. Now, I hate it when I cut into a cabbage head or break into a broccoli crown with little cabbage worms hidden inside, so I use this easy remedy, which I call Cabbage Worm Wipeout, starting when my cabbage begins to head. In addition to killing cabbage worms that eat the stuff, the powdery residue on the plants makes wanderers easy to spot and pluck.

... AND STAY OUT!

To keep cutworms from moving in next year, do what Grandma Putt did: Plant onions, garlic, or tansy among the culprits' favorite targets.

you can expect serious cutworm problems when growing plants in new beds that were previously covered with these plants. Prepare the bed in early spring. That way, you'll move the cutworms up close to the soil surface, where birds can spot them, zero in, and have the pesky pests for lunch. Robins, meadowlarks, blue jays, and blackbirds all consider cutworms to be gourmet chow.

Go for the Soft Underbelly

Cutworms don't like to slink across stuff that prickles their skin. So once your seedlings have outgrown their little collars, sprinkle the soil around each plant with one of these rib-ticklers:

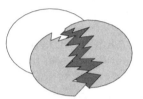

- **Chicken manure**

- **Eggshells**

- **Hair**

- **Wood ashes**

Collar 'em

Cutworms are the worst enemies a seedling ever had. Even if you have thrown a preplanting open house for the birds — and definitely if you haven't — your baby plants need protection. The best way to head off the varmints at the pass is to put a small barrier around each seedling. I sink my mini corrals 2 inches into the ground with about 3 inches showing above. Collars made from any of these materials will give young flower and veggie plants first-rate protection.

- **Aluminum foil**

- **Corrugated plastic or metal drain tile**

- **Linoleum**

- **Mailing tubes**

- **Paper or plastic cups with the bottoms cut out**

- **Tin cans minus the ends**

- **Cardboard tubes from wrapping paper, toilet paper, or paper towels**

Parsleyworms

Also known as celery worms and car-rot worms, these beautiful caterpillars have bright green and yellow bands across their backs. Unfortunately, they have killer appetites for dill, carrot, parsley, and parsnip leaves. After they eat their fill, parsleyworms pupate and, about 2 weeks later, emerge as beautiful black swallowtail butterflies.

Recycling Roundup

Don't toss your grapefruit rinds onto the compost pile. They make great traps for cutworms. Just scrape out the insides and set the rinds around the garden in the evening. When you go back in the morning, the bugs will be clustered inside and you can scoop them up, traps and all. Then squash the creeps, burn them, or dump them into hot soapy water. Also, when you're on a search-and-destroy mission, be sure to dig about 2 inches under the soil — they hide there, especially early in the morning.

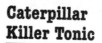

Timely Tonic

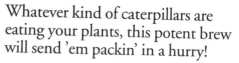

Caterpillar Killer Tonic

Whatever kind of caterpillars are eating your plants, this potent brew will send 'em packin' in a hurry!

½ lb. of wormwood leaves
2 tbsp. of Murphy's Oil Soap
4 cups of water

Simmer the wormwood leaves in 2 cups of the water for 30 minutes. Strain, then add the Murphy's Oil Soap and the remaining 2 cups of water. Pour the solution into a 6 gallon sprayer, and spray your plants to the point of run-off. Repeat this treatment until the caterpillars are history.

Control: Parsleyworms are so colorful that they're easy to handpick. And because I'm an old butterfly watcher from way back, I look for a clump of Queen Anne's lace (which is actually a wild carrot), and gently place the worms I collect on the foliage.

Sod Webworms

These nasty guys are grayish or tan caterpillars

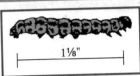
1⅛"

with black spots on their backs. They grow up into moths that prowl by night and sleep in your grass by day — except when you wake them up with your mower and they leap up to fly in zigzag patterns in front of you as you move across your lawn. Sod webworms will chow down on any type of grass, but they have a special hankerin' for Kentucky bluegrass and bent grass, and their favorite stomping, er, crawling, ground is America's heartland. You'll usually find the lowlifes concentrated in heavily thatched or dry areas of the lawn, where they create small, irregular dead patches of grass that slowly get larger and larger.

Jerry Baker Says . . .

"One clue that you've got sod webworms is if you see flocks of birds feeding on your lawn. They can't resist these tasty treats!"

GRANDMA PUTT'S OLD-TIME TIPS

TURN OFF THE MACHINE

Caterpillars are real leaf-eating machines. But you can keep them from eating your plants down to nubs and still make a haven for butterflies. Just do what Grandma Putt did: Plant crops of parsley, milkweed, and Queen Anne's lace for the larvae to munch on, and plenty of flowers that the jewel-toned grownups will flock to.

Control: Prevent their arrival by regularly aerating your lawn to remove thatch and improve water penetration. Once you've got 'em, apply *Bacillus thuringiensis* var. kurstaki (Btk), nematodes, my All-Season Clean-Up Tonic (see page 60), insecticidal soaps, or a pyrethrum-based insecticide. In extreme cases, reseed the lawn with endophytic lawn seed, which resists the creeps. Ask your Cooperative Extension Service to recommend a variety that performs well in your region.

Tent Caterpillars

The immature form of a brown moth, these are bluish, black, tan, or greenish hairy

1"– 1½"

caterpillars with spots or stripes. They build tents in the forks of their favorite trees.

Larvae in "tent"
on branch

During the day, they eat leaves. At night, they return to their tents. As the caterpillars get larger, their tents do, too. Their favorite menu items are apple and wild cherry trees, but they also chow down on cherry, peach, oak, willow, crabapple, and other trees. And chow down they do! These buggers can strip a tree bare of its leaves. Although a victim tree can produce a second set of leaves, the effort weakens it.

Control: In early spring, check your trees every 7 to 10 days for the signs. When you see them, remove the tents with a stick or high-pressure hose and drop them into a coffee can with about 2 inches of oil in the bottom. If you'd rather spray first and whack later, give the slimers a blast of my Caterpillar Killer Tonic (see page 215).

Hooray! They're Foiled Again!

To keep tent caterpillars from attacking your trees, follow this 3-step process.

Step 1 Wrap the lower section of each trunk with aluminum foil.

Step 2 Fasten the foil securely to the trunk at both top and bottom with electrical tape.

Step 3 Paint a ring of motor oil around the center of the foil strip, making sure that none of it gets onto the trunk.

FRISKY FLIES

The nasty flies that sneak into your house and send you running for the flyswatter won't hurt your yard, but they have several cousins that can really make a mess of certain plants. The adult flies lay their eggs on or near the plants they know their babies will like, and the larvae, which are always legless, squirmy little maggots, are often the real troublemakers. Here are four you are likely to encounter sooner rather than later.

Leaf Miners

These culprits don't kill plants, but they sure make a mess of 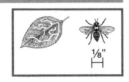 the leaves! Adult flies, which are usually very small and innocent looking, lay their eggs inside leaves, where the maggots feed, protected on both sides by the leaf surfaces. As they feed, they make meandering trails, so that the leaves look like they have been scribbled upon. Various leaf miner species attack larkspur, chrysanthemum, columbine, beets and spinach, and several shrubs.

Control: Because leaf miners feed inside leaves where sprays can't touch them, you can't control them that way. Instead, pick off leaves that show trails and destroy them. Besides sheltering a second generation, the damaged sections can become open invitations to diseases.

Root Maggots

If you've grown any member of the onion or cabbage family, you know what problems these guys can be. Adult flies lay  eggs in the soil around plants, and the larvae tunnel into the ground and eat the roots. If cabbage seedlings suddenly wilt and die, or onions simply stop growing, gently dig up a plant, swish the roots in a bucket of water, and look for little white maggots to float to the top.

Control: Rotate, rotate, rotate! Moving your plants around is a great defense against root maggots. This is especially important with winter-hardy onions, which are often damaged by maggots in the warm climates where they grow best.

Whiteflies

These teeny, tiny flying white insects damage plants by sucking juices from leaves and stems, and they usually take to the air in a cloud when disturbed. The eggs and larvae are too small to see, but you'll often notice leaves falling to the ground from plants that are badly infested. Whiteflies make themselves at home on a number of different plants, including beans, tomatoes, and cucumbers, as well as ageratum, basil, calendula, geraniums, and salvias.

Control: If you catch whitefly problems early, you can often dash their hopes for a happy summer by spraying your plants with anything soapy — including a good washdown with 2 tablespoons of baby shampoo or liquid dish soap per gallon of water. Be sure to thoroughly cover the undersides of leaves, because that's where the babies are found. In more serious situations, hit 'em hard with my Whitefly Wipeout Tonic. You'll get the best results by applying it first thing in the morning, before the dew dries and the whiteflies become airborne.

Fruit Flies

If you love to grow fruit, these guys are your arch enemies. Adults lay eggs in immature cherries, apples, or blueberries, and the resulting maggots proceed to eat their fill. Sometimes they also go after peaches, nectarines, pears, and plums.

Control: Call out the troops, namely braconid and ichneumon wasps, which polish off fruit flies by laying eggs inside them. If you grow plenty of flowers, these good guys will show up from near and far to sip the nectar. You can also hang up round red sticky traps and zap the fruit flies as they whiz by.

Timely Tonic

Whitefly Wipeout Tonic

1 cup of sour milk (let it stand out for 2 days)
2 tbsp. of flour
1 qt. of warm water

Mix these ingredients in a bowl and spray the mixture over any plants that are troubled by whiteflies.

Sap Suckers

These little terrors live their entire lives without ever eating solid food. Instead, they sink their little mouth parts into tender stems and leaves, and settle in to drink their fill. It's quite a trick, because even in dry weather, these critters don't have to worry about moisture. Here are three of the more important ones, and what to do when they show up in your yard.

Aphids

We old-timers used to call these pests plant lice. There are hundreds of species, and some of them can feed only on specific plants. Others have a number of different host plants. All aphids are small, pear-shaped critters, usually less than ⅛ inch long, and where you see one, you'll see a hundred, often clustered on stems so that they form a mass. Color varies with the species. They come in pink, yellow, black, and just about every shade of green.

Control: A few aphids are not a problem, but a lot of them are! Don't worry if they're widely scattered over plants, but do worry if they appear in hordes. I find that it's often simplest to pinch off leaves or stems that are covered with aphids, because they've usual-

Be Kind to the Ladies

Ladybeetles, a.k.a. ladybugs, that is. Ladybugs are big-time predators of many types of aphids. Their larvae have even bigger appetites — these little guys eat aphids like I eat popcorn! Look for these spiny, elongated red and black critters wherever you see aphids. Watching them work is quite a show!

ly been so badly damaged that they won't recover anyway. To protect plant parts that haven't been discovered yet, give them a thorough drench with my Lethal Weapon. The soap in the tonic often kills adult aphids, and the smelly garlic-and-onion juice repels others in search of a tasty liquid dinner.

Leafhoppers

With their powerful rear legs, these guys can jump like fleas. In fact, Grandma  Putt used to call them "flower fleas." These ⅛-inch-long insects have a distinctive wedge shape. You'll know you have a leafhopper problem if you see brown curled edges on the leaves of your plants. Their prime targets are asters, dahlias, and just about any veggie plant you can think of. When leafhoppers feed on asters, they also can transmit a disease called aster yellows, that makes the plants turn yellow and die.

Control: My Lethal Weapon will also do a number on leafhoppers, but make sure you spray the undersides of leaves very thoroughly — That's where the rascals like to hide. If there are still hoppers around a few days later, spray them with horticultural oil, mixed according to label directions, or a simple mixture of 2 tablespoons of vegetable oil and 1 tablespoon of baby shampoo mixed into a quart of water.

Timely Tonic

Lethal Weapon

3 tbsp. of garlic-and-onion juice*
3 tbsp. of skim milk
2 tbsp. of baby shampoo
1 tsp. of hot sauce
1 gal. of water

Mix all the ingredients together in a bucket, and pour into your 20 gallon hose-end sprayer, and spray on plants every 10 days.

*To make garlic-and-onion juice, chop 2 cloves of garlic and 2 medium onions. Blend in a blender with 3 cups of water, strain, and use remaining liquid. Freeze extra for future use.

Spider Mites

These little devils are so tiny you can't see them, but you can see the thousands of pinprick-sized yellow marks they make as they eat leaves. They're

Adult: less than 1/50"

most active in hot, dry weather, and they love beans, tomatoes, hydrangeas, roses, and just about any annual flower you can name.

Control: Spray your yard with my All-Season Clean-Up Tonic every 3 weeks during the summer (see page 60). Should the pests take you by surprise, surprise them back with my Super Spider Mite Mix (see page 188).

Baffling Bugs That Bite

You can have the most beautiful yard in the whole world, and end up suffering each time you try to enjoy it, if you're bothered by bugs that bite. Maybe ants ambush your footsteps, or mosquitoes make it impossible to relax and have fun. Even these guys have weaknesses that you can take advantage of to make your yard a more comfortable place to be.

Mosquitoes

If you live anywhere near fresh water or your climate is just plain rainy, you'll probably feel the sting of mosquitoes.  They can get you any time of day, though they're always worst at night. These thirsty little bloodsuckers genuinely need you for nourishment, so they are not easily discouraged.

In case you didn't know it, mosquitoes need fresh water in order to reproduce, because the larval stage is spent in water. They don't need much — an old pan left to collect rainwater that never gets emptied makes a fine skeeter nursery — so use your smarts and remove the secret water catchers around your yard.

Control: Some people find that growing lots of French marigolds makes mosquitoes go elsewhere, and it's a fact that bats love to munch on the foul things. I also think that skeeters like some people more than others. So if you're one of the unlucky ones, you'd better be ready to defend yourself with insect repellent. You can also reduce the numbers of culprits that call your yard home with my Mosquito Lemon Aid. Your yard will smell lemon fresh, but the skeeters will hate it!

Timely Tonic

Mosquito Lemon Aid

1 cup of lemon-scented ammonia
1 cup of lemon-scented dish soap

Put these ingredients into your 20 gallon hose-end sprayer and hose down everything in your yard 3 times a week, preferably early in the morning or late in the evening.

Princely Predators

When it comes to keeping mosquitoes where they belong — over the hills and far away — you couldn't ask for a better helper than a toad. Just one of these critters will put away hundreds of skeeters in a single night. And toads have plenty more than mosquitoes on their menu. They also chow down on sowbugs, gypsy moth larvae, slugs, cutworms, and all kinds of beetles. In fact, the scientists who study these things say that a single toad will pack away about 15,000 bugs in a single year.

It's a cinch to attract these helpful diners: Garden centers sell little houses specially made for toads, but it's easy to make your own toad abode from an old clay flowerpot. Just break a gap out of the rim to make a door, then set the pot upside down on top of some loosened soil in a quiet part of the yard (one that's safe from lawn mowers and family pets). Make sure there's a small body of water nearby, like a big birdbath sunk into the ground. Toads don't drink through their mouths; they absorb water through their skin, so they need a place that's deep

enough to jump into and soak in for a while. (This could be the excuse you've been waiting for to build a garden pond.)

Bat-er Up!

Like most folks, I used to turn purple at the thought of having a bat anywhere near my house. Then I learned that, though they're not the cutest critters on the face of the earth, they are one of the most valuable. They avoid humans like the plague, but they're the worst enemy a mosquito could ask for. They also zero in on the flying (and egg-laying) adult forms of cabbage worms, cutworms, assorted beetles, and corn earworms. Hard as it is to believe, every night, an adult bat puts away between 150 and 600 pests an hour. That's why I've bought bat houses at the garden center and hung them in my trees.

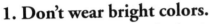

If there's anything more irritating than being dogged by buzzing bugs, I don't know what it is. The good news is that most of those buzzers won't hurt you — though I've been known to hurt myself by slapping at them so hard, I bruised my arm and my glasses fell off. Here are 5 simple ways to make yourself into a no-buzz zone when you're out working or playing in your yard.

1. Don't wear bright colors.
Wasps and bees aren't the brainiest critters on the face of the earth, but they sure know where their dinner comes from: brightly colored flowers! So don't go around looking like a bed of roses. Instead, try blending into the ground: Stick with beige or brown as your stock shades for gardenwear.

2. Avoid perfumes and colognes.
Just as you don't want to look like a bee's dinner, you don't want to smell like it, either.

3. Wear a broad-brimmed hat.
For some reason, the shade of a wide brim seems to discourage buzzing gnats, which can drive you nuts.

4. Swish aromatic herbs.
Before you start a yard project or launch into a game of Frisbee with the kids, pluck a few branches of basil, scented geraniums, or other aromatic herbs, and swish them in the air in the place where you'll be working or playing. Just a whiff of these spicy aromas seems to keep some insects away. And their loss is your gain, because the place will smell great to human noses!

5. Keep Avon Skin-So-Soft on hand.
Some days, the biting flies and no-see-ums are so persistent that you need to bring out the big guns. So slap on the lotion, and then sit back and smile.

Ants up Your Pants

There's no doubt about it: Ants can be annoying. But they have lots of important work to do, from tunneling around in the soil to help it drain better, to marching single file up a tree to tell us that rain is on the way.

Live and Let Live

Ants are fine most of the time; but when they decide to make a mound right beside your walkway or start scampering into the kitchen, here are 3 surefire ways to say "Scram!"

1. Pour boiling water onto the anthill — it'll turn it into a ghost town faster than you can say "Days of '49!" Just be sure to put safety first and carry that water in a container with a tight-fitting lid.

2. Lay sprigs of fresh mint where the little fellas are coming and going. Then, for good measure, brew up a batch of strong mint tea and spray it on their pathways. They'll hightail it outta there!

3. If all else fails, let 'em have it with either my Ant Control Tonic or my Ant Ambrosia. Don't use the first one if you have children or pets, because the boric acid will make them sick. But Ant Ambrosia won't hurt anybody but ants.

Timely Tonics

Ant Ambrosia

4–5 tbsp. of cornmeal
3 tbsp. of bacon grease
3 tbsp. of baking powder
3 packages of baker's yeast

Mix the cornmeal and bacon grease into a paste, then add the baking powder and yeast. Dab the gooey mix on the sides of jar lids, and set them near the anthills. The pesky critters will love it to death!

Ant Control Tonic

1 cup of sugar
3 cups of water
1 tbsp. of boric acid powder

Add the sugar to the water, and bring to a boil. Next, add the boric acid. Place the mix in jar lids, and set them in the middle of ant trails or near anthills. Store any extra in a child-safe container in a cabinet out of reach of children and pets.

Slugs and snails aren't insects, but they sure can bug your garden! Their favorite home is in damp shade, where they chomp on leaves of hostas and many other plants. But these guys can cause problems in any place they can hide from the sun — in mulches, under boards, or even in the folds of lettuce leaves.

Four Fine Ways to Slay Slugs and Snails

1. Clean up hiding places. Pick up pots and rocks that shelter them during the day, and go easy on mulch until you get your slimers under control.

2. Make 'em itch. Slugs and snails move by sliming along, and they are irritated by rough surfaces like sawdust or my favorite slug barrier, diatomaceous earth. This is a powder made from ground-up fossils, and its particles are so sharp that they cut into slugs and snails. Spread it around plants as a barrier, and be sure to reapply it after heavy rains.

3. Trap 'em. You can collect lots of slugs or snails by simply placing hollowed-out citrus rinds, or even upturned clay flowerpots in the

Timely Tonic

Slug It Out Tonic

1 can of beer
1 tbsp. of sugar
1 tsp. of baker's yeast

Mix these ingredients in a bowl, and let 'em sit for 24 hours. Then pour the mixture into shallow aluminum pie pans, and set the pans so the rims are just at ground level in various areas of your garden.

slimers' favorite stomping grounds. Set out the traps in the evening; come morning, pluck out any captives and drown them in a pail of salty water.

4. Bait 'em. Fill cat food cans with my Slug It Out Tonic. The slugs will slide in for a sip, and then go hog wild and drown themselves in it. Clean out and rebait your traps every other day.

CHAPTER 15

When the Culprit Is a Critter

Just when you think you've got your yard nicely settled in for the season, devastation strikes with all four paws! *Pow!* Animals large and small can wreak havoc in your yard, but there are some easy ways to outsmart every last one of them. Here's what you need to know to protect your yard from critters, whether they're your faithful old dog, dirt-digging rodents, hungry rabbits, or deer that tiptoe through the tulips.

PET PATROL

Some of the best friends I've ever had have been dogs and cats, but I learned the hard way that their ideas on gardening are different from mine. Dogs like to adopt soft planting beds as resting spots, while cats think that any well-cultivated spot (or pot) is a convenient bathroom. I also once had a dog who liked to pick off half-ripened tomatoes and eat them.

When you share your outdoor space with pets, it's smart to adopt a spirit of cooperation. If your dog likes to run along a certain fence to entertain passersby, or if he insists on taking his afternoon nap in a particular spot, you'll be fighting a losing battle if you try to grow flowers there. And since cats usually get what they want no matter what, it might be a good idea to give them a sandbox where they can romp without bothering your prized plantings.

Dogs Do It

Doggie damage in the landscape usually comes in one of three forms:

- Holes in your lawn and flower beds
- Sleeping spots where you don't want them
- Yellow spots in the lawn

But not to worry: I have easy solutions for all three, so it's not hard to have a beautiful yard and a happy dog!

Don't Give the Dog a Bone

A dog's sense of smell is 400 times as acute as ours, so naturally, he thinks that there's a bone to be found in planting holes that have bonemeal in them. The solution? If you share your yard with a digging dog, switch to another phosphorus-rich fertilizer. Colloidal phosphate, fish emulsion, poultry manure, rock phosphate, and seaweed are all great sources of the Big P.

They Won't Dig It!

Like people, dogs are sensitive to the capsaicin found in hot peppers, so I want you to make a habit of sprinkling my Dog-Be-Gone Tonic on newly cultivated soil where you don't want your dog to dig. After a few tries,

Fido will associate planting beds with a burning nose, and won't even try to dig where you've just planted — whether the pepper is there or not.

Go Bananas

She never did figure out why, but Grandma Putt knew that many dogs find the scent of bananas pretty disgusting, so she always laid banana peels in spots where she didn't want canines to camp out. And you know what? It worked! And that's not all: Those potassium-rich peels are like ambrosia to your plants, especially roses, which can never get their fill of the yellow wonders.

Bramble Beds

If your dog insists on sleeping on your prized clematis or smack dab in the middle of your hosta garden, stockpile pruned branches from roses, raspberries, and other thorny plants, and spread them over the area where you don't want him to sleep. Believe you me, he'll vacate that sleeping spot in no time flat!

Out, Out, Dog Spots

Yellowed doggie spots in the lawn are caused by excess nitrogen and salts in canine urine, both of which burn grass plants. To repair a dog-spotted lawn, first lightly sprinkle gypsum over and around each spot (it dissolves accumulated salts like magic). Then overspray your lawn with 1 cup of baby shampoo or liquid dish soap per 20 gallons of water. One week later, overspray the turf with my Lawn Saver Tonic.

Timely Tonics

Dog-Be-Gone Tonic

Keep dogs out by dousing your garden with this spicy Tonic.

2 cloves of garlic
2 small onions
1 jalapeño pepper
1 tbsp. of cayenne pepper
1 tbsp. of hot sauce
1 tbsp. of chili powder
1 tbsp. of liquid dish soap
1 qt. of warm water

Chop the garlic, onions, and pepper fine, and then combine with the rest of the ingredients. Let the mixture sit and "marinate" for 24 hours, strain it through cheesecloth or old panty hose, then sprinkle it on any areas where dogs are a problem.

Lawn Saver Tonic

½ can of beer
½ can of regular cola (not diet)
½ cup of ammonia

Combine these ingredients in your 20 gallon hose-end sprayer. Then spray your turf to the point of run-off.

Use Your Pooper Scooper, but . . .

Never put pet waste onto your compost heap, and remove it pronto from garden areas where you grow vegetables and herbs. Parasites that can make you sick are usually present in the waste of all carnivorous animals, and it's better to be safe than sorry.

Not Here, Kitty

It's no secret that cats are territorial creatures with minds of their own. You can train them to do all sorts of cute tricks, but you can't train them not to dig in newly seeded beds. Other people's cats can cause problems, too. For example, wandering toms have no respect for your interest in smelling your roses without the acrid aroma of cat tinkle wafting through the air.

If your porch, shrubs, or garden is regularly marked by cats, keep a squirt bottle of vinegar handy and regularly spritz places where cats tend to spray. The smell of vinegar confuses and repels them. Pine cleanser, mixed half-and-half with water, works well, too, and tends to last a little longer than vinegar.

Foil 'em Fast

There's another surefire way to keep cats where they belong — away from your prize plants — and it's as easy as 1, 2, 3. Here's what you should do.

Step 1 Fill empty 2-liter pop bottles half full of water.

Step 2 Put a couple of long, thin strips of aluminum foil into each bottle, and add a bit of bleach, just to prevent stinky algae from growing.

Step 3 Set the bottles strategically around the problem area.

GIVE A LITTLE Grandma Putt's way of heading off problems with frisky felines was to grow a big patch of catnip just for them. They'd be so busy romping and rolling in their own "garden" that they wouldn't even bother to visit Grandma's plants.

The foil's changing reflections will scare off any feline who tries to lay claim to your turf, and your catty problems will be a thing of the past.

Timely Tonics

Meow-va-lous Tonics

Cats are very scent oriented, and they can be just as finicky about what they smell as they are about what they'll eat. It's easy to persuade them not to dig in your flower and herb beds, or your newly planted vegetable garden: Just pick and choose between these two Tonics, and use them as a scent fence around your no-cats-wanted territory.

Tonic #1: Mix ½ cup of Tobacco Tea (recipe on page 61) or oil of mustard and ¼ cup of liquid dish soap in 2 gallons of warm water.

Tonic #2: Add 1 clove of garlic (crushed), 1 tbsp. of cayenne pepper, and 1 tsp. of liquid dish soap to 1 qt. of warm water, and puree the heck out of it.

Scat Cat Solution

To keep cats from digging in container plants, indoors or out, dribble this elixir lightly over the top of the soil's surface.

5 tbsp. of flour
4 tbsp. of powdered mustard
3 tbsp. of cayenne pepper
2 tbsp. of chili powder
2 qts. of warm water

Mix all of these ingredients together and sprinkle the solution around the perimeter of the areas you want to protect.

Don't You Dare Eat My Pals!

Some of the best friends we have are birds. Not only do they entertain us with their songs and their antics, but they also gobble up a ton of pesky bugs that cause endless amounts of yard and garden damage. But the archenemies of birds are — as we all know — cats. Now, don't get me wrong: I love cats (especially my own), but I've learned that when it comes to prey on the wing, there's no way to reason with them. The best way to keep yard-worker birds safe and happy on the job is to keep your cat inside. If your neighbors' cats are on the prowl and gunning for the birds in your yard, lay chicken wire on the ground under the nesting areas. Ornery felines will keep their distance.

WATCH IT

Don't Let 'em Pine Away

If you use a pine cleanser as a cat chaser, make sure you spray it only on hard surfaces or in places where plants don't grow, because it can poison their roots.

Rodent Roundup

One look at the long front teeth of chewing rodents, and you know that these are critters you don't want in your garden. Sometimes, it's not hard to simply poison pesky rodents, but you never know what will become of the dead ones. Dogs, cats, and birds can easily be poisoned by eating poisoned rodents — and you sure as shootin' don't want curious kids stumbling across the foul things! So I'm going to concentrate on control methods that are both effective and safe for people, pets, and plants.

GETTING AFTER GOPHERS

After hearing for years and years about gardeners' problems with gophers, I've about decided that there's a difference between country gophers and city gophers. The ones that live out where it's peaceful and quiet get spooked by small things, such as the vibrations from whirligigs set into the ground around the garden, or the regular footsteps of a gopher-getting dog. But city gophers are much bolder, and quickly become accustomed to the noise of lawn mowers, traffic, and the comings and goings of people and pets. Naturally, they're a tougher sort to keep out of your garden.

Get a Positive I.D.

Because defending your garden from gophers can be a lot of work, first make sure it's gophers you've got rather than moles. You'll know it's a g-man at work if:

✔ You see loose mounds of earth that are crescent or horseshoe shaped. (Moles always make round mounds.)

✔ Turnips, carrots, and other root crops get popped out of place by being pulled from below.

✔ You find 2-inch-wide tunnels about 6 to 12 inches below the surface.

Go Below

I admit it's a big job to tackle, but if you live where gophers are causing trouble everywhere, your best option — in fact, maybe your only option — is to defend your territory with a secure gopher fence. Most of the structure goes underground, because that's where gophers travel. To erect your barrier, bury a length of chicken wire or hardware cloth 18 inches below the surface, leaving 6 to 12 inches rising above ground level. In addition to protecting your plants, a gopher fence is your best defense against the toothy critters chewing into water lines and other buried utilities. And if that happens, you'll have real trouble!

Act Fast!

When you know a gopher is setting up housekeeping on your property, act fast before your problem multiplies. First, I highly recommend that you stick several wind-powered whirligigs as close to the tunnel as you can get them. Meanwhile, make up a batch of my Gopher-Go Tonic and dribble it in all the places where you suspect that the gophers are carrying on. If the culprits are staging all-out warfare on your yard, spring for a battery-operated sound device that will send them flying. They're available through catalogs and in some garden centers.

Good-bye to Moles

Moles are much smaller than gophers, but they can still do a lot of damage tunneling about under your lawn, where they eat lots of white grubs and other bugs. In fact, wherever moles travel, they tunnel right through plant roots, making them susceptible to new problems with drought and soilborne diseases.

The Farewell Party

I once had a little dog who loved to dig up moles, but the holes she dug were bigger than the ones made by the moles! So instead of depending on a dog for mole control, here's the 3-step program I want you to follow.

Step 1 Walk over every mole tunnel you see to push the grass back into place so it can take root and grow again. Use colorful golf tees to mark mole runs that pop up again and again. Give these runs a good dose of my Mole-Chaser Tonic.

Step 2 When you find an open mole hole, drop in a piece of unwrapped Juicy Fruit chewing gum and a clove of garlic that's been partially crushed. The critters' little pink snouts will turn red with confusion!

Step 3 Note all areas where you suspect that moles have been carrying on, and overspray the spots with my Move On Moles Tonic (see page 128). Any moles who have not yet made up their minds about hitting the road will quickly decide that your yard is not such a good place to be after all!

Timely Tonic

Mole-Chaser Tonic

This potent potion will give moles a taste they won't soon forget!

1½ tbsp. of hot sauce
1 tbsp. of liquid dish soap
1 tsp. of chili powder
1 qt. of water

Mix all of these ingredients, and pour a little of the mix into mole runways to make those moles run away!

VOLE CONTROL

Voles, which are close kin to mice, are pests in the winter, when they run in mole runs and eat any roots they come across. They can make a mess of flower beds, lawn, young trees, and shrubs. Fortunately, if you try this trio of tricks in the fall, chances are the vile villains will pack up and spend the snowy season elsewhere.

1. Mix diatomaceous earth and Bon Ami cleansing powder with your fall lawn food. You'll make the varmints vamoose and pep up the grass at the same time.

2. Sprinkle the mix in planting beds and around trees and shrubs.

3. Put a dusting of plain ol' Bon Ami into planting holes before you set in spring-flowering bulbs.

Tim-*ber!*

Voles can do extensive damage to young trees in winter, often under snow. To protect your tender, woody plants from those fiendish teeth, try the following.

✔ Circling the trunks with fine mesh wire or hardware cloth from the ground up to above the typical snow line.

✔ Drenching the area around all young trees with my All-Purpose Pest Prevention Potion just before the snow flies.

✔ Trapping voles that may be hiding out in your woodpile or nearby brushy areas. Set regular mousetraps (baited with peanut butter) in milk cartons or coffee cans, positioned so that children and pets can't be harmed.

Those Darn Rabbits

Rabbits are cute as all get-out — until they get into your garden and nibble your lettuce down to nubs, or strip your young shrubs of every last leaf. Fortunately, there are lots of creative ways to outwit rabbits by offending their sense of smell, spooking them with sound, or fencing them out with chicken wire.

Scent Fences

A fast-moving cat or dog can catch a rabbit, so the smell of your pets naturally puts bunnies on edge. You never want to put used cat litter on soil used to grow edible plants, but depositing some outside your garden will form a scent fence that rabbits will think about twice before crossing. Draping dog blankets around bushes or small trees works the same magic.

Recycling Roundup

The same milk cartons you use to protect plants from frost will keep them out of reach of rabbits. Cut off the bottom of each jug, and make a V-shaped slit in the top of the handle. Poke a stick down through the handle and into the ground to hold the jug steadily in place.

No Nibbling!

In winter, when there's not much around to eat, rabbits may nibble on the trunks of tender young trees. Protect the trunks with chicken wire or a wrapping of hardware cloth. Branches pruned from trees left lying on the ground may be of more interest to rabbits than tree trunks, especially if those branches hold tender twigs and buds.

Bottle Blowers

You know that deep bass fiddle sound you can make by blowing across the top of a soda pop bottle? That sound is *not* music to the ears of rabbits. In fact, it scares them off pronto. So bury soda pop bottles around the edge of your garden up to their necks, and let the wind do the whooshing.

Rabbitproof Fencing

A rabbit fence isn't hard to build, and it can even be an attractive addition to your landscape. To enclose a small vegetable or flower garden, here's all you need to do.

Step 1 Mark the outline of the plot you want to protect.

Step 2 Dig a 6-inch-deep trench all the way around it.

Step 3 Install 2-foot posts 6 feet apart in the trench.

Step 4 Attach chicken wire so that it reaches to the bottom of the 6-inch trench and extends at least 18 inches above the ground.

Step 5 Fill in the soil around the base of the fence.

Step 6 Install panels of picket fencing around the outside, attached to the same posts, along with a matching gate. As long as you remember to latch the gate, rabbits will have to drool over your lettuce and carrots from afar!

Jerry Baker Says . . .

"If you're plagued by rabbits as well as gophers, follow the directions for the gopher fence on page 233 and keep both pesky pests at bay."

Is It a Rabbit or Is It . . . ?

There's no doubt that rabbits love to sink their chops into your plants (Yum!). But so do plenty of other critters. If you're not sure who your diners are, do a little detective work and examine the damage. Rabbits make clean edges and leave behind the crowns of the lettuce, poppies, or whatever plants they've enjoyed as a predawn breakfast. Also, look around for the rabbit droppings — small piles of dark brown nuggets that look like Trix cereal only smaller. (If you do find that a rabbit has left behind little calling cards, scoop them up and scatter them around your plants: Rabbit droppings make fabulous fertilizer!)

If you have big shade trees around your house, then you probably have a dandy crop of squirrels to go with them. A hundred years ago, when squirrel stew was a practical and popular dish, squirrel populations actually dipped pretty low. But as cities became larger and people took to eating fancier stuff, squirrels figured out how to coexist with humans with great success. As a result, many towns are now teeming with the little gray bushy-tails.

But They're So Cute!

Yep. The problem is that while a few squirrels are usually satisfied with acorns and other wild foods, things go haywire when too many squirrels try to live in a small space. If they get hungry enough, they will eat any kind of seeds they can find, dig up tulip, crocus, and several other bulbs, and even start in on your shrubs. Even worse, when they run out of nesting sites in trees, squirrels are prone to moving into attics, basements, and unused chimneys.

Chicken Wire Boxes

Squirrels are so acrobatic that you can't fence them out of your whole yard, but you can fence them out of a certain bed or a collection of containers. Build a wood box frame, staple chicken wire onto it, and pop it over beds or pots you want to keep out of the reach of squirrels. To protect a small tomato patch, fasten chicken wire to wood stakes and encircle your plants. When you're not using it, you can roll up your squirrel fence for easy storage.

WATCH IT

Don't Feed the Squirrels

Although it may seem like a good idea, don't feed squirrels unless it's the only way you can lure them away from gnawing at your house. And then provide plain corncobs rather than more nutritious nuts, seeds, and corn. Giving squirrels a steady, nutritious diet frequently causes an increase in litter size, which leads to serious overpopulation problems.

Protecting Plants

Like other mammals, squirrels get burned by anything that contains capsaicin, the hot stuff in hot peppers. That's what makes my Squirrel Beater Tonic work so well. Squirrels are usually hungriest in the spring, so be ready to fight back if they start stealing flower buds and tender young shoots from perennial flowers.

It's for the Birds!

I don't know about you, but it makes me mad as a hatter to look out the window and see a squirrel helping himself to the chow in my bird feeder. But I've made a discovery: Squirrels have to be close to starving before they'll eat birdseed that's coated with cayenne pepper; but birds can't even taste it. Here's how to give wily squirrels a snack they won't like one bit.

Step 1 Find a 2-gallon plastic jug with a screw-on lid (some birdseed and dry cat food come packaged this way).

Step 2 Fill the jug two-thirds full of birdseed, and dump in a heaping tablespoon of cayenne pepper.

Step 3 Put on the lid and shake well, then pour the seed into your bird feeder.

Birds can't taste the stuff, but squirrels sure can! Whenever handling cayenne pepper, wear gloves or wash your hands promptly, and don't breathe in the dust or let it get into your eyes.

They'll Just Say No

Even if they're starving, squirrels leave these plants alone, so plant them to your heart's content.

- broccoli
- daffodils
- hot peppers
- morning glories

Recycling Roundup

To keep squirrels from climbing the pole to your bird feeder, cut holes in the bottoms of 2- or 3-liter plastic soda bottles and thread them onto the pole. Then, to make them even more slippery, slap a little petroleum jelly on the bottles.

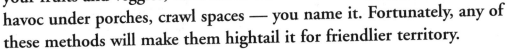

Chip 'n' Dale didn't become superstars by accident — there's not a cuter critter out there than these bushy-tailed tykes. On the flip side, there aren't many that get up to as much mischief in your yard. They'll unearth your plants, nibble on your fruits and veggies, then move on to wreak havoc under porches, crawl spaces — you name it. Fortunately, any of these methods will make them hightail it for friendlier territory.

Move 'em Out

To make 'munks hightail it:

- Sprinkle dog or cat hair around their stomping grounds.
- Put mothballs or flakes into their runs and holes, or where they enter and exit buildings.

Timely Tonic

All-Purpose Varmint Repellent

2 eggs
2 cloves of garlic
2 tbsp. of hot chili pepper
2 tbsp. of ammonia
2 cups of hot water

Mix all of these ingredients in a bucket, let the mixture sit for 3 or 4 days, and then paint it on fences, trellises, and wherever else unwanted varmints are venturing.

- Sprinkle dried blood meal in your bulb beds — besides keeping the 'munks out, this will feed your bulbs.
- Lay wire mesh over bulbs after you plant them.

Travelin' On

If the chipmunk population is bordering on the ridiculous, live-trap the critters and transport them deep into the woods. Any of these baits will work like a charm.

- **Cereal**
- **Corn**
- **Molasses on crackers or whole wheat toast**
- **Peanut butter**
- **Rolled oats**
- **Sunflower seed**
- **Unroasted peanuts**

As far as I'm concerned, there's nothing endearing about these pesky pests. They help themselves to your food — whether it's in your garden, your kitchen cabinets, or your root cellar — then demolish your belongings and leave droppings all over the place. What's even worse, the vile villains often carry a whole host of parasites and diseases.

Wanted Dead or Alive?

Trapping and poisoning are the classic control methods, but both are unpleasant and messy. What's more, dealing with the results can be downright dangerous, exposing you (and your pets and grandkids) to tapeworm, ringworm, salmonellosis, and, in the case of rats, trichinosis and even rabies. The good news is that there are better methods for dealing with these wily characters — you just need to outwit 'em.

Don't Touch Those Plants!

To protect your bulbs from mouse and rat damage, circle the bed belowground with fine mesh netting that extends 3 to 4 inches aboveground. And don't mulch until after you know the ground has frozen solid.

They're Wired

To protect fruit trees from those sharp little teeth, get yourself some 1 x 2-inch boards. Cut them into 1-foot lengths and set them against the tree trunks. Then wrap rat wire tightly around the boards. For good measure, cut up prickly branches and scatter them liberally around the base of each tree trunk. Those toothy culprits will keep their distance!

WATCH IT ⚠️

Think Thin

Come wintertime, there's almost nothing a mouse likes better than snuggling under a nice deep blanket of mulch. To keep the rascals from bedding down around your trees, keep the mulch layer on the thin side.

Roll On, You Rascals!

These are my basic guidelines for keeping rats, mice, and other rodents from taking over your turf.

✔ Keep your yard clean and free of debris. Get rid of boxes, pipes, stacks of scrap wood — anything they can use for cover and nesting sites.

✔ Have refuse carted off promptly and, in the meantime, keep it in tightly sealed containers.

✔ Store all food — both pet and human — in rodent-proof containers.

✔ Keep your compost pile turned so that it cooks properly. Better yet, invest in a few plastic compost bins. Not only will they keep your fruit and veggie scraps well removed from prying paws, but compost will reach the done stage considerably faster than it does in an uncovered pile.

✔ To keep the critters from coming and going through holes in wood or drywall, clean out all

openings and pack them with steel wool or fine copper mesh. Then seal them closed.

✔ Enlist their enemies — adopt a cat or, better yet, get a ferret or a deodorized skunk. Cats vary greatly in their mouse-hunting prowess, but ferrets and skunks are world-class performers.

✔ Sprinkle ground cayenne pepper liberally at likely entry and exit points and along runs. (It's easy to spot them — just look for fecal pellets.)

✔ Try one of the ultrasonic devices sold in hardware stores and mail-order catalogs. They repel rodents by creating stress on their bodies, but they don't bother most household pets.

These critters can do whale-sized damage, but they're less likely to come calling if you follow my basic rodent-control guidelines.

How Corny Can You Get?

Nothing starts a raccoon's heart to pitter-patterin' as much as a big patch of corn. Keeping the rascals out can take some doing, but I like to think of it as good exercise for my imagination. Here are some of my better ideas.

- Prop old screens or bushel baskets against the cornstalks.

- Cover the silks with panty-hose toes dabbed with perfume.

- Lay crumpled newspaper on the ground between rows.

- Drape strings of blinking Christmas-tree lights in and among the stalks.

- Sprinkle dog droppings, blood meal, fox scent, or coyote urine around the base of each plant.

- Spray both the stalks and the ground with my All-Purpose Varmint Repellent (see page 240).

Don't Squash 'em

Since long before Grandma Putt's day, lots of folks have kept raccoons out of the corn patch by planting squash or pumpkins among the corn. The theory is that 'coons don't like to get all tangled up in the vines on their way to the corn, so they usually just give up and go away.

Well, I've tried that method, and I've found that it has one little flaw: It works just fine if you're growing field corn or popcorn, which stays on the stalks until the end of the summer, when the kernels are good and hard, but it's another matter altogether with sweet corn, which you harvest earlier in the season. When you're trying to get to your corn, you'll get as tangled up in the vines as the 'coons would, and you'll probably squash a few squashes in the process.

Skunks: Friend or Foe?

A skunk can be good news or bad news. The good news is that, adopted young and deodorized, these friendly, pretty critters make great pets — and useful ones. A skunk can eat his weight in snails, slugs, grubs, and mice in a single night.

The Bad News

Wild skunks can destroy your lawn in the process of getting to their food. (You'll know they've been at work if you find your lawn riddled with 2- to 3-inch holes.) They also go after berries and vegetables, especially corn. Then there's the aroma. . . .

It's fairly simple to exclude skunks from their living quarters, which forces them to seek shelter elsewhere. Here's a trio of tactics.

1. Sprinkle flour around suspected entrances. When you spot tracks leading out, seal up the hole with dirt, concrete, or a big boulder.

2. Scatter mothballs or set pans of ammonia around the entrance holes.

3. Shine light on living areas.

Timely Tonics

Banishing the fragrance of eau de skunk, from either pets or property, takes powerful medicine. Fortunately, I have 2 Tonics that will do the job pronto.

Skunk-Away Pet Bath

With the help of this potion, you can deliver first aid fast to a cat or a dog who's had a run-in with the wrong end of a skunk.

1 qt. of 3% hydrogen peroxide
¼ cup of baking soda
1 tbsp. of liquid dish soap

Mix these ingredients in a bucket and wash your pet with the solution. Rinse thoroughly, then follow up with another bath using a moisturizing pet shampoo.

Skunk-Odor-Out Tonic

1 cup of bleach or vinegar
1 tbsp. of liquid dish soap
2½ gal. of warm water

Mix these ingredients and thoroughly saturate walls, stairs, or anything else your local skunk has left his mark on.
Caution: Use this Tonic only on nonliving things — not on pets or humans.

The Problem with Deer

I'll be the first to agree that deer are beautiful animals, but in some places, there are just too darn many of them! It's a wildlife management problem, but gardeners end up fighting the war. How strong is the enemy? It depends. The number of deer and the availability of food add up to what's called deer pressure. Where deer pressure is severe (lots and lots of very hungry deer), you have two options: Fence them out or grow only plants that deer don't like to eat.

The good news is that if your deer problem is relatively minor, there are lots of easy ways to keep the hungry rascals from eating up your yard. So don't give up!

Severe Deer

Installing a reliable deer fence is a big project. To declare your yard a garden oasis in the midst of a deer population that's out of control, one surefire option is to surround it with an 8-foot-high fence topped with 3 strands of barbed wire.

It's less expensive to go with an electric fence, and how extensive that fence needs to be depends on the desperation levels of local deer. If there are plenty of other places for them to go and find something to eat, you may get good protection with a single strand of electric fencing installed at knee height. But in some places I've heard about, it takes 3 strands (or even 5) to keep deer from busting through for dinner!

Timely Tonic

Deer Buster Eggnog

2 eggs
2 cloves of garlic
2 tbsp. of hot sauce
2 tbsp. of cayenne pepper
2 cups of water

Put all of these ingredients into a blender and puree. Allow the mixture to sit for 2 days, then pour or spray it all over and around the plants you need to protect.

Deterring Deer

Let's say deer aren't bad enough to fence out, but they do come around to browse on certain plants again and again. Picky eating habits are a sign that deer aren't exactly famished, which means you can probably get good results using deterrents that rely on the critters' sense of smell. Here's a roundup of the most effective ones I've found. Scatter any of these around the deer's stomping ground, and they'll head for friendlier territory.

✔ Perfumed or deodorant soap

✔ Smelly socks, dirty diapers, or old shoes

✔ Athlete's foot or baby powder, sprinkled on a cotton cloth

✔ Dog or human hair

✔ Big-cat droppings (ask your local zoo for some cougar or bobcat feces)

✔ My Deer Buster Eggnog (see page 245)

Flowers Deer Really Dig

Locate these plants where deer are known to travel, and you're asking for trouble.

Azalea	Hydrangea
Black-eyed Susan	Lily
Candytuft	Pansy
Crocus	Rose
Hosta	Tulip

Flowers Deer Don't Like

As long as deer aren't starving and these plants are not right in their path, they usually leave them alone.

Coreopsis	Iris
Daffodil	Purple coneflower
Dianthus	Vinca
Dusty miller	Yucca
Foxglove	Zinnia

Bid Birds Farewell

There's no doubt about it: Birds are some of the smartest critters you'll ever come across. That's why it's so much fun to watch them when they're hard at work making nests or flitting around getting food for their young 'uns. It's also why you can drive yourself crazy trying to keep the hungry devils from snatching a harvest out from under your very eyes.

The Plan

I have to admit that it hasn't been easy, but I've come up with a few scare tactics that actually do send the wily wingers on their way (most of the time). Here's my basic 4-part strategy.

Part 1. Make it colorful. Birds see in color, just as we do. Bright colors stand out better and look scarier than earthy tones, which blend in with the scenery. Pinwheels and small, colorful flags are a good bet. Buy a few dozen at a discount store, and set them around your garden.

Part 2. Make it noisy. Birds usually steer clear of sounds they're not used to. But don't put on loud music or tapes of booming cannons. As long as the birds can hear it when they get close to their target, they'll turn tail and head elsewhere. Try bells, wind chimes, wooden sticks tied together — anything that makes a little noise when a breeze comes up.

Part 3. Make it look dangerous. Birds are coming to your garden to *have* dinner, not to *be* dinner. If they look down and see the enemy, they'll hightail it out of there. Many garden centers sell statues of cats, owls, foxes, and dogs just for bird-scaring purposes.

Part 4. Keep it moving. Because they are so smart, birds catch on in a hurry when you're trying to pull the wool over their eyes. Whatever scare tactic you use, move it to a new spot every few days.

Trouble on the Wing

Most of us enjoy the company of birds in our yards — that is, until they start snapping up our sprouts, seeds, and berries. If your bird population is high, then you should spend a few dollars to buy some polyester bird netting. This lightweight plastic mesh will keep birds away from anything you cover with it. If you handle it gently, you can switch the netting around as needed to protect young corn sprouts in spring, ripening tomatoes in summer, and berries, grapes, and tree fruits whenever they need it.

If birds cause aggravation on only a few plants, like a little cherry tree or a pair of blueberry bushes, you can discourage feeding by spritzing the plants with my Bye-Bye, Birdie Tonic between rains.

Keep Your Kool

If pesky birds pluck up your corn seed as soon as you plant it, sprinkle the soil over the seeds with grape Kool-Aid®, straight from the packet. Birds dislike it so much that they'll go elsewhere for lunch.

Take 'em by Surprise

Birds do most of their damage in the morning, so whatever scare devices you rig up, move them around in the evening. That way, when the birds show up for breakfast, they'll have a surprise in store.

Jerry Baker Says . . .

"When you gather up your arsenal of bird-chasing gizmos, use a combination of objects, not just one, and change them frequently, so the birds don't get to thinking of them as simply part of the green scene."

Timely Tonic

Bye-Bye, Birdie Tonic

1 tbsp. of baby shampoo
1 tbsp. of ammonia
1 gal. of water

Mix these ingredients together, and between rains, spray the potion on your trees when they're full of fruit.

CHAPTER 16

Dastardly Diseases

Just like people, plants sometimes get sick. But also like people, the
healthier and happier plants are to begin with, the less likely they
are to be devastated by common diseases. Unfortunately, though,
you can do everything right for your plants and every now and then,
problems will still crop up. In this Chapter, we'll look at the most common diseases that bother landscape plants, along with easy ways to prevent or cure sick plants and bring them back into the pink of health.

GO ON THE OFFENSIVE

The first step in fighting diseases in your yard is to get them before
they have a chance to get you. You'll be well on your way to winning
the war against plant germs if you choose plants that were born (or
bred) to thrive in your climate, give them good soil and the right
amount of sunlight, and keep them well fed and watered. Then, when
any disease does rear its ugly head, you can follow through with the
routines outlined in this Chapter.

MILDEWS AND LEAF SPOTS

Because leaves and stems are the plant parts we see, diseases that cause leaves to develop unsightly patches and spots usually get our attention right off the bat. Most of these are caused by fungi — microscopic life forms that exist as parasites on our beloved plants. Disease-causing fungi invade plant tissues, destroy cells, and sap leaves of their energy, and then release thousands of spores that germinate and grow on other leaves.

Make Mine Morning

Just as with seeds, the germination of fungal spores takes time and usually requires moisture, so leaves that stay wet for a long time are usually the first ones to show signs of disease. This is one of the reasons why I recommend watering your garden in the morning. When you must water in the evening, do it with soaker hoses, so that the foliage stays dry.

The Old Eagle Eye

The best way to stop mildews and leaf spots in their tracks is to keep a close watch on your plants and keep them well supplied with my All-Around Disease Defense Tonic (see page 177). If you notice sickly leaves and pluck them off right away, there will be far fewer spores floating around, waiting for their opportunity to come to life on healthy plant leaves.

BATTLING BLIGHTS

A number of different diseases that cause dark spots to form on leaves until they wither and die are called blights. As far as this bit of nastiness is concerned, there's bad news and good news (more or less).

The bad news is that blights can spread like lightning when conditions are favorable.

The good news is that blights tend to affect only closely related plants. For example, early blight of tomato, which causes the lowest leaves to shrivel to brown, can also infect potatoes, but it won't bother other vegetables or flowers. In similar style, English ivy blight won't spread to other plants.

More Bad News

Once you've seen blight in your garden, you'll probably see it again. The spores can exist for a long time in weeds, tree crevices, and even dirt. Plus, if your neighbor's garden plants have a touch of blight, it takes only one flitting bug to carry a few spores across the fence to your place.

STOP BLOSSOM END ROT

Those dark patches on the tail ends of your tomatoes look like a disease, but they're not. Blossom end rot is really a nutritional disorder that develops when tomato plants are growing so fast and furiously that they just can't get enough calcium to the far ends of the fruits. Fortunately, there's a simple way to prevent this pesky problem: When you plant your seedlings, just put a trowelful of my Rot Go Tonic into each hole. Then, each time you water, sprinkle ground-up, dried eggshells around the base of each plant, and water them in well.

My One-Two Blight-Busting Punch

I recommend 2 ways to stop blight in its tracks.

1. Do your best to prevent blight from getting started on your plants by spritzing them regularly with Compost Tea (see page 27). It's loaded with helpful microorganisms that nurture plants while putting them on high alert to defend themselves from the bad guys.

2. If you're just unlucky and blight gets a foothold anyway, pick off the speckled leaves, and then drench your plants with my Fungus Fighter Tonic (see page 174). It'll go to work right away, picking up where the Compost Tea left off.

Timely Tonic

Rot Go Tonic

1 heaping shovelful of compost
1 tsp. of gypsum
1 tsp. of Epsom salts

Mix these ingredients in a bucket. Then, when you plant your tomato seedlings, add a trowelful to each planting hole.

PITIFUL POWDERY MILDEW

It's the most common plant disease on earth, so sooner or later you will no doubt see the telltale patches of white on leaves that are the evidence of powdery mildew. From bee balm to phlox to lilacs to dogwood trees, it's possible to see this disease on many different plants. But don't get the idea that all powdery mildews are exactly the same. They're not, so they can't spread between unrelated plants. However, the conditions that favor one strain also favor another. So whenever days are warm and nights are cool, powdery mildew might just rear its ugly white head in your lawn, your shrubs, *and* your flowers.

Stop It in Its Tracks

Older leaves are usually the first ones to show symptoms. Once a leaf is infected, you can't rub or spray away the mildew, because it is actually rooted in the leaf. But you can stop the mildew from spreading with my Powdery Mildew Control Tonic (see page 155). Before

applying the tonic, use your hose turned on full force to give your plants a vigorous shower. This step will knock lots of spores to the ground, where they are often filtered into oblivion by mulch and soil.

The Resistance Movement

Plant breeders are always trying to improve the ability of plants to stand up to powdery mildew, especially very susceptible ones like cucumber, lilac, garden phlox, and zinnia. Whenever you can, look for varieties or cultivars with the words "mildew-resistant" on the seed packet or plant tag.

ERADICATING RUST

When you run into a problem with rust, you know it in a hurry. This is one colorful disease, in that infected plants show deposits of bright orange powder on the undersides of the leaves. Those are the spores, and by the time the disease has gone this far, it's already done a lot of damage. Rust also tends to strike fast. One spell of rainy weather is all it takes to turn a tiny outbreak into an infection that runs rampant through your bean patch, blackberries, corn, or hollyhocks, or paints entire viburnums or willows with orange dust.

Jerry Baker Says . . .

"Once leaves have been infected by rust, they never really recover, but you can at least strike a blow against next season's problems by treating plants with an all-purpose fungicide such as Fung-onil. Be sure to get 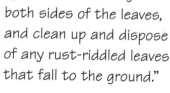 both sides of the leaves, and clean up and dispose of any rust-riddled leaves that fall to the ground."

LAWN PATCH PROBLEMS

Two different diseases cause brown patches to form in lawns, and both are caused by fungi gone out of control. In northern areas where bluegrass reigns supreme, small spots the size of a silver dollar often follow on the heels of prolonged rainy spells. This is called dollar spot disease. In warm, humid climates, much larger spots and patches are evidence of brown patch, which can ruin the appearance of a beautiful lawn.

You can't stop the rain that often opens the door to these diseases, but you can do other things to discourage them.

✔ Rake out excess thatch, which is often an invitation to disease. Follow up with my Thatch Buster Tonic (see page 108).

✔ Never water at night.

✔ Choose resistant varieties (many bluegrass varieties resist dollar spot).

✔ Aerate the lawn to help fertilizers penetrate better and get air to the turf's roots.

✔ Treat spots promptly with my Lawn Fungus Fighter Tonic (see page 117).

DOWN WITH DAMPING-OFF

If you start plants from seed, sooner or later you will see what's called damping-off. Seedlings only a few days old suddenly shrivel and die, or perhaps they fall over first. If you investigate the problem with a magnifying glass, you will see that one of two things happened. Either the roots rotted, causing the seedling to collapse, or a dark spot of rot developed on the main stem, just above the soil line, girdling the baby.

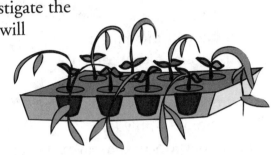

WATCH IT

Damping-off is caused by several different fungi, but it's entirely preventable. If you follow the steps below, your encounters with damping-off will be few and far between.

1. Thoroughly clean seedling containers before planting, using lots of warm, soapy water. The fungi that cause damping-off can easily live from year to year in containers.

2. Use soilless seed-starting medium, fresh from the bag. The primary ingredients in these products, vermiculite and milled peat moss, simply don't host damping-off fungi.

3. Use small containers for small plants, and move them to roomier quarters as they grow. Damping-off fungi are foragers, so a little seedling in a large pot is easy prey.

4. Whenever you can, water seedlings from the bottom rather than flooding them from the top. Surface moisture invites problems with damping-off.

5. Give seedlings intense light and a little air movement. You can even blow on them gently as you water them. It will help the stems grow tough and strong.

6. Mist all of your seedlings with my Damping-Off Prevention Tonic (see page 15). They'll love you for it!

Fighting Fusarium

This is a strange soilborne disease that gets into plants through breaks in the roots — and not only the breaks that gardeners cause. There are lots of harmless underground critters that bump into or accidentally tear through plant roots all the time. If the right strain of fusarium is present to infect the plant that happens to be growing there, the fungus will quickly spread through the plant's vascular system (its blood-stream) and clog it up. Tomatoes stricken with fusarium wilt turn a noticeable buttery yellow color as they slowly die, so in tomatoes, this disease is sometimes called fusarium yellows. The strain of fusarium that infects cabbage makes it turn yellow, too, but parsley or basil simply wilt when stricken with this disease, and peas with it basically struggle to grow at all.

Once you know that a certain strain of fusarium is present in your soil, your best defense is to grow resistant varieties. Resistant tomatoes have a capital F after their varietal name, and seed catalogs will tell you if a certain variety of cabbage is resistant.

Round and Round

Sometimes fusarium (and other soilborne fungi) live on plant roots, but the populations are so low that the plants prosper anyway. However, if you put the same plant in the same place next year, those fungi are ready and waiting, and they will dash your hopes of a great crop of beans, basil, parsley, or peas. Planting a different crop in that soil deprives the fungi of the host plant they require, so they perish. Rotating your plantings from place to place is an easy way to win the war with all sorts of fungi that infect plant roots.

THE TINIEST TERRORS: VIRUSES

Do you know what it looks like when plants get the flu? Plants infected with viruses don't sneeze or suffer stopped-up noses. Instead, new growth becomes distorted, leaves show odd textures and colors, and plants that are supposed to grow tall look short and stunted.

Unlike fungi, viruses can't blow around in the wind or be carried from place to place in droplets of rainwater. They must have a live host, usually an insect, which spreads the virus from plant to plant as it feeds. Leafhoppers, aphids, and thrips are the usual culprits, and it takes only one little bite to infect a susceptible plant with a virus.

Get 'em Outta There!

No matter what kind of virus is bugging you, what you need to do about it is the same — you need to get rid of the infected plants! Just as you don't want to hang around with someone who has the flu, you don't want to keep sick plants around where they can share their germs with everything in your yard. At the first sign of a viral disease, pull out the infected plants and dump them into the garbage. (Don't put them onto the compost pile — your trouble will only multiply.) Then just keep your fingers crossed that you caught the disease before it became an epidemic.

Jerry Baker Says . . .

"The best way to head off viruses and all other kinds of nasty germs is to keep your plants well supplied with my All-Around Disease Defense Tonic (see page 177)."

Five Viruses Worth Watching

When it comes to viruses, these are some of the vilest villains around.

1. Bean mosaic virus is common, but not as lethal as many other plant viruses. When bush beans are infected, leaves become streaked and puckered with yellow and dark green, but the plants may produce decent crops anyway. Pole beans are often not so lucky, and respond to the virus by producing huge clusters of infertile flowers. Grow resistant varieties whenever you can, and pull out infected plants.

2. Cucumber mosaic virus is pretty common, and it can be hosted by several unrelated plants, including cucumbers, tomatoes, petunias, and even lilies. Leaves may become brittle and mottled with varying shades of green, and plants struggle to grow. Many modern hybrids are resistant, but if you grow heirloom varieties of tomato and pepper, this is a virus you need to know about. When tomatoes or peppers are infected, leaves become thin and stringy,

and the plants never produce well. Pull them out right away to keep aphids from spreading the disease to other plants.

3. Pea enation virus is mostly a problem in the West, where it is spread by several species of aphids. Leaves develop yellow spots followed by blisters on their undersides, and new growth is twisted. If you live where pea enation virus is prevalent, grow only resistant varieties.

4. Raspberry mosaic virus is often the reason raspberries grow very slowly, show little vigor, and produce berries that fall apart in your hands. Leaves of infected plants often have curled edges, and may also show dark green mottled patterns. Sorry, there is no cure. The best strategy is to get rid of an infected patch and start a new one in a new location. Always buy plants from a reputable nursery to make sure you don't import this disease.

5. Tobacco mosaic virus is best known for infecting tomatoes and its close relatives in the vegetable garden, eggplants, peppers, and potatoes — and, of course, tobacco. But it can strike other vegetables and several flowers, including petunias, Iceland poppies, and one of my all-time favorites, Nicotiana, a.k.a. flowering tobacco. The disease can be spread by insects or by human touch, and usually arrives in a garden on infected plants. Symptoms include thickened leaves that are mottled with various shades of green, slow growth, and greatly reduced fruit set. Many hybrid tomatoes and a few peppers are resistant.

WATCH IT

No Smoking, Please

Once tobacco mosaic virus (TMV) shows up in your garden, it's the dickens to get rid of. It often arrives courtesy of tobacco from a cigarette, but you can also carry it in on contaminated plants or even containers they've come into contact with. The nasty stuff lives in the soil for as long as 5 years, and during that time, there's no telling where it could pop up. If TMV has attacked your garden, don't grow anything but resistant varieties for at least 3 years. You'll know you've spotted a winner when you see a capital T after the variety name in a catalog description or garden center label.

The Milk of Plant Kindness

Nobody's figured out why, but milk seems to neutralize the tobacco mosaic virus. If you know this villain is lurking somewhere in your garden, just waiting to attack, try this tactic: When you're working near a likely target — which is any plant in the tomato family — keep a bowl handy that's filled with a half-and-half mixture of milk and water. Then, every few minutes, dip your hands and tools into the liquid. It'll stop those sniveling cowards dead in their tracks!

NASTY NEMATODES

Do you know that your garden is full of nematodes? Most of them are important (though virtually invisible) members of your soil's natural community of life forms. Nematodes, a.k.a. eelworms, are microscopic worms that swim and wiggle through the soil, and many species prey on insect larvae and other nematodes. You can actually buy these guys at garden centers and use them to control cutworms and other pesky pests.

But not all nematodes are nice guys. Especially in warm climates, several species are plant parasites that infect roots and even stems. As they multiply inside plants, they clog them up and make it very hard for the plants to take up the water and nutrients they need to grow.

Nematode-infested roots (size varies)

Be a Nematode Detective

How can you tell if a plant has fallen victim to nasty nematodes? Here's my 5-point checklist for all you nematode detectives.

1. Do plants seem thirsty, no matter how much you water them?

2. Is midday wilting very severe, but plants perk up overnight and wilt only a little on cloudy days?

3. When you dig up a plant, do you see knobby growths on the roots?

4. Are the root tips forked like a snake's tongue?

5. If you don't see knots on the roots, have all the deep roots disappeared, leaving only a thick tangle of surface roots?

Knocking Out Nematodes

Nematodes make life miserable for gardeners in warm-climate regions. Here's how to fight back.

✔ **Feed their sweet tooth.** Spread 5 pounds of sugar over every 50 square feet of planting area. The nematodes will choke on the stuff.

✔ **Starve 'em out.** Grow *only* French marigolds in the soil for one season. Nematodes can't infect French marigold roots, so the culprits starve to death.

✔ **Saturate the planting area with my No, Mo' Nematodes Tonic.** It'll deliver the final one-two knockout punch!

Solar Power: Seven Steps to Cleaner Soil

If pests and diseases are causing big-time trouble in your yard, get help from ol' Sol. Solarizing your soil heats it up to 150°F or so and kills fungi, nematodes, most insect larvae, and even weed seeds. For the process to work, you need to do it during the hottest part of the year, which in most places is July and August. Here's the routine:

Step 1 Dig up a plot of soil that's about 10 feet square.

Step 2 Work in a 1- to 2-inch layer of fresh manure.

Step 3 Rake the soil into planting beds or rows.

Step 4 Water well, then let everything settle overnight.

Step 5 Cover the plot with a sheet of clear 3- to 6-mil plastic, and pile soil around the edges to keep it in place. Make sure the cover has some slack in it so it can puff up (instead of blowing away or bursting) when the heat starts rising.

Step 6 Wait about 6 weeks — longer if the weather's cool.

Step 7 Take off the cover, water, and plant away. But don't cultivate or you'll bring up untreated soil.

CHAPTER 17

Natural Disasters

As the old saying goes, everyone talks about the weather, but nobody does anything about it. But gardeners do! We watch the weather, come up with dozens of special tricks to help our plants survive the challenges that stressful weather brings, and when real disasters develop, we get creative and make lemonade out of nature's lemons. That's what this Chapter is all about — turning bad luck into good luck in your yard and garden.

HIDE-AND-SEEK WITH FROST

Two of the biggest turning points in any growing season are the coming of the first and last frost. You can get the approximate dates of these events from your Cooperative Extension Service, or rely on your favorite TV weatherman (good luck!). Either way, you will know only part of the story, because as far as your garden plants are concerned, there's a huge difference between light frost, heavy frost, and a hard freeze (sometimes called a hard frost).

How to Entertain Jack Frost

Different kinds of frost require different kinds of action. Here's a rundown on what you can expect ol' Jack to offer up and how your plants want you to respond.

Light frost occurs when temperatures hover right at the freezing mark. Because cold air sinks, plants in low spots will get a heavier dose of frost than those growing on higher ground. Plants that have tropical ancestry — tomatoes, peppers, basil, and zinnia, for example — host bacteria on their leaves that actually promote frost damage. Hardier plants have little trouble with light frost, and may even benefit from the light chilling that frost brings.

Bedders on the Move

Keep transplants in a wheelbarrow or wagon so you can easily move them in and out of your garage during the changeable weather of spring and fall. This is an easy way to "harden off" greenhouse-grown bedding plants to get them ready to face strong sun, chilling winds, and other stresses they'll face in the outdoor world.

What to do: Keep a supply of old sheets, blankets, and even newspaper on hand to cover plants overnight through the first fall frost, and also use them in spring if a late frost threatens early plantings. You can also use buckets, cans, flowerpots, or baskets to cover plants that might be damaged by light frosts. If more than one frosty night is likely, leave the covers in place until the mild weather returns.

Help 'em Out

Just before you transplant your flower or vegetable seedlings, do what Grandma Putt did: Water them with a solution of 2 ounces of salt or baking soda per gallon of water. This will temporarily stop growth and increase their strength so they can stand right up and say "boo" to the changing conditions they'll face outdoors.

Heavy frost is likely when temperatures drop into the high 20s and the air is moist enough to promote heavy dew. Most tender plants will be seriously damaged by heavy frost if they are not given good protection.

What to do: Double up on blankets or other covers to nurse tender plants through heavy frost. The afternoon before heavy frost comes, water plants thoroughly so they will be well supplied with moisture. Move plants in containers to a protected place, such as your garage or a cold frame or tunnel, if you have one. Wait several hours after the frost has gone to touch or move plants that may have been partially frozen by heavy frost.

Hard freezes result  when temperatures are at or below 26°F for more than 6 hours. Plant tissues actually freeze, and unless they are cold-hardy species, they may not recover. Leaves of tender plants blacken and drop following a hard freeze, while hardy plants usually perk up after they thaw.

What to do: Give plants in cold frames and tunnels extra protection by covering the enclosures with heavy blankets or straw. Pull up and compost plants that are seriously damaged. Once hard freezes become frequent, mulch over the soil to keep it from freezing and thawing over and over again (see Chapter 3 for the complete lowdown on mulches).

Jerry Baker Says . . .

"If a late freeze threatens the flowers on your spring-blooming shrubs and trees, spray them lightly with water, so that the buds will be protected by a thin layer of ice. You  may still lose some blossoms, but later ones should emerge in all of their splendor."

Season-Stretching Structures

You can add several weeks to your growing season by setting up special places where you can expose plants to strong sunlight while insulating them from low temperatures and frigid winds.

Cold frames can be as plain as an enclosure made from 4 bales of hay with clear plastic stretched over the top, or as sophisticated as the ones used by European gardeners — brick-lined raised beds topped with windowpanes that open and shut on hinges. Any box-type structure with a clear or translucent lid will do. The only essentials are that you can close the lid when it's cold and windy, and open it in warm weather to keep the plants inside from cooking.

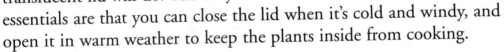

Recycling Roundup

Here's another device that says "Phooey!" to frost — and chances are there's at least one in your refrigerator: a plastic milk jug. Just cut off the bottom, set it over a tender plant, and sink the bottle a couple of inches into the ground, so it won't blow away in the breeze.

Tunnels work just like cold frames, with the advantage of being portable and quick to assemble. My favorite setup consists of a black plastic garbage bag spread over the ground, with an arch of concrete-reinforcing wire over it. I cover the wire arch with clear plastic, slide flats of seedlings or container-grown plants inside, and secure the edges of the plastic with bricks. In less than 15 minutes, I have a season-stretching structure that the plants inside think is an unheated greenhouse.

TAME THE WIND

Once spring gets under way, temperatures may be fine for your plants, but the wind can be just too much. A little wind is good for plants; it encourages stems to grow tough and strong, and moving air keeps leaves dry and free from disease. But too much wind leaves plants battered and bruised, so taming things down is definitely the kind thing to do.

Give 'em Shelter

When a cold, harsh wind whips in, or the weather forecast predicts one, you need to rush to the aid of young plants. Here's how.

✔ **Seedlings and new bedding plants.** Cover them with bottomless plastic milk jugs or upside-down flowerpots. Sink the jugs into the soil a couple of inches, so they won't blow away. If the pots are plastic, put a brick or heavy stone on top of each one.

✔ **Newly planted roses or other shrubs.** Surround each plant, or group of plants, with wooden stakes, then staple on burlap to make a screen.

Recycling Roundup

If you don't have burlap on hand when the wind kicks up, don't worry: Just reach for some old towels, over-the-hill flannel sheets, or sturdy fabric remnants. Stapled to wood stakes, they'll make dandy wind fences for tender shrubs.

Shingle Shields

Is your garden hit by strong winds that tend to come from one direction in the spring? Make a practice of installing wind shields each time you set out a seedling. Wood roofing shingles are ideal, or you can use foot-long sections of lumber or 12- by 14-inch pieces of corrugated fiberglass. Set the shields in the soil 4 inches deep alongside your seedlings. You can leave your wind shields in place all season, or pull them out when your plants get tough enough to stand on their own.

The Case for Windbreaks

A site that's way too windy is tough on plants and the people who grow them. Persistent wind often keeps plants constantly thirsty, and makes it harder for you to enjoy your landscape. Why not plant a windbreak? To determine the angle from which heavy winds blow, tie ribbons or strips of cloth to wood stakes. Then, plant a row of stocky evergreen trees or shrubs to block the gusts.

Jerry's TOP TEN

Plants for Windbreaks

When you're planning a living windbreak, keep the size of your yard in mind. Go with shrubs or dwarf trees if your yard is small. Large properties can handle taller, fuller trees. Set the plants close enough so they'll just touch when they're fully mature. For extra protection, plant two alternating, overlapping rows.

- **Arborvitae** *(Thuja occidentalis)*; 6 to 25 feet, Zones 3 to 7
- **Canada hemlock** *(Tsuga canadensis)*; 40 to 70 feet, Zones 4 to 8
- **Foster holly** *(Ilex × attenuata* cv. Foster); 25 to 40 feet, Zones 6 to 9
- **Frazier's photinia** *(Photinia × frazeri)*; to 15 feet, Zones 6 to 9
- **Leyland cypress** *(Cupressocyparis leylandii)*; to 60 feet, Zones 6 to 8
- **Ligustrum** *(Ligustrum japonicum)*; 12 to 18 feet, Zones 7 to 10
- **Norway spruce** *(Picea abies)*; 40 to 60 feet, Zones 2 to 7
- **Red cedar** *(Juniperus virginiana)*; to 40 feet, Zones 2 to 9
- **Swiss stone pine** *(Pinus cembra)*; to 35 feet, Zones 4 to 8
- **Wax myrtle** *(Myrica cerifera)*; 10 to 20 feet, Zones 7 to 9

WHEN THE RAINS DON'T COME

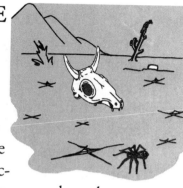

Late summer and early fall are often dry seasons, but drought can strike at any time of year. All plants need water, and if they get less than a half inch of rain weekly, they're probably stressed.

Providing water is the logical solution, but sometimes this is neither practical nor legal. During severe droughts, many communities impose watering restrictions, which means you must find other ways to keep your plants happy until the rains return.

Drought 911

When Mother Nature's tears of joy dry up, don't throw in the trowel. With just a little extra TLC, you can see your yard and garden safely through the emergency. Just follow this checklist.

✔ **Double up on mulches.** The less moisture that evaporates away, the better off your plants will be (see page 271).

✔ **Treat shrubs with an anti-transpirant.** It'll form a polymer coating around plants that reduces moisture loss through the leaves by up to 50 percent.

✔ **Watch plants closely for signs of spider mites** (see page 221). These minuscule pests tend to flourish magnificently under drought conditions!

✔ **Keep vegetables picked and deadhead flowers often.** The less fruit plants hold, the less water they'll need to stay alive.

✔ **Install shade covers over vegetables and flowers.** An old sheet or a piece of lattice attached to 4 wood stakes will do the trick.

GO NATIVE
When you're shopping for plants, look for old-timers that are native to your territory. As Grandma Putt knew, they're better equipped to deal with nature's whims than either newfangled hybrids or plants that hail from other parts of the country.

OF FLOOD AND MUD

Usually, gardeners pray for rain, but every once in a while, it rains so much that we pray for it to stop. That's because once the soil becomes saturated, most of the air gets pushed out of it, and plant roots can't get the oxygen they need to survive. Fortunately, though, most plants can endure waterlogged conditions for a short time without serious damage.

SAVE THOSE WORMS!

When soil becomes very wet, earthworms move to the surface to avoid drowning. There they become easy prey for robins and other worm-eaters. Grandma Putt knew the important work worms do in adding organic matter to the soil and opening up drainage holes, and there was no way she was going to let a single one of her helpers perish. So after a rain, she'd go out and scoop up all the worms she could find and give 'em a safe haven in her compost pile.

Feet Off!

The most important thing to do when rains drown your yard is to be patient. Avoid walking around out there as much as you can, because your footsteps will squeeze out what little air is left in the soil. And never *ever* attempt to cultivate very wet soil. It will turn into a gloppy mess that will dry into hard, root-killing chunks.

If you need to gather herbs, vegetables, or flowers when the ground is muddy, lay old boards over the ground and use them as a temporary walkway. Besides keeping your shoes clean, the board-walk will distribute your weight and limit the amount of soil compaction caused by your footsteps.

After the Deluge

A long period of steady rain can be especially hard on the grass in your yard. But don't let the showers dampen your spirits — or drown your lawn! Maybe you can't shut off Ma Nature's faucet, but you can restore your lawn to health once the heavy rains stop. Just follow these timely tips.

- Try to stay off the grass until all traces of standing water disappear. Otherwise, your footsteps could leave the "wrong impression" or tear up the turf and make a mud bath.

- Strap on your aerating lawn sandals or golf shoes, and walk around the area. This will help water percolate into the soil.

- In the worst cases, dig a series of small, deep holes in out-of-the-way parts of your yard. They'll give the excess water a run-off route.

- Then apply gypsum at a rate of 50 pounds per 2500 square feet of yard. This will loosen the soil, encouraging better drainage — almost like an army of little rototillers going to work in the soil.

- One week later, apply a natural organic lawn food at the recommended rate.

- In the fall, feed your lawn with my Fall Lawn Food Mix (see page 117). Then overspray this mix with my Thatch Buster Tonic (see page 108) or All-Season Green-Up Tonic (see page 27).

PROBLEM and SOLUTION

The Big Washout

Problem: It seems that every year, just after I've seeded my beds, the spring rains come and wash the seeds away. Do you have a solution? G.B., Zone 6

Solution: I sure have! Snip some old mini-blinds into 6-inch pieces. Then slip them into the soil between your rows of seeds to make little edgings, so the rain won't wash the seeds from one part of the bed to another.

Preventing the Ravages of Winter

Most plants need a winter rest, but winter is still a mean season. Count yourself lucky if the ground gets blanketed with at least 6 inches of snow. Winds may howl as air temperatures dip well below zero, but soil temperatures beneath snow usually hover at a comfortable 20 to 25°F.

In cold winters without snow, it helps to erect burlap fences around shrubs to protect them from drying winter winds. And even with snow, exposed plant parts are easy prey for hungry rabbits and mice. Check shrubs and trees regularly, and use the methods described in Chapter 15 if critters start chomping on your plants.

As winter approaches, give your trees, shrubs, and plants a final wash-down with my Fall Clean-Up Tonic. It'll keep all your green friends healthier, so they can fend off nasty weather problems.

Before winter hits, apply a thick coat of a good anti-transpirant. This handy product protects plants from drying winds. In fact, it reduces moisture loss through the leaves by up to 50 percent.

PROBLEM and SOLUTION

Save That Grass

Problem: In my part of the country, winter is just one snow and ice storm after another. My town is Johnny-on-the-spot with its salt truck, but come spring, my grass is a mess where the lawn meets the road. How can I keep it looking good? M.L., Zone 5

Solution: Before the first snow arrives, you need to liberally sprinkle gypsum on all grassy areas that border streets, sidewalks, and driveways — anyplace that will be treated with salt or snow-melting chemicals. Then apply my Winter Walkway Protection Tonic. It'll keep your lawn in great shape all winter long!

Fall Clean-Up Tonic

1 cup of baby shampoo
1 cup of antiseptic mouthwash
1 cup of Tobacco Tea (recipe on
   page 61)
1 cup of chamomile tea

Mix all of these ingredients in a
bucket, and then add 2 cups of it to
your 20 gallon hose-end sprayer, filling the balance of the sprayer jar
with warm water. Overspray your
turf, trees, shrubs, beds, and so on
when the temperature is above 50°F.

Winter Walkway Protection Tonic

1 cup of liquid dish soap
½ cup of ammonia
½ cup of beer

Mix all of these ingredi-
ents in your 20 gallon
hose-end sprayer, and
then apply it liberally
over the gypsum.

Mulch Magic

Give trees a thick mulch in early
winter, especially young ones that
have been in the ground less than
3 years. Keep the mulch about 2
inches away from the main trunk
to discourage mice. This security
blanket will prevent drought
stress that often comes in early
spring, when air temperatures are
warm but the ground remains
frozen and plants' roots have
trouble taking up moisture.
Beneath a cozy layer of mulch,
though, the soil remains warm
enough so that water can move
through it easily — and right
into your trees' roots.

Ice Isn't Nice

Snow may be a
blessing to your
garden in winter,
but ice can be a
nightmare. It's so
heavy that it often
breaks off branches, and
any attempts you make to lighten
the load by knocking off the ice
can only make matters worse. But
you can help small, ice-encrusted
shrubs by throwing lightweight
covers over them so that when sun
shines through the ice, it doesn't
burn the plant tissues inside. This
is a perfect job for sheets that are
too old for bedtime duty.

Give Heaving the Old Heave-Ho

Water expands as it freezes and contracts as it thaws. So when soil freezes and thaws over and over again, it often heaves up, breaking plant roots in the process. To keep perennials and shrubs from suffering this kind of damage, apply a loose mulch over the soil *after* the soil freezes in early winter. And when you're done with your Christmas tree, cut off the branches and lay them onto the bed as well. The idea is to keep the soil frozen, reducing the risk of damage to plant roots.

Recycling Roundup

These days, lots of folks buy bales of straw to decorate their yards for Halloween, and then put the bales out with the trash. It's a great time to collect them, for free! Put that weathered straw to good use as mulch around your plants or as a protective covering on your walkways.

Think Ahead

To save time and hassle next spring, it pays to give your annual flower and vegetable beds a little pre-winter care. Here's the bedding-down routine I follow:

Step 1 Clear out all plants and toss them onto the compost pile.

Step 2 Loosen the subsoil with a garden fork. By doing this chore in the fall instead of waiting until spring, I give the earthworms time to repair the damage it does to their tunnels.

Step 3 Dig my Bedtime Snack into the soil (see page 334).

Step 4 Spread a thick layer of leaves over the soil and top it off with straw. I've found that this combo keeps the worms warm and busy all winter long, enriching the soil with their castings. Come spring, my planting beds are well fed and all set to grow.

Step 5 Overspray the mulch with a good healthy dose of my Sleepytime Tonic (see page 324).

Part IV

BEYOND GREENERY: WALKWAYS AND FENCES

Plants are the part of a yard that stir the soul of a gardener like me, and it's no secret that I get a big charge out of helping folks solve problems with all my green, growing friends. But there are other things that go into making a yard, sweet yard. Two of the most important, at least to my way of thinking, are the things that get us from one place to another — paths, walkways, and stairways — and those that enclose the yard and make it private, cozy, and secure — walls and fences.

Now, these nonliving structures are not subject to most of the pests and diseases that plague plants, but that doesn't mean they're problem-free. In this section, I'll clue you in on what to do when trouble strikes the stuff designers call "hardscape" — and how to keep it from striking in the first place!

CHAPTER 18

Down the Garden Path

Is your biggest garden-variety headache a backyard that's so steep you've spotted mountain goats prancing around in it? Do you have a hard-packed strip of dirt where the kids, the neighbors, and the mailman have cut across the lawn to your back door for the past five years? Does everyone in the family avoid going into the backyard because . . . well . . . it's just not inviting? If so, then here's the answer to those problems and plenty more besides: paths, walkways, and even stairways, in all shapes, sizes, and materials.

THEY WORK FOR THEIR KEEP

Durable paths, walkways, and stairways help get you where you want to go in your yard, safely and comfortably, regardless of the weather. But they do more than that: They also add to your property's value. Every pathway in your yard has an important job to do, and the more serious that job, the more solid and dependable the pathway needs to be.

Hares and Tortoises

Having trouble deciding what kind of pathway you need? Here are my basic guidelines:

- Major corridors, such as those leading from the sidewalk to your front door, or the one that carries you from your car to the kitchen with armfuls of groceries, should be so wide, safe, and level that people can move along at a good, fast clip, without looking down. For this reason, very hard surfaces such as concrete, brick, or mortared stone are usually the best materials for the job.

- In other places, such as paths that meander from one part of your yard to another, speed doesn't matter so much. In fact, you may want a pathway material that slows you down just a tad, so you can relax and take a good look at the green scene. Loose materials, such as finely shredded mulch or pebbles, may be just right, or you can install stepping-stones flush with your grass so that you can mow right over them.

How Wide Is Wide?

A path or walkway that's too narrow for the job at hand can be a major pain in the grass — and sometimes it's even dangerous. Here are my rules of thumb for deciding how wide a path or walkway needs to be.

✔ Paths meant for slow and easy strolling can be as little as 2 feet wide.

✔ Where you'll need to get through with a wheelbarrow or mower, make sure the pathway measures at least 3 feet wide.

✔ Major walkways, like the one that leads to your front door, should be the widest of all. A 4-footer will let two or three people walk comfortably, and it'll make your entrance look like a million bucks, besides!

Slope or Steps?

Let's say the place where you need a pathway involves a bit of a climb. Should you let the pathway follow the natural slope or level it slightly and install steps? Here are 3 ways to help you decide.

1. If you want to preserve visual flow within the site, opt to work without a step, but use a material that's not slippery underfoot, such as textured concrete or bricks.

2. If a single step can accommodate the elevation change, go for it! Just make sure you build the step using a material that's easy to see, such as light-colored stone.

3. If you need two or more steps, make them lead to something, like a shapely lawn, a flower garden, or a bird feeding station.

WATCH IT

Lighten Up

Any walkway in a naturally dark place is an accident waiting to happen unless you light it up at night. This goes double for pathways made of uneven materials such as rough stone, or those that include steps. If you can't adjust your existing outdoor lights to illuminate walkways, consider putting in a low-wattage lighting system along the edges. These are widely available as kits at home supply stores and are very easy to install.

Jerry Baker Says . . .

"Whatever you do, make sure your steps aren't too difficult to climb by making them a reasonable size. The height (or rise) between steps can be as little as 4 inches, but should never be more than 8. And the step itself needs to be at least 12 inches deep to accommodate a full, solid footfall."

Step Basics

When you think about how and where you can use a short run of steps in your landscape, keep in mind that they don't have to head straight up your slope. A change in direction is often nice, and it makes steps appear less intimidating, too. Or you can have a step or two, a broad landing with a place to sit, and then another step above that.

PAVING WITH BRICK AND STONE

Although costly at first, brick or stone walkways are usually well worth the investment. For one thing, they'll last for years with little or no maintenance — and, as any real estate agent will tell you, their good looks will be a big plus when the time comes to sell your house. Even in an area like a narrow side yard, where the most common activity is wheeling your garbage cans out for collection, a solid surface underfoot makes the job safe, sure, and maybe even enjoyable.

Pros and Cons

Whether you go with brick or stone, you have a choice of two building methods.

1. Mortaring the pieces in place gives you a walkway that needs little upkeep, but cracking is often a problem in climates that are very cold or very wet, or in sites where tree roots are present and ready to push up toward the surface.

2. Unmortared walkways are easy to build and fast to repair, but weeds often make themselves at home in the crevices if you don't fill them with little plants.

So the amount of time, money, and effort needed to maintain it are all things you need to consider before building a walkway.

Using Old Bricks

Old bricks salvaged from houses or ancient walkways make a fine paving material for rustic paths, but to avoid cracks and crumbled spots, it's wise to give them a little special handling. Here's what to do.

Step 1 Clean them up as best you can. I like to use warm water and a wire brush.

Step 2 Lay them out in a sunny spot to dry.

Step 3 Before you start placing them in your walkway, dip them in a waterproofing solution (you'll find several to choose from at building supply stores).

Not on the Level

One of the reasons we create paved walkways is to have a safe, level walking surface, but good walkways are not level at all. Rather, they have a very slight pitch from the high side to the low side, so that water will run off of them quickly. This pitch should be so slight that you can hardly see it, such as a difference of only ¼ inch between the high and the low sides of a 2-foot-wide walkway. But you should be able to see it when you use a board-mounted level to check the level of your walkway.

What Lies Beneath

Water can't filter through solid paving materials like concrete or mortared bricks. Paving over plain soil can create a swimming pool effect, so that your walkway sits in water after heavy rains. This will make it prone to sinking, cracking, or heaving in the winter when the ground freezes hard. To prevent these problems, always plan for enhanced drainage before you build a walkway.

The simplest plan is to excavate the area where the walkway will be, and fill it with a bed of well-compacted crushed stone that's at least 2 inches deep. That way, water that accumulates under the walkway has a place to go until the ground below has a chance to absorb it.

Keep 'em Out

To keep pesky weeds from invading your unmortared walkway, include a piece of geotextile liner between the foundation layers. Place it on top of your bed of crushed rock, and then cover it with 1 inch of rock dust or construction sand. Besides making weeds feel unwelcome, the liner will help keep the walkway stable.

Pop Goes the Walkway!

The freeze-and-thaw cycles that make plants pop up out of the ground can do the same damage to brick or stone walkways. To keep walkways from popping to pieces in the winter, mulch over them with 6 inches of weathered hay soon after the ground freezes. It makes a decent walking surface, and when spring comes, you can quickly gather up the mulch and dump it onto your compost pile. And while you're at it, protect the grass around those walkways with a healthy dose of my Winter Walkway Protection Tonic (see page 271).

> ### Jerry Baker Says . . .
>
> "Once you've installed a new brick or stone walkway and the mortar has cured, take an hour or so to roll over the surface with a sealant. It will keep the pavers from absorbing water, make them easier to keep clean, and deepen their color ever so slightly."

FUN WITH CONCRETE

What's more fun than a barrel of monkeys? A barrel of concrete that you pour into rigid plastic molds to create walkways that look like stone blocks or cobblestones. You can buy molds that turn this project into child's play. In fact, if you liked making mud pies as a kid, you'll love working with concrete path-making kits! Here's my 7-step process for making a path that's solid and trouble-free.

Step 1 Mark off the area where you want a pathway, and dig out the grass, weeds, and tree roots. Get the surface as level as you can, but don't dig up the soil any more than is absolutely necessary. You want the base for your walkway to be as solid as possible, so the more compacted the soil is, the better.

Step 2 Buy ready-made concrete molds at a building supply store, or make your own by nailing boards together into the size and shape you want.

Step 3 Because concrete sticks to any surface, you can install a molded concrete walkway on plain soil, but it's better to excavate down an extra inch and fill the base with crushed stone or sand, with a piece of weed barrier sandwiched in the middle. Tamp it down to make it as level as you can.

Step 4 Mix dry ready-mix concrete with water in a sturdy wheelbarrow or a big plastic pail. Be sure to measure your water, because concrete that's too wet is prone to crumbling after it has cured. Start with 3 quarts of water per 60-pound bag of ready-mix. If it's just right, the mixture will be gloppy but not quite sloppy.

Step 5 Place the mold on the prepared site, pour or shovel in the wet concrete, and use gloved hands and a concrete trowel to mash it into the mold so that it fills every corner. Smooth the surface, spritzing on a little water, if needed, to make it smooth. The concrete will begin to set after only a few minutes, so you can pull up the mold and go onto the next section.

Step 6 When you're done, lightly spray your new molded walkway with water, and then cover it with a sheet of clear plastic to make the concrete dry slowly. Repeat daily for 3 days. The idea is to make the concrete cure very slowly, which makes it harder in the long run.

Step 7 Use clean play sand to fill the crevices in your walkway. This is easy to do by dumping small amounts of sand along the walkway and working it into crevices with a stiff broom. Then wet down the sand to make it settle, and repeat until it is almost to the top of the sections of molded concrete.

WATCH IT ⚠️

Cover Up

Wet concrete can irritate your skin like nobody's business. So when you're handling it, always wear heavy gloves, long pants, and long sleeves. And if some of the stuff does get onto your skin, make sure that you wash it off right away.

MORE MASONRY MARVELS

If you like the looks of a pebble or gravel walkway, but you don't like all that shifting about underfoot, here's the solution: Frame up the walkway, fill it with pebbles or gravel, and install stepping-stones down the middle. Again, it's a good idea to put a weed barrier under the gravel.

Save Your Achin' Back

Whether you buy them or make them yourself, stepping-stones can be heavy, and toting them around can take a toll on your muscles. Here's how to lay out a new path without even breaking a sweat.

Step 1 Trace the outline of a stepping-stone on cardboard, and cut it out with a utility knife.

Step 2 Make several more templates the same way. (If you're really ambitious, make as many as you'll need for your whole path.)

Step 3 Arrange and rearrange the cardboard "stones" until you get exactly the configuration you want.

Step 4 When each template is in the right spot, cut around it with a small spade.

Step 5 Remove the sod, and take out the soil to a depth of about twice that of your stone (the real one, not the template!).

Make a Great Impression

You can use all kinds of things to make decorative impressions in fresh concrete, including leaves, shells, hands, and feet. To make sure you get a clean impression, spray the object with an all-purpose lubricant, such as WD-40® or cooking spray, before you press it into the wet concrete.

Step 6 Add a thin layer of sand or gravel and level it, checking the depth of the hole against the thickness of the stone.

Step 7 Set the stone into the hole, and you're done, with no sore back or scraped knuckles to show for it!

TROUBLESHOOTING WALKWAYS

Walkways don't have problems with pests and diseases the way plants do, but that doesn't mean that they're totally carefree. Sometimes they need repairs, which are always best done at the first sign of trouble. Whatever you do, don't let a worrisome walkway turn into a safety hazard. If popped-out bricks or cracks make *you* stumble, they're sure to trip up a stranger who doesn't know to be watching his step!

Cracked Concrete

Problem: My front walkway has a couple of mysterious cracks in it that seem to be getting worse. One of them is just a small open crack, but the other one is bigger, with a slight difference in height between the two edges. Can I just fill these with a concrete crack filler, or is there something else I should do? D.J., Zone 6

Solution: Get after both of those cracks as soon as you can, because the longer they're left open, the bigger they'll get. Water seeping through the cracks will cause a little shifting, and frozen water is even worse. To repair your small crack, use a stiff brush to clean out debris, and fill it with concrete crack filler, mixed with water according to label directions. With your big uneven crack, use a chisel and hammer to remove the concrete until the crack is about 2 inches wide. Get out all the debris and brush the crack clean, and then fill it with a crack filler product made especially for large cracks. Use gloved hands to firmly press the filler in place, and add more, if needed, to smooth out the new seam.

Jerry Baker Says . . .

"When you're finished patching your walkway, you'll still be able to see the repair, but at least nobody will trip over it!"

Messed-Up Mortar

Problem: My front steps are made of brick, and along one edge the mortar has cracked so that the brick is nearly loose. How do I go about fixing this problem? N.P., Zone 5

Solution: Cracks in mortar are bad news, because they trap water that causes more cracks, and can even make the mortar that's left crumble as though it's rotten. Fortunately, this is an easy problem to fix. Here's what you should do.

Step 1 Use a cold chisel and hammer to knock out the seam of mortar that's cracked, working all the way back to bare brick if you can. You may need a vacuum cleaner to get all the little pieces out of the hole.

Step 2 Spray the cleaned crevice with water and let it dry for at least a couple of hours.

Step 3 Buy a small package of mortar at a home supply store, and mix it according to label directions.

Step 4 With a trowel, pack the mortar into the crevice, being careful not to get any on nearby bricks. If you do drop some, wipe it up right away. When you're finished, run a gloved finger down the seam to make a slight curved indentation. This will help it shed water.

Step 5 Let the repair cure for a few days, and then give your steps a good cleaning. When they are dry, apply a sealant to keep this kind of problem from developing again.

WATCH IT

Handle with Care

Some stains are all but impossible to remove from concrete, including those made by paint, oily substances, and lawn fertilizers that include weed killers. So when you use any of these near a concrete surface, proceed with extreme caution.

Crowded Corridor

Problem: My concrete front walkway runs parallel to my foundation shrubs, which are so big that they take up space meant for walking. What's worse, they're prickly hollies, so when you brush into them, they scratch. Can I prune these back without killing them? They're pretty, and replacing them would be a huge job that I don't think I want to take on. I.P., Zone 7

Solution: Your hollies can be pruned pretty hard, but that's not going to solve your problem. They'll keep growing back with amazing speed, because once big shrubs have big root systems, they bounce right back from hard pruning. But for now, have at 'em with heavy-duty electric pruning shears, which will make the job go fast. And if you're determined to keep those big hollies, why not widen your walkway on the other side by adding a row of bricks held in place with a frame of treated wood? That way, you and your shrubs can coexist peacefully.

Tilted Walkway

Problem: I have a narrow concrete walkway that is divided into panels with open seams between them. One of the square panels has sunk on one side so that it's tilted, but the others are fine. Is there an easy way to correct this, or should I call a professional? Y.B., Zone 5

Solution: If you have a couple of friends with strong backs and crowbars, you can fix this problem yourself in only a few minutes. The operation involves lifting the low side with crowbars and propping it up with a block of wood long enough to spread a little gravel or coarse sand underneath to raise it up. Then pull out the wood, ease the panel of concrete back into place, and, like magic, it should be level again.

Empty Spaces

Problem: I'm planning to build a flagstone walkway between my patio and my herb garden, and I've heard that you can fill the spaces between stones with little plants. Do you have any suggestions for plants that work especially well when used this way? G.Y., Zone 6

Solution: Since you like herbs, my first suggestion is to try creeping thyme *(Thymus praecox)*, which grows only 3 inches tall and spreads into little mounds. Another little plant that's almost mosslike in appearance is pearlwort *(Sagina subulata)*, and it's definitely worth a try. If the spot is sunny and you'd like some color, it's hard to beat creeping phlox *(Phlox subulata)*. Shadier spots, especially along the edges of the walkway, are perfect places to try vigorous *Mazus reptans*, which even blooms a little in midsummer.

Jerry Baker Says . . .

"After you plant your herbs in your walkway, keep 'em sleek and sassy with my Happy Herb Tonic (see page 198)."

Washout

Problem: Last year, I built a brick walkway and filled the crevices between the bricks with sand. Every time it rains, a lot of the sand disappears, so I guess it's being washed away. What can I do to stop this from happening? N.F., Zone 6

Solution: Sounds like you're using very fine sand, which goes into crevices easily but comes back out just as fast. Switch to a coarser material, such as rock dust, which is often sold as paver base. In addition to fine sandy particles, rock dust includes small jagged pieces that should stay put once you get them wedged into those crevices. Use a flat chisel or the side of a mason's trowel to really stuff those crevices tight, and they should stay packed through the heaviest rains.

CHAPTER 19

Do Fence Me In

When it comes to solving problems in the yard, fences and walls are some of the hardest workers I know. Whether you need to carve out some privacy, keep kids and pets from wandering far and wide, add more planting space, keep a hillside from caving in, or block out something you'd rather not look at, the right fence or wall can come to your rescue. What's more, you don't have to wait around for these superstructures to grow to the size you want, as you do with trees and shrubs. You just put 'em up and — bingo! — problem solved!

MAKE A MATCH

A fence or wall works best when it blends with the style of your house. Rustic wood fences work well with houses that have exteriors made of wood or vinyl siding, but a formal brick home calls for a more sophisticated approach, like you might get with brick or iron. (Just think what New Orleans would be like without all those gorgeous cast-iron balcony trimmings!) A good landscaping eye is important, and if you don't have one, call in a professional to help.

Materials for Fences

Here's a quick guide to fence makings you'll find at any large home supply store.

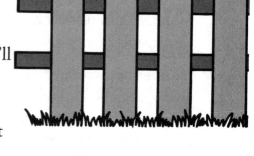

✔ **Wood** fencing comes in endless variations, and wood fences are not difficult to install. The three parts of a wood fence are the posts, rails, and siding, which may be called pickets or infill. Weather-resistant redwood, cedar, or locust can be stained or left to weather, but to avoid deterioration problems, softer pine needs to be pressure treated and sealed with a good waterproofing product. And painting is always an option with wood.

✔ **Vinyl** looks like wood, but it never needs painting — only cleaning every couple of years to remove dirt and algae. Lightweight and easy to install, white picket fences made of vinyl look exactly like their wood counterparts but require much less maintenance. Vinyl fencing is also available in beige, green, and black.

✔ **Chain link** is affordable, and there's no better way to keep Spot from wandering the neighborhood. Chain link must be

Paint Your Chain Link

Don't like the cold, stiff look of your silver chain-link fence? Paint it dark green or black to make it blend right into the yard. Paint stores sell special weather-resistant paints for this job. To make fast work of painting chain link, recruit a partner and use rollers to paint against each other from opposite sides of the fence. You'll still need to go back with a brush to fill in joints and crevices, but if you feed your helper well, maybe he'll stick around and help out with that part, too!

stretched tight, so getting pros to install it is usually money well spent.

✔ **Iron,** either wrought or cast, is costly, but there's nothing like it for historic old houses or courtyards where you want an antique effect. Check with recyclers if you need only a short panel of iron fence to frame a patio or small outdoor living area. Iron fencing combines beautifully with low brick walls. To use iron on a budget, see if you can find a great-looking iron gate that will work well with a wood fence.

✔ **Stucco** walls can be made of concrete block, or they can be wood frames that are then covered with stucco. You can do the construction work yourself and then have a stucco installer come to handle the last step. In the Southwest, stucco is often the best material for echoing the style of the house it is meant to enhance.

✔ **Brick or stone** walls always add a feeling of heavy permanence to the landscape. They look best when their texture is repeated in other parts of the yard, such as in your patio or walkways (see Chapter 18). You will need to hire a professional brick mason to build a brick wall, but many people enjoy doing stonework themselves. I'll explain the basics later in this Chapter.

WE'RE A LITTLE OLD-FASHIONED
Call me old-fashioned, but I'm always charmed by a white picket fence like the one Grandma Putt had, and so are plenty of other folks. If you have a flower bed that doesn't look quite finished, put a run of picket fence behind it and, like magic, it will become a traffic-stopping masterpiece!

WOOD FENCE BASICS

Wood fences are the most popular choices of do-it-yourself landscapers, and you'll be amazed at what you can accomplish with simple tools and ready-to-go kits. Installing a wood fence is pretty straightforward, especially if you're working with preassembled panels from a home supply store. Here's how it's done.

Step 1 Mark off the location of the fence with string tied to stakes. Measure where posts will go, starting from any walls or other fixed features that will be attached to the fence. Depending on the fence, posts may be up to 8 feet apart, though 6 feet apart is the usual distance with wood fences.

Step 2 Set the posts in concrete (see page 290), making sure they are absolutely plumb. If necessary, hold them in place with diagonal pieces of scrap lumber while the concrete cures.

Step 3 Install horizontal rails. Picket fences and fences that are less than 4 feet tall usually have only 2 rails. A third rail is needed to support 6-footers.

Step 4 Roughly sand vertical pickets or infill before securing them in place. If you're using preassembled panels, check nails and screws before you attach the panels to the posts to make sure they're nice and tight.

Step 5 Wipe the fence with a clean cloth and then apply a sealant to protect the wood. When it's started to absorb water — usually in 2–3 months — complete the job by applying any type of finish that you like.

WATCH IT

Rusty Nails

Besides making unsightly streaks in wood fencing, nails can actually encourage wood to rot as they rust. You can prevent this problem by using aluminum or galvanized nails or screws in any type of wood fence.

Permanent Posts

If you want to keep your fence on the up-and-up, and safe from insect damage, you need to set the posts in concrete. If you've never worked with concrete, that may sound a tad intimidating, but don't worry: It's as easy as 1, 2, 3. Here's how it's done.

Step 1 With a posthole digger, dig a hole that's 18 inches deep and 2 inches wider on all sides than the diameter of the post.

Step 2 Place 2 inches of dry gravel in the bottom of the hole, and set the post in place. Use a level to make sure the post is perfectly plumb (perpendicular to the ground). Have a helper hold the post in place, or use pieces of scrap lumber to build a temporary support frame.

Step 3 Mix up a batch of concrete, and shovel it into the space around the post, filling to about an inch above the soil line. Let the concrete cure for at least 2 days before putting the post to work supporting a fence.

Gardening on the Up-and-Up

Here's a riddle: How do fences make a small garden larger? The answer: by creating places for vertical gardening with tall upright flowers, vines, and even slender trees and shrubs. So if limited space is a problem at your place, go hog wild with plantable fences and trellises. Your yard will look better, and you'll have many new opportunities for having fun with plants.

Good-Neighbor Fences

If you want to put a fence right on the property line between your house and that of your neighbor, shake hands and work together from the outset. Your neighbor may share your enthusiasm and even want to share expenses. There are several designs of wood fencing in which the rails are installed on alternate sides of the posts, so that both sides look the same. So a true good-neighbor fence has no right or wrong side, only two good ones!

Transform an old fence gate into a garden centerpiece. Just dig holes for supporting posts on either side, attach the gate to the posts, and plant a climbing rose or other vine at the bottom. Presto! — you've got what designers call a "focal point."

Don't Cross City Hall

Before building any wall or fence, head off big-time trouble by checking local zoning ordinances. Many communities have restrictions on how tall fences or walls can be, and even the materials you can use to build them. In most cities, fences are expected to be no more than 6 feet tall, and some towns require a building permit for any type of fence. Take no chances with your property lines, either. If you're not sure exactly where they are, have your place surveyed *before* you start digging those postholes!

Fence 'em Out

I hope I don't have to tell you that if you have something potentially dangerous in your yard, such as a swimming pool, trampoline, or maybe a flying trapeze, you need a fence that will keep curious kids from getting inside when you're not at home. This is just common sense, but it's also the law in most areas. Gates should be self-latching from the inside, and the fence itself should be difficult or (better yet) impossible to climb.

Onward and Upward

If you already have a fence or a wall in place, but it's not tall enough to screen out a view or create privacy, make it taller with sprawling vines. Train wisteria, grapes, or climbing roses to grow over the top of the fence, and you'll easily add a foot or more to its height.

Open Lattice

When most of us think of lattice, we think of the wood panels made of diagonal strips of thin lumber. But there are many variations on the theme. Lattice can be any structure with lots of open spaces, from woven bamboo to plastic pipe fastened to posts. A string or net trellis is lattice, too. Unless you really need a sturdy enclosure, lattice can have a number of advantages over a standard fence. For instance:

✔ **Fast results.** Lattice can go up and come down in a hurry, so it's the perfect solution when you need to screen a view right now, or when you want a structure that can move with you.

✔ **A balanced budget.** Unless it's made of solid gold (or a reasonable facsimile thereof), lattice is all but guaranteed to cost less than even the least expensive fence of comparable size. That's a good deal, for my money!

✔ **Fresh air.** Unlike most fences, lattice gives you privacy, shade, and air circulation at the same time — and good air circulation is a must for fending off diseases in your plants, especially those caused by fungi.

✔ **Less bulk.** Because a lattice has a much lighter, less imposing appearance than a solid fence, it's often the best way to turn a small space into an outdoor room that feels cozy, not cramped.

Jerry Baker Says . . .

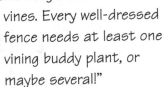

"I've described what I think are the 20 finest vines in Chapter 12, and it's hard to imagine a fine wall, fence, or lattice without a vine to keep it company. If you have trouble thinking beyond the big three — clematis, honeysuckle, and wisteria — go back and check out my favorite long-lived perennials and single-season annual vines. Every well-dressed fence needs at least one vining buddy plant, or maybe several!"

SUPER STONE

Problems don't have to be major to be irksome. For instance, maybe one of your garden-variety woes involves a yard that slopes just a tad too much. Or perhaps you have a nice view — say off into some shady woods — but it seems a little boring.

Well, my friends, I've got the answer to both of those problems: a low stone wall. There is no prettier way to define such a boundary, and building a stone wall that's less than 2 feet tall is a snap — and fun, too! It does take time, though, because building with stone is like painting a picture. Every few feet, you need to stand back and look at your work, and maybe shift the stones around a bit to make them fit together just right.

Go Low

A tall fence is not the only way to create privacy. Instead, you can use a low fence or wall to define a boundary, and then plant the area behind it with large shrubs or small trees. This is an especially nice-looking combination arranged in 3 layers: Use evergreens to make a tall, dark background, place a modest fence in front of them, and then plant light-colored flowers in the foreground.

All Stacked Up

Stone for building walls is called stacking stone, and it comes in many forms. Most often it is either sandstone or limestone that has been broken, or "faced," so that it's flat on at least two sides. Stacking stone is sold by the ton, and how much you'll need depends on how much wall you intend to build. For a simple 18-inch-tall wall, figure on 1 ton of stone per 20 feet of wall. But don't guess about quantity: Let a contractor who sells stacking stone help you figure out how much you need — and ask him to deliver it, too.

From the Ground Up

A stone wall set on the ground is usually unstable, so I strongly recommend that you take the time to excavate a level foundation for your wall. If it's at the bottom of a slope, dig out a few inches of soil, and make the foundation tilt slightly backward, so that your wall angles toward the hillside. Otherwise, the force of soil and water from behind the wall may eventually make it come tumbling down.

Sit on It

Humpty Dumpty fell from his wall, but you won't topple if you let a low wall do double duty as a sitting area. Lay flat capstones atop a low wall, and people will feel inclined to sit a spell.

Use your largest, flattest stones for the lowest tier of your wall. After the base tier is in place, begin stacking stones as artistically as you like. Do make certain that crevices are offset from one tier to the next, and fill small openings with small stones. Also use little rocks as shims beneath larger stones that don't fit just right.

As you work, place each tier of stones ever so slightly behind the one below it, so that your wall tilts back into the slope. When you're done, firmly pack soil into the open space behind the wall, using a rod or shovel handle to work loose soil into all open crevices.

GETTING INTO GATES

I don't know about you, but the last problem I want to worry about in my yard is a flimsy gate that can easily be broken by rambunctious grandchildren or a large, excited dog. That's why the only gate worth having is one that's sturdy and dependable. Because a gate is only as strong as the posts (or wall) to which it is attached, do whatever you must to make the mountings immovable. Wood gates need to be reinforced with at least one diagonal brace to keep the corners tight.

Don't skimp on hardware. Use heavy hinges for mounting a gate, and include a spring pull to help the gate swing itself shut. There are dozens of kinds of gate latches to consider, but it's important to choose one that can be locked if you're concerned with security.

Size 'em Up

Before you erect any gate, make sure it's wide enough to handle whoever or whatever will need to get through it — you don't want to order a load of brick for a patio, only to find that the delivery truck can't get through the gate to the backyard! My rule of thumb is to decide the widest possible vehicle that a gate might have to accommodate, and then add 5 inches of clearance on either side for good measure.

GATING GOING

Who says you have to have a fence to have a gate? Grandma Putt had beautiful, fancy iron gates on posts that snuggled right up to the big, bushy shrubs that enclosed her yard. She called those gates her "doors into wonderland" — and you wouldn't wonder why if you'd ever seen her yard!

Bright and Light

A gate can be put to work bringing both color and unity to your yard if you paint it just the right color. For example, matching the color of a front entry gate to your front door magically brings the two of them together, especially if it's a bold bright color like wine red or forest green. In a similar way, you might use blue or gray to link the color of a backyard gate to the cushions on your outdoor furniture or the color of the siding or trim on your house.

TROUBLESHOOTING FENCES AND WALLS

If a fence isn't standing strong, it's not doing its job. You can repair many small fence problems, and make a plain fence look better with a few small improvements. Give your fences the same care and attention that you give to your house, and your troubles should be few and far between.

Willing Wallflowers

Problem: Part of the property surrounding our home had a tumbled-down stone wall, which I'm slowly rebuilding. I've seen pictures of flowers actually growing in the crevices of stone walls, and I wonder if I can do this, too. Most of the wall is in sun, but it's not very tall and there are lots of crevices near the top of it, which I assume I would fill with soil or something before poking in the plants. Please steer me in the right direction. Y.B., Zone 6

Jerry Baker Says . . .

"You will need to provide water to help your wallflowers become established. After the first season, this probably won't be as much of a challenge, because the flowers that do well in stone crevices have natural talents for finding damp pockets with long, searching roots. Plus, they are water misers by nature."

Solution: As long as you are restacking your wall, leave some crevices as large as you can, and fill them with a mixture of soil, peat moss, and sand. Plants that will flourish in this situation include basket of gold *(Aurinia saxatilis),* a perennial that blooms yellow in early spring, and usually forms a cascade of foliage and flowers that's just perfect for the highest section of your stone wall. Lower down, where there's a little shelter, try moss pink *(Phlox subulata),* which comes in many shades of pink and blue. In the long run, you will probably find that the strongest survivors in rock crevices are various sedums — a varied group of hardy succulents that usually bloom once a year. Supertough *Sedum acre* produces its yellow blooms in spring, while other species bloom later in the season. Finally, the pert pink blooms of an ancient herb called soapwort (*Saponaria ocymoides*) are always pretty when used to fill crevices in stone walls.

Rotted Rails

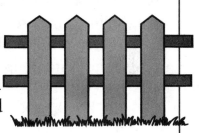

Problem: My backyard is surrounded by a cute wood picket fence that I would very much like to keep. However, at one corner, the rails have rotted where they are attached to the post, and I'm afraid that a strong storm will tear it apart. Is there an easy way to fix it? P.C., Zone 6

Solution: There is a good reason why the joints where rails attach to posts are often the first places to rot on a wood fence. Rainwater runs down the rails and accumulates in the joints, where it soaks up into the cut ends of the rails and takes forever to dry out. Inspect the rails closely, and see if you can saw out the rotten parts and screw patch pieces of lumber to the rails at least 4 inches into the sound sections of the old ones. It may also help to use a wood patch to reinforce that part of the post where the rotten rails were attached. That way, you will be nailing new wood to new wood, which will make the repair job sturdy and long lasting.

Wobbly Posts

Problem: Two sides of my backyard are enclosed by an old wire fence attached to cedar posts that are set in the ground rather than in concrete. Although I don't think the bases of the posts are rotten, they are somewhat loose in the ground, which makes the whole fence a little wobbly. What's the easiest way to reinforce wobbly posts without digging them up and replacing them? W.B., Zone 5

Solution: You can try using splints, which is the same idea behind the wood splints that old-time doctors once used to set broken bones. Use a narrow plumber's spade to dig out the soil on two sides of your wobbly posts, leaving the other two sides firmly packed, so that the posts don't shift out of place. Dig at least 12 inches deep, and then place 24-inch-long splints of treated lumber alongside the posts, nailing them in firmly. Backfill the soil and firm it in well, and your posts should stand up straight and tall for several more years.

Green Pickets

Problem: Eight years ago, we put in a wood privacy fence, and I'm sure that it was treated wood. Over the years, it has weathered to gray, and the parts of it that get shade in the summer show a greenish color. I thought it looked okay until our neighbors put in a new wood fence, which makes ours look old and moldy. Is there a way to restore it so that it looks better? It's still nice and sturdy, but it sure looks tired. R.T., Zone 7

Solution: Count yourself lucky that your fence has stood the test of time and has not yet started to decay. The chemicals in treated wood leach out over time, so after a few years, it is only semitreated at best, especially in high-rainfall areas. I think the time has come to paint your fence, which will make it look fresh and new. If the trim on your house is a neutral beige or gray, match your fence color as closely as you can. Also, to make your paint job last longer, put down a coat of sealer before you paint it with a good exterior enamel paint.

Part V

PUTTING IT ALL TOGETHER

Well, we've romped through the big adventure of planting your yard, sweet yard, learned how to fend off pesky pests and dastardly diseases, and even cast a weather eye or two on Ma Nature's practical jokes.

Now, in this section, we'll pull together all the nitty-gritty grow-how that you'll need to keep your outdoor living areas in tip-top shape. Chapter 20 is my Calendar of Care that will tell you what needs doing in your yard and when you should be doing it. I've also included a USDA Plant Hardiness Zone Map (see page 328) to help you select plants that will grow up happy and healthy in your neck of the woods.

Then Chapter 21 collects in one handy place all of the Timely Tonics that are scattered throughout this book, so you can refer to them anytime you want to whip up whatever you need to get your plants off to a good start, send bad-guy bugs packing, or even protect your walkways from the ravages of Old Man Winter. Folks, it doesn't get any easier than this, so enjoy yourself as you're spraying your troubles away!

CHAPTER 20

Calendar of Care

I don't think I'm any more absent-minded than most folks, but I still forget to do things that need doing in my yard. I try all sorts of tricks — keeping a garden calendar, making lists on scraps of paper, and even setting out tools one day to remind me of what I want to do the next. But timing can still be confusing. That's why I've put together this Calendar of Care — so you and I will never have another excuse for not getting after those chores.

MEET ME HALFWAY

Now, because this country is so darn big and varied, you're going to have to do a little adjusting to find your rightful place on my calendar. For example, if you live in a very cold climate, you might want to push the to-do lists back a month, or move them ahead if you live where winters are short and summers are long. See the USDA Plant Hardiness Zone Map on page 328. I'll mention USDA Zones here and there to help you find your way, but please meet me halfway by doing a little of the thinking for yourself. (If you're new in town, or new to gardening, call your closest Cooperative Extension Service; they'll clue you in on what you can expect Mother Nature to serve up, and when.)

All-Season Tonics for All Seasons

Before we begin, I want to remind you that the most important thing that you can do for your yard to keep problems to a minimum is to regularly apply my All-Season Green-Up and Clean-Up Tonics (see pages 333 and 332). These two extra-special tonics will keep bugs, slugs, and other thugs away while giving your plants the proper nourishment they need to keep on growing strong.

JANUARY

Start Keeping Records

When wall calendars get marked down to half price, buy one just for your yard and garden. Use it to write down the first and last projected frost dates, planting times, and when your favorite plants bloom, along with measurements you want to remember. That way, you won't have to figure out, over and over again, how much fertilizer it takes to feed your front lawn, and you'll become an expert on the best time to get your favorite plants, such as petunias or tomatoes, into the ground.

Make Plans

While the nights are long and cold, start thinking about your yard and what changes you might want to make. To get some good ideas, pick up a few gardening books

and magazines, and note the pictures that appeal to you. By the time the weather becomes suitable for working outside, you'll know exactly what you want to tackle in your yard.

Pick Up Sticks

Ma Nature prunes trees in winter with her strong winds and heavy loads of ice and snow. As soon as you can, gather up the limbs and sticks that have fallen to the ground. Besides helping out your resting lawn, you won't run the risk of tripping over these unexpected obstacles the next time you're taking a stroll.

Collect Catalogs

Seed and nursery catalogs are like dream books, and I don't ever get tired of thumbing through them. Besides, this time of year, catalog shopping for seeds, plants, or pretty garden accents sure beats watching reruns on TV!

Spoil Your Houseplants

When you can't garden outdoors, keep things green and growing indoors. Besides making great companions in any room, houseplants help clean up polluted indoor air, and some of them even produce flowers when the days become longer in late winter. Watch out for little pests on your houseplants, especially mealybugs and aphids.

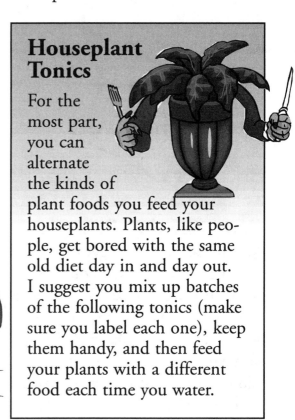

Houseplant Tonics

For the most part, you can alternate the kinds of plant foods you feed your houseplants. Plants, like people, get bored with the same old diet day in and day out. I suggest you mix up batches of the following tonics (make sure you label each one), keep them handy, and then feed your plants with a different food each time you water.

Timely Tonics

General Foliage Plant Food

½ tbsp. of ammonia
½ tbsp. of bourbon
½ tbsp. of hydrogen peroxide
¼ tsp. of instant tea granules
1 vitamin tablet with iron
1 gal. of warm water

Add 1 cup to each gallon of water used to feed your plants. For flowering houseplants, use vodka instead of bourbon.

Natural Plant Food

1 tbsp. of fish fertilizer
4 tsp. of instant tea granules
½ tsp. of liquid dish soap
1 gal. of warm water

Use at full strength when you water.

Balanced Plant Food

1 tbsp. of instant tea granules
1 tsp. of 15-30-15 fertilizer
½ tsp. of ammonia
½ tsp. of liquid dish soap
1 gal. of warm water

Use at full strength when you water.

Lighten the Snow Load

Snow does a great job of insulating the ground, but its weight can be too much for trees, shrubs, and evergreens to bear. Shovel off a little bit if you can, and watch where you pile the snow that you remove from walkways. High, sunny spots are better than low spots, where mud persists for a long time.

Collect Containers

If you plan to grow flowers for cutting next summer, set aside plenty of containers you can use as vases to share your bounty with family and friends. Anything goes: I save beer and wine bottles, and scout around flea markets for great old jars. Believe you me, you can never have enough old jars and bottles in shapely shapes and interesting colors!

FEBRUARY

Start Pruning

Begin pruning your trees and vines on those rare days when you can smell spring in the air. Make sure that you seal all cuts with my Pruning Wound Bandage Tonic (see page 346). But keep your hands off birches and maples for now, because they often bleed sap when pruned this time of year. Wait until late summer or early fall to trim those trees.

Recycling Roundup

If you grow peas in your vegetable garden, collect good trellis branches as you prune your trees. A good trellis branch is about 4 feet long and splits into several sturdy stems. Stuck into the pea row so that they barely overlap, it's just the kind of support peas need!

Trim Back Your Ornamental Grasses

Good old hand hedge clippers that work like giant scissors are my favorite tools for trimming back the tops of big ornamental grasses. Cut them back to where new blades will emerge, which is usually 6 to 12 inches above the ground, but may be higher for giant grasses such as pampas grass.

Let In the Light

Begin uncovering your perennials, especially if you live in a climate where spring comes early. But don't get rid of ever- green boughs or old blankets just yet. You may need them to protect plants from a late-winter blizzard.

Get Rich Quick

Even if you can't dig your soil because it's frozen or just plain wet, dump compost or manure onto the surface in places you intend to work into beds later in the spring. The organic matter will weather nicely, and under the piles, earth- worms and tiny critters will enjoy a sneak preview of spring.

MARCH

Turn Your Compost

As soon as your compost pile thaws, get after it with a digging fork, and turn and mix it as best you can. When combined with the rising temperatures, the slicing, dicing, and mixing should get your compost going. To really get it cooking, overspray it with my Compost Feeder Tonic.

Dig In When It's Dry

Whenever your soil isn't frozen and is dry enough to dig, you can begin setting out new perennials, shrubs, and trees. Early planting is especially smart in Zones 7 and 8, where spring doesn't last long and the plants need to be well rooted by the time the hot summer weather comes around.

Timely Tonic

Compost Feeder Tonic

Just like your plants, your compost pile needs a boost now and then. Once a month, spray it with this Timely Tonic.

½ can of beer
½ can of regular cola (not diet)
½ cup of liquid dish soap

Mix these ingredients in the jar of your 20 gallon hose-end sprayer and apply generously.

Recycling Roundup

In Zones 6 to 9, you can start setting out annuals and vegetables that like cool weather, but they'll fare better if you protect them from cold winds with cloches. These can be anything ranging from plastic milk jugs, with their bottoms cut off, to overturned flowerpots, to old cardboard boxes. Or make your own plastic tunnels by stretching clear plastic over wire arches.

Plan a Moving Day

If you have a shrub or two that you want to move to a different place, go around them with a spade and slice a circle into the ground as deep as you can. What you're doing is root pruning, so that the plants have a chance to get ready for moving day (see page 77 for details). The best time to actually dig up and move a misplaced shrub is just as it begins to show new growth.

Prune Back Overgrown Shrubs

If you have huge, old shrubs that are blocking your windows, arm yourself with a pruning saw and pruning loppers, and cut back those bushes by about one-third of their size. You can be even more aggressive if you like, but I've found that the one-third guideline is a good one to begin with.

Control Crabgrass

Declare war on crabgrass by applying a preemerge crabgrass control at just the right time. In the North, do it when the forsythias bloom. In the South, dogwood blossoms mark the best time to attend to this task.

Feed Summer Bloomers

March is prime time for feeding shrubs and perennials that bloom in the good old summertime. Rake back the mulch, serve them up a square meal, then put the mulch back into place. Bear in mind, though, that flowering shrubs and perennials hanker for slightly different kinds of chow. The shrubby fellas like to dip their roots into my Super Shrub Tonic, while perennials will bloom their darndest when they get a taste of my Perennial Passion Powder.

Timely Tonics

Super Shrub Tonic

You'll have the happiest, healthiest, bloomingest shrubs in town if you add this elegant elixir to their diet.

½ can of beer
½ cup of fish fertilizer
½ cup of ammonia
¼ cup of baby shampoo
1 tbsp. of hydrogen peroxide

Mix all of these ingredients in your 20 gallon hose-end sprayer jar. Then feed your flowering shrubs in very early spring, and every 3 weeks throughout the growing season.

Perennial Passion Powder

Your perennials will bloom like champs when you put this powerful powder onto their training table.

2 lbs. of dry oatmeal
2 lbs. of crushed dry dog food
1 handful of human hair
½ cup of sugar

Mix all of these ingredients in a bucket, and spread a trowelful around each of your perennial plants in early spring.

Start Seedlings Under Lights

Now's the time to set up an indoor garden under lights custom-made for growing special vegetables or flowers from seed. As the plants get taller, adjust the height of the light so that it's always 2 to 3 inches above the tops of the leaves.

WATCH IT

Not Yet!

Don't feed your azaleas and rhododendrons just yet: Wait until *after* they bloom. Then give them a fertilizer that's specially formulated for plants that prefer acid soil. And don't forget to throw your coffee grounds around these blooming beauties!

APRIL

Increase Your Bounty

Daylilies aren't the only perennials that grow so well that you need to dig and divide them. As soon as green shoots emerge from the ground, consider multiplying your collection of astilbe, bee balm, catmint, coreopsis, heuchera, hosta, sedums, and yarrow as well. If you dig, divide, and replant all in the same day, you will lose very few divisions.

Jerry Baker Says . . .

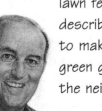

"Warming temperatures will kick your grass into high gear, especially if you give it plenty of good stuff to grow on. Follow my step-by-step lawn feeding program described on page 109 to make your gorgeous green grass the envy of the neighborhood!"

Set Roses Free

Folks in cold climates can finally remove the winter protection from around their roses. Give the plants a week or two to respond to the feel of the sun, and then inspect the canes for signs of new buds. When those buds begin to swell, prune off the tips of any canes that appear to be dead and budless. Stop when you hit healthy green wood and an outward-facing bud. Feed your established rose bushes initially in the spring with my Robust Rose Food to get them growing great. They'll love you for it!

Timely Tonic

Robust Rose Food

5 lbs. of garden food
2 cups of bonemeal
1 cup of Epsom salts
1 cup of sugar
4 pulverized (dried) banana peels

Mix all of these ingredients together, and sprinkle a handful or two around the base of each plant.

Plant Cool-Season Vegetables

Most salad veggies grow best in cool weather, though you may need to protect them from late frosts with cloches or an old blanket. Cold-hardy vegetables that benefit from an early start include broccoli, cabbage, lettuce, parsley, radishes, and spinach.

Spring Mower Maintenance Checklist

Before the mowing season gets into full swing, have your mower serviced or do it yourself.

- Sharpen or replace the blade.
- Install a new spark plug.
- Clean the air filter.
- Change the oil if you didn't do it last fall.
- Get a fresh supply of gas.
- Check the pull cord for wear, and replace if it's badly frayed.

Keep Spring-Flowering Shrubs Well Fed

Keep spring bloomers, like forsythia and lilac, happy with an organic or controlled-release fertilizer and a dusting of lime to help keep the soil in the neutral range. Sprinkle ¼ cup of Epsom salts for every 3 feet of plant height on the ground, out at the tips of the farthest branches. This will deepen the color, thicken the petals, and increase root structure. You'll have the best-looking shrubs, and folks will be wondering what kind of miracle food you've been using.

Protecting Your Babies

Young trees, especially dogwoods, beeches, and maples, have very delicate bark that can very easily get sunburned!

To protect them from the sun, wrap the trunks from the base to the lowest branches with burlap, foil, cheesecloth, or tree wrap. Spiral the tape up the trunk, overlapping the layers by about an inch to keep water out. Keep the wrap on the tree for about 2 years to give the bark time to toughen up.

Get Ground Covers

Celebrate shade by planting spreading ground cover plants beneath trees or in shadowy spots that are difficult to mow. Be sure to provide water to help your plants get off to a running start. The faster they fill in, the less weeding you'll need to do!

Jerry Baker Says . . .

"Young trees that got bent or twisted by winter winds may need stakes to help them regain their good posture. Follow the routine I outline on page 54. Remove the stakes as soon as possible — because trees grow strong new roots in the spring, they should be standing firmly on their own 'feet' in no time at all!"

MAY

Plant Your Summer Vegetables

As soon as the last frost has passed, fill out your vegetable garden with plants that like warm weather, including beans, cucumbers, melons, peppers, squash, and tomatoes. Just before you're ready to do your transplanting, water them with a solution of 2 ounces of salt or baking soda per gallon of water. This will temporarily stop growth and increase their strength so they can stand right up and say "Boo" to the changing conditions they'll face outdoors. If your climate is on the cool side, you can keep planting more lettuce and other great greens for summer salads.

Set Out Colorful Annuals

Adopt all of the bedding plants you can get your hands on, and use them to fill beds, pots, baskets, and window boxes. Just about any annual you can name is ready to plant now, including the big five — geraniums, impatiens, marigolds, petunias, and zinnias.

Create Container Bouquets

As you set out bedding plants, plan ahead to have a few orphans to plant together in container bouquets. Fill large containers with potting soil, and then plug in your bedders. Place those with an upright growing habit in the center, and tuck sprawling or cascading plants just inside the rims of the pots.

Get Into Herbs

Your garden will smell just great if you include aromatic herbs like basil, lavender, rosemary, and thyme. These nose pleasers will also help keep bad-guy bugs away from your flower and vegetable plants. Container grown plants are widely available now, and they're sure to thrive with just a little TLC. When you plant them, make sure that you add some of my Herb Soil Booster Mix to the soil to get them off to a rip-roarin' start. Then, every 6 weeks during the growing season, give them a drink of Happy Herb Tonic (see page 341).

Timely Tonic

Herb Soil Booster Mix

5 lbs. of lime
5 lbs. of gypsum
1 lb. of 5-10-5 garden food
½ cup of Epsom salts

Work this mix into each 50 square feet of herb garden area to a depth of 12 to 18 inches, and then let it sit for 7 to 10 days before planting.

Prevent Floppy Phlox

And keep other plants from lying down on the job, too! Many flowering plants stand right up there until the blossoms open. Then they get either blown over by the wind or pulled down by the weight of their flowers. Use interlocking metal plant stakes to help peonies and garden phlox hold their heads high. Taller plants, such as delphinium, foxglove, and hollyhock, do best with tall, slender stakes. (You'll find plenty of both types of supports at any garden center.)

Pinch Back Fall Bloomers

Use your fingers or small pruning shears to pinch back asters, chrysanthemums, and dahlias. Pinching makes the plants grow bushier, which means more flowers to color up your yard when autumn comes.

WATCH IT

Leave 'em Be!

Even if the leaves are in your way, allow the foliage of daffodils, tulips, and other spring-flowering bulbs to stay until it naturally turns yellow and collapses. As long as the leaves are green, the bulbs will benefit from a light application of a bulb fertilizer. If you don't like the way the foliage looks, fold it over and rubber-band it into place, or plant a bunch of daylilies around them; the daylilies will just be emerging as the bulb foliage is dying back, making them the perfect camouflage!

Shear Hedges

Get out your electric pruning shears to shape up hedges and shrubs that you want to grow into a tight shape. Leave old flower clusters intact on plants that produce berries, or you won't have colorful fruits to brighten up your garden and delight wild birds.

Time to Mow!

When you start mowing your lawn again, let the grass grow a little taller than the recommended growing height before cutting. This gives the lawn a jump start and makes it stronger. Set the mowing deck to trim the grass back by about one-third, then gradually lower the mowing deck height until you're mowing at the recommended height for your type of grass. Then wash your grass down once a month with my Terrific Turf Tonic to help the plants recover faster from the mowing shock.

Trim Flowering Shrubs

Many of the prettiest spring-blooming shrubs need only a little pruning, so trim them only if they need it to keep them healthy and shapely. You can thin crowded branches from shrubs that bloom in the summer, but be careful not to remove too many buds or you won't get many flowers.

Timely Tonic

Terrific Turf Tonic

Keep your lawn looking its best by washing it down once a month with this Tonic after you mow.

1 cup of baby shampoo
1 cup of ammonia
1 cup of weak tea

Pour the ingredients into your 20 gallon hose-end sprayer and fill the balance of the sprayer jar with warm water. Then apply it to your lawn to the point of run-off.

JUNE

Mow Slow

You will probably need to mow your lawn once a week, but always wait until the grass is dry to start your engine. Also, vary the pattern you follow from week to week — an easy way to help your grass grow evenly, so that the turf is as smooth as green velvet.

Refresh Mulches

Except for roses, which need clean mulch every year to help prevent diseases, you can simply cover old, thin mulches with an inch or two of fresh material. If you haven't fertilized trees, shrubs, or perennials that are getting a fresh helping of mulch, scratch some all-purpose fertilizer into the old mulch before you cover it with a fresh, new layer. Then overspray it with my Mulch Moisturizer Tonic to give it a little extra kick.

Jerry Baker Says . . .

"Is your lawn turning a whiter shade of pale? Sick yellow or brown? Do you see bare ground? If so, then you may be scalping it. Don't cut it so deeply, or so often!"

Bring Out Your Dead

Clip off faded flowers from annuals, perennials, and shrubs to make your yard look neater and to help the plants send energy to the newer buds growing a little farther down the stem. Pull up plants that mysteriously wither and die. In warm climates, annuals grown through the winter, such as pansies, naturally melt away in early summer.

Timely Tonic

Mulch Moisturizer Tonic

1 can of regular cola (not diet)
½ cup of ammonia
½ cup of antiseptic mouthwash
½ cup of baby shampoo

Mix these ingredients in your 20 gallon hose-end sprayer, and give your mulch a nice long, cool drink.

Water, Water Everywhere

Always consider efficiency as you make plans to keep thirsty plants adequately supplied with water. A sprinkler is best for lawns, but soaker hoses work better in flower beds and vegetable gardens, and drip buckets are better for widely spaced trees and shrubs. You should always water your shrubs with soaker hoses, which allow water to bubble out on top of the ground, rather than run off. Also, the soil is not disturbed by a huge, high-pressure volume of water.

Keep Your Eyes Open

Patrol your yard regularly to catch insect or disease problems early. Use Part III of this book to help identify common pests. You'll stand the best chance of winning the battle against slugs and other habitual offenders if you trap them fast, before they can reproduce. If you need to call out the artillery, mix up a batch of my Squeaky Clean Tonic, and let 'em have it!

When to Say When

How can you tell if you've soaked the soil long enough? Scoop up a handful of soil about 3 inches down. If you can shape it into a tight ball, chances are your soil is wet all the way down to the roots. If not, then you need to water some more.

Timely Tonic

Squeaky Clean Tonic

This is a more potent version of my All-Season Clean-Up Tonic, and no matter what bad-guy bugs are buggin' your plants, it'll stop 'em dead in their tracks.

1 cup of antiseptic mouthwash
1 cup of Tobacco Tea (recipe on page 61)
1 cup of chamomile tea
1 cup of urine
½ cup of Murphy's Oil Soap
½ cup of lemon-scented dish soap

Mix all of these ingredients in a bucket, then pour into your 20 gallon hose-end sprayer, and apply to the point of run-off. The Murphy's Oil Soap suffocates bugs on contact, and the lemon-scented dish soap contains a citrus odor that bugs just can't stand.

JULY

Mow High, Mow Often

When the weather is hot and dry, it's best to raise your mower blade a notch and cut your grass high and often. Tall grass withstands drought better, because the blades shade the soil, which also discourages weeds.

Gather Flowers While You Can

Cut flowers for indoor arrangements first thing in the morning, while the petals are full of water. If you can't work with them right away, put them in a cool, dark place in a tall container of water.

Gather flowers for drying in the middle of the day, when all the dew has dried from the blossoms. Gather the stems in bunches secured with a rubber band, and hang them upside down to dry. The colors will hold better if you dry the flowers away from direct sunlight.

Jerry Baker Says . . .

"Generally, a plant yields up its biggest, best harvest during its first few weeks of production. After that, the veggies tend to be smaller and take longer to mature."

Enjoy the Fruits of Your Labor

If you keep a vegetable garden, it's important to harvest your bounty regularly. Ripe fruits draw extra moisture from the plants, which makes them need more water. Pull up leafy greens that are past their prime, and replace them with more heat-tolerant crops.

Remember to Have Fun!

You'll be busy as a bee keeping up with everything you have growing and, of course, you need to watch out for pests and diseases through the summer. But don't forget to relax now and then, and enjoy the beauty of your backyard.

Whip Up on Weeds

Weeds that you missed when they were young may be too big to pull, especially if the soil is dry. The next best thing is to lop off their heads with a sharp hoe or mow them down with a mower or string trimmer. Whatever you do, don't let them shed their seeds in your garden, because, as my Grandma Putt used to say, "One year's weed is many years' seeds."

Repot Houseplants

Check your houseplants that are spending the summer outdoors to see if their roots have outgrown their containers. If they have, move any rootbound plants into containers that are only one size larger than the ones they grew in before. Use my Houseplant Repotting Mix to fill in around the edges. If you have to divide plants, give them a chance to recover from having their roots disturbed by keeping them in deep shade for at least a week.

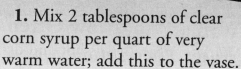

Keep 'em Goin'

Here are a few of my tricks for extending the life of cut flowers:

1. Mix 2 tablespoons of clear corn syrup per quart of very warm water; add this to the vase.

2. Add a cube of sugar per pint of water, and put a copper penny into the vase.

3. Use any one of the cut flower preservatives or Christmas tree extenders sold in flower shops.

4. To hold blossoms longer, spray the cut flowers with hair spray after they've been cut for a day or so.

Timely Tonic

Houseplant Repotting Mix

- 1 lb. of potting soil
- 1 lb. of professional potting mix
- ¼ cup of Epsom salts
- ¼ cup of bonemeal
- 1 tbsp. of instant tea granules

Thoroughly mix all ingredients, and then sprinkle it around the root mass of your transplants. *Don't* pack it in.

AUGUST

WATCH IT

Give 'em a Drink

Keep your hanging baskets and other containers growing by feeding them with my Container Plant Food Tonic. And since they frequently dry out in the middle, restore moisture by soaking parched containers in a large tub of water for half an hour. Or you can soak a number of plants by putting 4 inches of water into a kiddie pool and then putting your plants in for a swim.

Water, Water Everywhere

This is the peak of the hot, dry season, so your plants may need water more than anything else. If watering is restricted due to short supplies, concentrate on getting moisture to newly planted trees and shrubs. A thick mulch will ensure that you don't lose a drop.

Five Steps to a Happy Harvest

When you're out there bringing in the bounty, follow these guidelines:

Step 1 Pick veggies in the morning, when their sugar content is the highest.

Step 2 Never harvest (or do any other garden work) when plants are wet: You're likely to spread diseases then.

Step 3 Work carefully. Bruised or scratched vegetables spoil quickly, and damaged plants are sitting ducks for pests and diseases.

Step 4 Use your fingers to pick thin-stemmed vegetables like peas and beans, and ones that slip easily from the vine, like tomatoes.

Step 5 Use clippers or a sharp knife to cut tough- or brittle-stemmed crops. Vegetables like cabbage, peppers, broccoli, eggplant, and squash, can be damaged badly if you try to pull or tear them from their stems.

Tree and Shrub TLC

Never feed your trees, shrubs, or evergreens after August 15: You'll encourage new growth that may not have time to mature before winter. Give hedge plants a good shearing late in the month, but don't follow up with food or water. That way, you'll discourage new growth from forming, and any that does emerge will have time to harden off before winter.

If the Pot Fits . . .

When it comes to choosing pots for your herbs, one size does not fit all. Use these general guidelines:

- **4-inch container:** ideal for basil and sweet marjoram seedlings and young thyme divisions
- **6-inch container:** best for mature basil or clumps of chives, oregano, summer savory, and thyme
- **8-inch container:** your best bet for marigolds, dill, and sage
- **2-inch container:** home, sweet home for scented geraniums, catnip, fennel, lavender, mints, and young rosemary plants
- **14-inch or larger container:** just right for bay trees or lemon verbena and mature rosemary

Timely Tonic

Container Plant Food Tonic

To water your container plants, make this marvelous master mix of fortified water.

1 tbsp. of 15-30-15 fertilizer
½ tsp. of gelatin
½ tsp. of liquid dish soap
½ tsp. of corn syrup
½ tsp. of whiskey
¼ tsp. of instant tea granules

Mix all of these ingredients in a 1 gallon milk jug, filling the balance of the jug with water. Then add ½ cup of this mixture to every gallon of water you use to water all of your container plants.

Pot Up Herbs

You don't need to take them in just yet, but if you pot up herbs you want to grow indoors this winter, they'll have ample time to get settled into their containers. Rosemary, thyme, and tarragon are excellent candidates for this procedure.

SEPTEMBER

Bulb Bonanza

Plant spring-flowering bulbs north of Zone 6 after you've had a good, hard frost. In warmer climates, wait until late October to early November to plant daffodils, hyacinths, and tulips.

Before you order or buy any bulb, make sure you consider all of the following:

1. The color of the flowers.

2. The months they will bloom.

3. How tall they will get.

4. How deep to plant them.

Set Out Pansies

As soon as you see pansies at garden centers, take some home and plant them, so they'll have time to develop reliable roots before the soil gets cold. Fall-planted pansies often survive winter as far north as Zone 6.

Overseed Cool-Season Lawns

This is the perfect time to reseed thin areas in a bluegrass, tall fescue, or other cool-season lawn. Make sure the seed is in firm contact with the soil, and keep seeded spots moist for 2 weeks. And don't forget to promptly rake up leaves that fall onto baby grass plants, because they need all the light they can get.

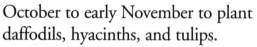

Jerry Baker Says . . .

"To head off trouble with cutworms and other bad guys next spring, zap egg-laying bugs now with my Winterizing Tonic."

Timely Tonic

Winterizing Tonic

1 cup of Murphy's Oil Soap
1 cup of Tobacco Tea (recipe on page 61)
1 cup of antiseptic mouthwash

Mix these ingredients in a 20 gallon hose-end sprayer, filling the balance of the jar with warm water. Saturate your lawn and garden, and they'll be rarin' to grow come next spring.

Feed Your Lawn

As the nights get longer, your lawn will get hungry. Treat it to another round of my Fabulous Fertilizer Formulas (see page 109), especially if you have a warm-season grass. Because cool-season grasses keep growing well into the fall, you can wait to fertilize your lawn until just before rain is expected, even if it's next month before the dry weather breaks.

Dig New Beds

While the weather's fine and the soil is dry, dig new beds that you want to plant next year. Besides getting a head start on next season, you'll turn up insects that hide in the soil — many of them will be eagerly snapped up by hungry birds.

Install New Hardscapes

Take advantage of mild, dry weather to build new walkways, patios, or other hard surfaces. Work quickly if your projects involve mortar or concrete, because they don't set well in very cold weather.

WATCH IT

Keep Their Cool

Now's the time to divide perennials and clumps of multiplying bulbs like daffodils. But September afternoons can still get hot, and that's not good for uprooted plants. Try to do your digging and dividing on a cool, overcast day, or early in the morning. If you can't replant your divisions right away, keep them in a cool, shady place, covered with a damp cloth. And don't forget to soak your transplants in my Transplant Tonic before you tuck them into their permanent beds.

Timely Tonic

Transplant Tonic

When dividing perennials, soak the best rooted pieces in this Tonic for about 10 minutes just before replanting them.

1 can of beer
¼ cup of instant tea granules
2 tbsp. of liquid dish soap
2 gal. of water

When you're finished transplanting, use a small pail to scoop up any leftover Tonic and dribble it around the new transplants.

OCTOBER

Rake Leaves

Rake up fallen leaves so they don't block light to your lawn. If your lawn mower has a bagger attachment, you can use it to shred and gather leaves at the same time. Shredded leaves mixed with grass clippings make a fine addition to your compost pile.

WATCH IT !

Rout Out Stowaways

Numerous pests and diseases live from one year to the next in dead leaves, stems, and roots, so it makes sense to do a good job of cleaning up your garden and beds. Cut back the foliage from faded perennials, pull up spent annuals, and chuck the skeletons of vegetables onto your compost pile.

What's Your pH?

This is an excellent time to check your soil's pH. See Chapter 1 for step-by-step instructions on testing your soil, and for tips on how to change the pH if you need to.

Vegetable Garden Clean-Up

Remove all dead, dying, or spent plants to your compost pile. Then cover your garden with some of the grass clippings/shredded leaves mixture, and overspray it with my Fall Garden Bedtime Tonic. A week to 10 days later, lightly spade this material in, and then let your garden sit for the winter.

Set Out Shrubs

In the mild winter climates of Zones 7 and 8, set out container-grown trees and shrubs. Evergreens, in particular, benefit from winter rains, and from the chance to develop extensive roots before summer. And to fend off trouble, give each plant a dose of my Shrub Pest Preventer Tonic.

Timely Tonics

Fall Garden Bedtime Tonic

When you put your vegetable garden to bed for the winter, give it this nightcap.

1 can of regular cola (not diet)
1 cup of liquid dish soap
¼ cup of ammonia

Mix these ingredients in your 20 gallon hose-end sprayer, filling the balance of the jar with warm water. Saturate the layer of mulch that's on top of the soil.

Shrub Pest Preventer

1 cup of baby shampoo
1 cup of antiseptic mouthwash
1 cup of Tobacco Tea (recipe on page 61)
1 cup of chamomile tea

Mix these ingredients in a bucket, and then add 2 cups of it to your 20 gallon hose-end sprayer, filling the balance of the sprayer jar with warm water. Overspray your shrubs until they are dripping wet whenever the temperature is above 50°F.

Winter Wonders

In the mild winter climates of Zones 7 to 9, this is the time to plant veggies and annual flowers that thrive in cool weather. Any of this bunch will give you plenty of bang for your buck:

Flowers
- Annual dianthus
- Dusty miller
- Pansies
- Snapdragons

Vegetables
- Brussels sprouts
- Carrots
- Cauliflower
- Lettuce and other greens

Fertilize Fescue

In shady lawns in Zones 6 and 7, where tall fescue reigns supreme, this is the prime month for over-seeding and fertilizing. Also, check the soil's pH, and apply lime if it has become very acidic.

Recycling Roundup

To light up your walkway for trick-or-treaters, make a batch of lanterns. Just punch holes in the sides of empty soup cans, place a candle inside each one, and line them up on either side of your path for a great evening glow.

November

Keep Raking

Don't hang up your rake until the last leaves and pine needles have fallen. Even though lawns rest in winter, they are able to use whatever winter sun comes their way.

Tool Time

Clean, sharpen, and organize your tools. I hang my long-handled tools on the inside wall of my garage, where I won't trip over them, and they always stay dry. Clean your garden gloves and hand tools, too, and spend a few minutes putting sharp new edges on your garden knife and pruning shears.

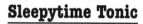

Timely Tonic

Sleepytime Tonic

When Old Man Winter is just around the corner, you should tuck in your beds with a thick blanket of mulch. This mixture feeds the mulch that slowly feeds your garden until it's time to wake up next year.

1 can of beer
1 can of regular cola (not diet)
1 cup of baby shampoo
½ cup of ammonia
¼ cup of instant tea granules

Mix these ingredients in a separate bucket, pour them into your 20 gallon hose-end sprayer, and saturate the mulch in flower beds, around shrubs, and under trees.

Jerry Baker Says . . .

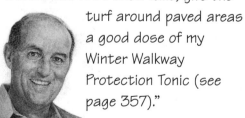

"Salt and other snow-melting chemicals can do a real job on grass. Before the first snow falls, give the turf around paved areas a good dose of my Winter Walkway Protection Tonic (see page 357)."

Put Your Mower to Bed

After the last mowing, get the mower ready for winter by draining the gas tank, replacing the engine oil, checking the spark plug for wear, and sharpening the mower blades. Give your weed trimmer and other gas-powered tools the same end-of-season TLC. You may even want to have them all tuned up so they'll be rarin' to go come spring.

DECEMBER

Gather Greenery

If you need extra greenery for holiday decorations (and who doesn't?), now's the time to raid the backs of your trees and shrubs. Just get out the pruners and borrow a few branches of boxwood, yew, fir, or any kind of pine. Tie your evergreen bouquet with a bright ribbon, and you've got a mighty fine arrangement for any holiday table!

Enjoy a Rest

The days are too short and cold to push to do things outdoors. So enjoy your well-deserved rest, get ready for Santa Claus, and warm your feet by the fire!

Adopt a Poinsettia

Few plants are more colorful and festive. Place your poinsettia near a warm, sunny window, but don't let it touch the glass. Check the soil every day, and water when it's dry to the touch. Don't allow the soil to either dry out completely or remain soaking wet.

If you want to enjoy your poinsettia for another season, stop watering and store it in a cool, dry place when the leaves fall off. In the spring, water it again and cut the stems back to 6 inches tall. Keep the stems pinched back, as the new leaves begin to form, to make a short, compact plant. From early October until blooming starts, place the plant in a dark closet for 12 hours each night, say from 8 P.M. until 8 A.M. Keep the plant in a sunny window or under grow lights for the other 12 hours of the day, and you should be rewarded with bright, beautiful blooms!

WATCH IT !

No Eating!

Keep poinsettias well out of reach of pets and toddlers who might be tempted to treat them as food. Poinsettias are not lethal poisons, but they are severely irritating to the stomach, and a few nibbles could result in a trip to the emergency room.

Jerry Baker Says . . .

"Use extra care when transporting your holiday plants. Cover them with newspaper before taking them outside, if the temperature is below 50°F. Warm up the car and park as close to the door as you can to keep the plants from being outdoors too long. You don't want them to catch a cold!"

Feed Warm-Season Grasses

For you folks living in relatively mild climates, where snow is almost as rare a sight as a zebra walking down the road, wintertime is feeding time. But I want you to use a good, balanced, all-purpose fertilizer, like a 10-10-10.

Those of you in the Sunbelt should feed your turf now, too. But use a regular lawn food at half the recommended rate, adding 1 pound of Epsom salts per each 25 pounds of lawn food. In either region, follow up with my Stress Reliever Tonic to keep your lawn relaxed through the winter.

A Bird's-Eye View

Now that winter has settled in, keep a close eye on your bird feeders, and make sure they're well stocked with sunflower seed, thistle, suet, and all the other good things our fine feathered friends need to chow down on to carry them through until spring.

Recycling Roundup

Bugs won't call the soil of your houseplants "home" after this trick: Simply sprinkle pencil sharpening shavings onto the soil, or place a 3-inch slice of cedar pencil in the soil for every 3 inches of pot diameter (for example, a 6-inch-diameter pot would need 2 cedar pencil-slices, and so on).

Timely Tonic

Stress Reliever Tonic

1 cup of baby shampoo
1 cup of antiseptic mouthwash
1 cup of Tobacco Tea (recipe on page 61)
¾ cup of weak tea
¼ cup of ammonia

Combine all of these ingredients in your 20 gallon hose-end sprayer and apply to the point of run-off.

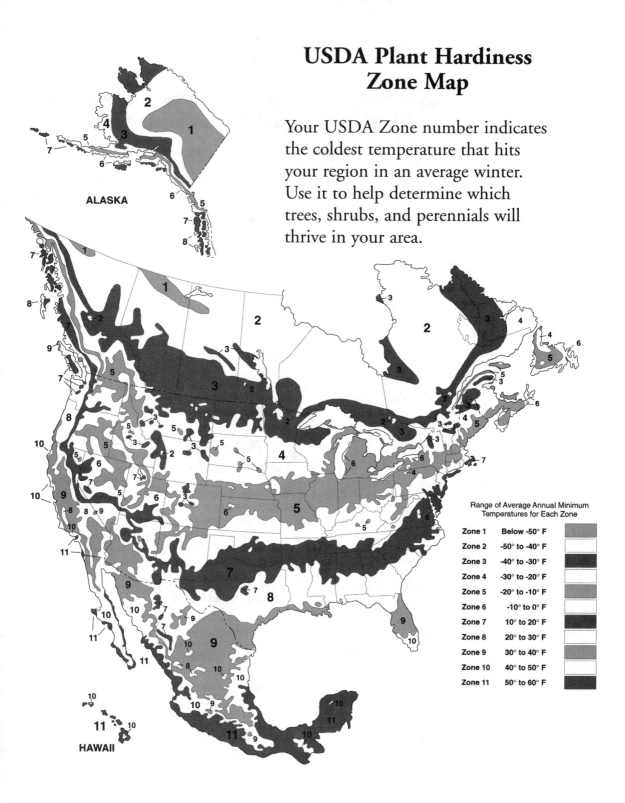

USDA Plant Hardiness Zone Map

Your USDA Zone number indicates the coldest temperature that hits your region in an average winter. Use it to help determine which trees, shrubs, and perennials will thrive in your area.

ALASKA

HAWAII

Range of Average Annual Minimum
Temperatures for Each Zone

Zone 1	Below -50° F
Zone 2	-50° to -40° F
Zone 3	-40° to -30° F
Zone 4	-30° to -20° F
Zone 5	-20° to -10° F
Zone 6	-10° to 0° F
Zone 7	10° to 20° F
Zone 8	20° to 30° F
Zone 9	30° to 40° F
Zone 10	40° to 50° F
Zone 11	50° to 60° F

CHAPTER 21

Jerry's Timely Tonics

By now you've heard me say over and over again that you can use my timely tonics to solve all kinds of problems in your yard. Well, guess what? I've gathered all of my marvelous mixers, fixers, and elixirs together right here in one handy-dandy place, so you can refer to 'em quickly if trouble strikes on your home turf.

MISSION IMPOSSIBLE?

For over 40 years now, I've been a-mixin' and a-fixin' my tonics using common household products like baking soda, baby shampoo, and mouthwash. You may be asking yourself, "How can these things possibly help my plants grow bigger and stronger?" And you're probably wondering how they can *possibly* keep pesky bugs and crafty critters from doing their dirty work in your yard. Well, when you mix 'em and use 'em according to my directions, these tonics really do work, honest injun! And every single one of my ingredients is there for a very important reason.

Here's the Lowdown

Here's a quick review of the major ingredients in my Timely Tonics and the role that each one plays in your fight against backyard problems of all kinds — from sending ornery critters packing to keeping your walkways safe from Ol' Man Winter's shenanigans.

AMMONIA is actually a readily available source of nitrogen that'll help encourage leafy plant growth. Watch out — this is very potent stuff! To avoid burning your plants, always dilute it as specified in my tonic recipes. Ammonia can burn you, too, so wear gloves when you're working with it, and don't get it anywhere near your eyes. And *never, ever* combine it with vinegar or bleach (or products containing either one). The resulting chemical reaction releases toxic fumes.

ANTISEPTIC MOUTHWASH does the same thing in your garden that it does in your mouth. Yep, it actually destroys those disease germs that can cause big-time trouble if you don't get after 'em.

BABY SHAMPOO and ***LIQUID DISH SOAP*** help soften soil and remove dust, dirt, and pollution from your plants so that osmosis and photosynthesis can occur more easily. They also send bugs packing — one taste and they'll be doing the Green-Apple Shuffle to the bug bathroom quicker than you can say "Holy tomoley!"

BEER helps release the nutrients that are locked in the soil and puts 'em to work making your plants grow stronger, healthier, and better able to nip any problems in the bud.

COLA helps feed the good bacteria that condition your soil. Just be sure you stick with the real thing; bacteria need sugar, not the artificial sweeteners in diet drinks.

EPSOM SALTS deepens the color, thickens the petals, and improves the root structure of your plants — and healthy roots mean strong, healthy plants that can join you in the fight against pests, diseases, and even nasty weather.

SUGAR, MOLASSES, *and* **CORN SYRUP** stimulate chlorophyll formation in plants and help feed the good soil bacteria.

TEA contains tannic acid, which helps plants digest their food faster and more easily. As I always say — a well-fed plant is a healthy plant!

TOBACCO is pretty nasty stuff — it poisons bugs when they ingest it or when they simply come into contact with it. It does the same thing to some of the germs that cause plant diseases.

URINE from any source (your choice) has a powerful — and frightening — smell that will send critters like deer and gophers galloping off to find friendlier territory.

WHISKEY, whether it's Scotch, bourbon, or the plain old rot-gut variety, provides nutrients and is a mild disinfectant that'll keep bugs and thugs away.

WATCH IT ⚠

Always Remember — Safety First!

Even though my tonic ingredients are natural substances and, for the most part, are safe when used as directed, some can irritate your eyes or skin, especially if you have allergies. So always take the proper precautions when you use these products. Be sure to label each tonic clearly — so that no one mistakes it for a product for human consumption — and keep all ingredients safely stored away in a locked cabinet, well out of reach of children and pets.

All-Around Disease Defense Tonic

1 cup of chamomile tea
1 tsp. of liquid dish soap
½ tsp. of vegetable oil
½ tsp. of peppermint oil
1 gal. of warm water

Mix all of these ingredients together in a bucket. Mist-spray your plants monthly before the really hot weather (75°F or higher) sets in. This elixir is strong stuff, so test it on a few leaves before spraying the whole plant. Stop spraying when summer really heats up in your area. (For related text, see page 177.)

All-Purpose Bug & Thug Spray

3 tbsp. of baking soda
2 tbsp. of Murphy's Oil Soap
2 tbsp. of canola oil
2 tbsp. of vinegar
2 gal. of warm water

Mix all of these ingredients together in a handheld sprayer and mist-spray your plants until they are dripping wet. Apply in early spring, just when bugs and thugs are waking up. (For related text, see page 207.)

All-Purpose Pest Prevention Potion

Ornery critters will take off when they get a whiff of this potion.

1 cup of ammonia
½ cup of liquid dish soap
½ cup of urine
¼ cup of castor oil

Mix all of these ingredients in a 20 gallon hose-end sprayer and thoroughly saturate all of the animal runs and burrows you can find. (For related text, see page 235.)

All-Purpose Varmint Repellent

Grandma Putt swore by this stuff for getting rid of just about any kind of unwelcome critter that came down the pike. It still works like a charm for me!

2 eggs
2 cloves of garlic
2 tbsp. of hot chili pepper
2 tbsp. of ammonia
2 cups of hot water

Mix all of these ingredients in a bucket, let the mixture sit for 3 or 4 days, and then paint it on fences, trellises, and wherever else unwanted varmints are venturing. (For related text, see page 240.)

All-Season Clean-Up Tonic

1 cup of baby shampoo
1 cup of antiseptic mouthwash
1 cup of Tobacco Tea (recipe on page 354)

Mix these ingredients in a 20 gallon hose-end sprayer, and give everything in your yard a good shower every 2 weeks during the growing season. (For related text, see page 60.)

All-Season Green-Up Tonic

1 can of beer
1 cup of ammonia
½ cup of liquid dish soap
½ cup of liquid lawn food
½ cup of molasses or clear corn syrup

Mix all of these ingredients in a large bucket, pour into a 20 gallon hose-end sprayer, and saturate your lawn, trees, flowers, and vegetables every 3 weeks throughout the growing season. (For related text, see page 27.)

Amazing Aphid Antidote

1 small onion, chopped fine
2 medium cloves of garlic, chopped fine
1 tbsp. of baby shampoo or liquid dish soap
2 cups of water

Put all of these ingredients into a blender and blend on high. Let sit overnight, and then strain through a coffee filter. Pour the liquid into a hand-held mist sprayer, and apply liberally at the first sign of aphid trouble. (For related text, see page 85.)

Ant Ambrosia

4–5 tbsp. of cornmeal
3 tbsp. of bacon grease
3 tbsp. of baking powder
3 packages of baker's yeast

Mix the cornmeal and bacon grease into a paste, then add the baking powder and yeast. Dab the gooey mix on the sides of jar lids, and set them near the anthills. The pesky critters will love it to death! (For related text, see page 226.)

Ant Control Tonic

1 cup of sugar
3 cups of water
1 tbsp. of boric acid powder

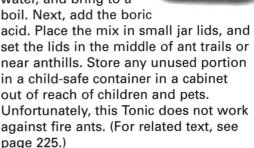

Add the sugar to the water, and bring to a boil. Next, add the boric acid. Place the mix in small jar lids, and set the lids in the middle of ant trails or near anthills. Store any unused portion in a child-safe container in a cabinet out of reach of children and pets. Unfortunately, this Tonic does not work against fire ants. (For related text, see page 225.)

Baking Soda Spray

2 tbsp. of baby shampoo
1 tbsp. of baking soda

Mix these ingredients in 1 gallon of warm water, and mist-spray your plants lightly once a week. (For related text, see page 85.)

Balanced Plant Food

1 tbsp. of instant tea granules
1 tsp. of 15-30-15 fertilizer
½ tsp. of ammonia
½ tsp. of liquid dish soap
1 gal. of warm water

Mix all of these ingredients in a plastic jug, and use the liquid at full strength when you water your plants. Be sure to label it! (For related text, see page 302.)

Beauty Bath for Bulbs

An hour or two before you plant your bulbs, soak 'em in this mixture to get 'em clean and ready to grow. Just don't peel off the papery skins! The bulbs use them as a defense against pests.

2 tsp. of baby shampoo
1 tsp. of antiseptic mouthwash
¼ tsp. of instant tea granules

Mix all of these ingredients together in 2 gallons of warm water. After your bulbs are planted, dribble any leftover Beauty Bath on the soil around your evergreen trees and shrubs. (For related text, see page 161.)

Bedtime Snack

Fall is a fine time to break new ground, because the soil has all winter to digest slow-acting amendments. This rich mixture works miracles in heavy clay.

25 lbs. of gypsum
10 lbs. of natural organic garden food (either 4–12–4 or 5–10–5)
5 lbs. of bonemeal

Mix all of these ingredients together, then apply them to every 100 square feet of soil with your handheld broadcast spreader. Work them into the soil and cover with a thick blanket of leaves, straw, or other organic mulch. (For related text, see page 7.)

Beetle Juice

Whatever kind of beetles are buggin' your plants, round up a bunch of 'em and whip 'em up into this potent potion.

½ cup of beetles (both larvae and adult beetles)
2 cups of water
1 tsp. of liquid dish soap

Collect ½ cup of beetles and whirl 'em up in an old blender with 2 cups of water. Strain the liquid through cheesecloth and mix in the soap. Pour about ¼ cup into a 1 gallon handheld sprayer and fill the rest of the jar with water. Drench the soil around new plants to keep the beetles from getting started. If they're already on the scene, spray your plants from top to bottom, and make sure you coat both sides of the leaves. Wear gloves when handling this mixture, and be sure to promptly clean your blender with hot, soapy water. (For related text, see page 201.)

Black Spot Remover Tonic

15 tomato leaves
2 small onions
¼ cup of rubbing alcohol

Chop the tomato leaves and onions into finely minced pieces, and steep them in the alcohol overnight. Use a small, sponge-type paintbrush to apply the brew to both the tops and the bottoms of any infected rose leaves. (For related text, see page 98.)

Bug-Be-Gone Spray

1 cup of Murphy's Oil Soap
1 cup of antiseptic mouthwash
1 cup of Tobacco Tea (recipe on
   page 354)

Mix all of the ingredients together in a
20 gallon hose-end sprayer and soak
your plants to the point of run-off. (For
related text, see page 210.)

Bulb Cleaning Tonic

When you remove your bulbs,
tubers, and corms from the ground
in the fall, wash them in this Tonic.

2 tbsp. of baby shampoo
1 tsp. of hydrogen peroxide

Mix these ingredients in a quart of
warm water and give your bulbs a
bath. Just be sure to let them dry thoroughly before you put them away for
the winter — otherwise, they'll rot. (For
related text, see page 165.)

Bye-Bye, Birdie Tonic

This timely Tonic will keep pesky
birds from getting to the fruit on
your trees or berry bushes before
you do.

1 tbsp. of baby shampoo
1 tbsp. of ammonia
1 gal. of water

Mix these ingredients together, and,
between rains, spray the potion on
your trees when they're full of fruit.
(For related text, see page 248.)

Cabbage Worm Wipeout

As your young cabbage plants develop heads, whip up a batch of this
terrific mixture.

1 cup of flour
2 tbsp. of cayenne pepper

Mix the ingredients together, and
sprinkle over your cabbage heads and
all over your broccoli and cauliflower to give them a good
coating. The flour swells up
inside the worms and bursts
their insides, while the
hot pepper keeps other
critters away. (For
related text, see
page 213.)

Caterpillar Killer Tonic

Whatever kind of caterpillars are eating your plants, this potent brew
will send 'em packin' in a hurry!

½ lb. of wormwood leaves
2 tbsp. of Murphy's Oil Soap
4 cups of water

Simmer the wormwood leaves in
2 cups of the water for 30 minutes.
Strain, then add the Murphy's Oil Soap
and the remaining 2 cups of water.
Pour the solution into a 6 gallon
sprayer, and spray your plants to the
point of run-off. Repeat this treatment
until the caterpillars are history. (For
related text, see page 215.)

Clematis Chow

5 gal. of well-cured horse or cow
  manure
½ cup of lime
½ cup of bonemeal

Mix all of the ingredients together in a
wheelbarrow and spread over the root
zone of your clematis first thing in the
spring. Then add a rich mulch of half-
rotted compost to make sure the soil
stays cool and moist. (For related text,
see page 184.)

Compost Feeder Tonic

Just like your plants, your compost
pile needs a boost now and then.
Once a month, spray it with this
timely Tonic.

½ can of beer
½ can of regular cola (not diet)
½ cup of liquid dish soap

Mix these ingredients in the jar of
your 20 gallon hose-end sprayer, and
apply generously to your compost pile.
(For related text, see
pages 8 and 305.)

Compost Tea

Compost tea is the most healthful
drink a plant could ask for. It delivers a balanced supply of important
nutrients — major and minor —
and fends off diseases at the same
time. Here's the recipe.

1½ gal. of fresh compost
4½ gal. of warm water

Pour the water into a 5-gallon bucket.
Scoop the compost into a cotton,
burlap, or panty-hose sack, tie it closed,
and put it into the water. Cover the
bucket and let it steep for 3 to 7 days.
Pour the solution into a watering can or
misting bottle, and give your plants a
good spritzing with it every 2 to 3
weeks. (For related text, see page 27.)

Note: You can make manure tea (another wonder drink) using this same recipe.
Just substitute 1½ gallons of well-cured
manure for the compost, and use the
finished product in the same way.

Container Plant Food Tonic

To water your container plants, make
this marvelous master mix of fortified water.

1 tbsp. of 15–30–15 fertilizer
½ tsp. of gelatin
½ tsp. of liquid dish soap
½ tsp. of corn syrup
½ tsp. of whiskey
¼ tsp. of instant tea granules

Mix all of these ingredients in a 1 gallon
milk jug, filling the balance of the jug
with water. Then add ½ cup of this
mixture to every gallon of water you
use to water all of your container
plants. (For related text, see page 319.)

Crabgrass Control Energizer Tonic

1 cup of baby shampoo
1 cup of hydrogen peroxide
2 tbsp. of instant tea granules

Mix these ingredients in your 20 gallon hose-end sprayer and saturate the turf to the point of run-off. The potent potion will jump-start the crabgrass control into action. (For related text, see page 107.)

Damping-Off Prevention Tonic

You can prevent damping-off disease in your young seedlings by using a sterile seed-starting medium and this quick Tonic.

4 tsp. of chamomile tea
1 tsp. of liquid dish soap

Mix these ingredients in 1 quart of boiling water. Let steep for at least an hour (the stronger the better), strain, then cool. Mist-spray your seedlings with this Tonic as soon as their little heads appear above the soil. (For related text, see page 15.)

Daylily Transplant Tonic

½ can of beer
2 tbsp. of liquid dish soap
2 tbsp. of ammonia
2 tbsp. of fish fertilizer
1 tbsp. of hydrogen peroxide
¼ tsp. of instant tea granules
2 gal. of warm water

Mix all of these ingredients together in a large bucket. Just before setting divided daylilies in their new planting holes, dip out 2 cups of the mixture and pour it into each hole. (For related text, see page 153.)

Deer Buster Eggnog

2 eggs
2 cloves of garlic
2 tbsp. of Tabasco sauce
2 tbsp. of cayenne pepper
2 cups of water

Put all of the ingredients into a blender and puree. Allow the mixture to sit for 2 days, then pour or spray it all over and around the plants you need to protect. (For related text, see page 245.)

Dog-Be-Gone Tonic

Keep dogs out by dousing your garden with this spicy Tonic.

2 cloves of garlic
2 small onions
1 jalapeño pepper
1 tbsp. of cayenne pepper
1 tbsp. of Tabasco sauce
1 tbsp. of chili powder
1 tbsp. of liquid dish soap
1 qt. of warm water

Chop the garlic, onions, and pepper fine, and then combine with the rest of the ingredients. Let the mixture sit and "marinate" for 24 hours, strain it through cheesecloth or old panty hose, then sprinkle it on any areas where dogs are a problem. (For related text, see page 228.)

Double Punch Garlic Tea

If thrips and other bugs are driving your plants buggy, don't pull any punches. Spring into action with this powerful brew.

- 5 unpeeled cloves of garlic, coarsely chopped
- 2 cups of boiling water
- ½ cup of Tobacco Tea (recipe on page 354)
- 1 tsp. of instant tea granules
- 1 tsp. of baby shampoo

Place the chopped garlic in a heatproof bowl, and pour boiling water over it. Allow it to steep overnight. Strain through a coffee filter, and then mix it with the other ingredients in a hand-held mist sprayer bottle. Thoroughly drench your plants to thwart those thrips. (For related text, see page 168.)

Drought Buster Tonic

Your lawn should sail through the hot weather with flying colors if you overspray it once a week during hot weather with this timely Tonic.

- 1 can of beer
- 1 cup of Thatch Buster Tonic (recipe on page 354)
- ½ cup of liquid lawn food
- ½ cup of baby shampoo

Combine all of these ingredients in a 20 gallon hose-end sprayer jar, and apply to the point of run-off. Apply this Tonic in the early-morning hours to minimize evaporation and give the grass plants ample time to digest it. Then, in addition to your normal watering, water for 10 minutes at noon and again at 4 P.M. for optimum results. (For related text, see page 112.)

Fairy Ring Fighter Tonic

- 1 cup of baby shampoo
- 1 cup of antiseptic mouthwash
- 1 cup of ammonia

First, sprinkle dry laundry soap over the problem area. Then mix all of these ingredients in your 20 gallon hose-end sprayer, and overspray the area to the point of run-off. (For related text, see page 130.)

Fall Clean-Up Tonic

Fend off snow mold, fungus, and other wintertime nasties with this excellent elixir.

- 1 cup of baby shampoo
- 1 cup of antiseptic mouthwash
- 1 cup of Tobacco Tea (recipe on page 354)
- 1 cup of chamomile tea

Mix all of these ingredients in a bucket, and then add 2 cups of it to your 20 gallon hose-end sprayer, filling the balance of the sprayer jar with warm water. Overspray your turf, trees, shrubs, beds, and so on when the temperature is above 50°F. (For related text, see page 270.)

Fall Garden Bedtime Tonic

When you put your vegetable garden to bed for the winter, give it this nightcap.

1 can of regular cola (not diet)
1 cup of liquid dish soap
¼ cup of ammonia

Mix all of these ingredients in your 20 gallon hose-end sprayer, filling the balance of the jar with warm water. Saturate the layer of mulch that's on top of the soil. (For related text, see page 322.)

Fall Lawn Food Mix

1 50 lb. or 2500 sq. ft. bag of lawn food
3 lbs. of Epsom salts
1 cup of dry laundry soap

Mix all of these ingredients together, and apply at half of the recommended rate with your handheld broadcast spreader or drop spreader. (For related text, see page 117.)

Fantastic Flowering Shrub Tonic

1 tbsp. of baby shampoo
1 tsp. of hydrated lime
1 tsp. of iron sulfate

Mix all of these ingredients in 1 gallon of water. For an extra "kicker," add 1 tablespoon of Liquid Iron to the mixture. Then spray the elixir on your flowering shrubs. (For related text, see page 87.)

Flower Flea Fluid

"Flower fleas" was Grandma Putt's name for leafhoppers. When she spotted any of these feisty little guys bugging her veggie garden or her prize asters and dahlias, she'd let the tiny culprits have it with this powerful stuff.

1 cup of Tobacco Tea (recipe on page 354)
1 tbsp. of baby shampoo or liquid dish soap
1 qt. of water

Mix all of these ingredients together in a handheld mist sprayer, and apply liberally to leaves until they're dripping wet on both sides. (For related text, see page 157.)

Flower Power Tonic

1 cup of beer
2 tbsp. of fish fertilizer
2 tbsp. of liquid dish soap
2 tbsp. of ammonia
2 tbsp. of whiskey
1 tbsp. of corn syrup
1 tbsp. of instant tea granules

Mix all of these ingredients with 2 gallons of warm water in a watering can. Drench annuals every 3 weeks to keep them blooming strong all summer long. (For related text, see page 134.)

Flower Soil Prep Mix

Here's a flower planting mixture that'll really energize the soil and produce big, bright, beautiful blooms.

4 cups of bonemeal
2 cups of gypsum
2 cups of Epsom salts
1 cup of wood ashes
1 cup of lime
4 tbsp. of medicated baby powder
1 tbsp. of baking powder

Combine all of these ingredients in a bucket and work the mixture into the soil at planting time. (For related text, see page 134.)

Fungus Fighter Tonic

½ cup of molasses
½ cup of powdered milk
1 tsp. of baking soda
1 gal. of warm water

Mix the molasses, powdered milk, and baking soda into a paste. Put the mixture into the toe of an old nylon stocking, and let it steep in a gallon of warm water for several hours. Then strain, and use the liquid as a fungus-fighting spray for your perennials. (For related text, see pages 152 and 174.)

Garlic Tea Tonic

When thrips zero in on your prize roses, give 'em a taste of this elixir.

5 cloves of unpeeled garlic, coarsely chopped
2 cups of boiling water
1 tsp. of baby shampoo

Place the chopped garlic in a heatproof bowl, and pour the boiling water over it. Steep overnight. Strain through a coffee filter, and pour the liquid into a handheld mist sprayer bottle along with the baby shampoo. Store at room temperature. (For related text, see page 99.)

General Foliage Plant Food

½ tbsp. of ammonia
½ tbsp. of bourbon
½ tbsp. of hydrogen peroxide
¼ tsp. of instant tea granules
1 vitamin tablet with iron
1 gal. of warm water

Add 1 cup to each gallon of water used to feed your plants. Mix in a jug. For flowering houseplants, use vodka instead of bourbon. (For related text, see page 302.)

Get-Up-and-Grow Tonic

To energize my dry Spring Wake-Up Tonic, overspray it with a mixture of the following.

1 cup of shampoo
1 cup of ammonia
1 cup of regular cola (not diet)
4 tbsp. of instant tea granules

Mix all of these ingredients in your 20 gallon hose-end sprayer, and apply to the point of run-off. (For related text, see page 109.)

Gopher-Go Tonic

I've had amazing results with this Tonic, and so have other folks who have tried it.

4 tbsp. of castor oil
4 tbsp. of liquid dish soap
4 tbsp. of urine

Combine all of these ingredients in ½ cup of warm water, then stir them into 2 gallons of warm water. Pour the mix over the infested areas. (For related text, see page 233.)

Grass Clipping Dissolving Tonic

If you don't pick up your grass clippings, give your lawn an inexpensive "facial" to help it breathe better. Spray it with this terrific Tonic twice a year.

1 can of beer
1 can of regular cola (not diet)
1 cup of ammonia
1 cup of liquid dish soap

Mix all of these ingredients in a bucket, and pour them into your 20 gallon hose-end sprayer. Apply to your yard to the point of run-off. This'll really speed up the decomposition process for any clippings left littering your lawn. (For related text, see page 114.)

Grass Seed Starter Tonic

This nifty Tonic will guarantee almost 100% grass seed germination every time.

¼ cup of baby shampoo
1 tbsp. of Epsom salts
1 gal. of weak tea

Mix these ingredients in a large container. Drop into your grass seed and put the whole shebang into your refrigerator for 2 days. The shampoo softens the seed shells, and the Epsom salts and tea provide nourishment to the emerging plants. The chill makes the seeds think that it's winter, so when they wake (warm) up, they'll be rarin' to grow. (For related text, see page 118.)

Ground Cover Starter Mix

3 parts bonemeal
1 part Epsom salts
1 part gypsum

Mix all of the ingredients together, and place in the planting hole and on the soil surface when planting ground covers. (For related text, see page 123.)

Happy Herb Tonic

Grandma Putt grew plenty of herbs, and she kept 'em healthy and chipper with this nifty elixir.

1 cup of tea
½ tbsp. of bourbon
½ tbsp. of ammonia
½ tbsp. of hydrogen peroxide
1 gal. of warm water

Mix all of these ingredients together in a bucket. Feed your herb plants with it every 6 weeks throughout the growing season. (For related text, see page 198.)

BOURBON
WHISKEY

Herb Soil Booster Mix

When you plant your herbs, add some of this marvelous mix to the soil to get the plants off to a rip-roarin' start.

5 lbs. of lime
5 lbs. of gypsum
1 lb. of 5-10-5 garden food
½ cup of Epsom salts

Work this mix into each 50 square feet of herb garden area to a depth of 12 to 18 inches, and then let it sit for 7 to 10 days before planting. (For related text, see page 311.)

Hot Bite Spray

There's nothing squirrels enjoy more than munching on tulips. But they'll stay away from yours if you spray the plants with this timely Tonic.

3 tbsp. of cayenne pepper
2 cups of hot water
1 tbsp. of hot sauce
1 tbsp. of ammonia
1 tbsp. of baby shampoo

Mix the cayenne pepper with the hot water in a bottle, and shake well. Allow the mixture to sit overnight, then pour off the liquid without disturbing the sediment at the bottom. Mix the liquid with the other ingredients in a hand-held sprayer bottle. Keep a batch on hand as long as new tulip buds are forming, and spritz the flower stems as often as you can to keep them hot, hot, hot! (For related text, see page 169.)

Hot Bug Brew

3 hot green peppers (canned or fresh)
3 medium cloves of garlic
1 small onion
1 tbsp. of liquid dish soap
3 cups of water

Puree the peppers, garlic, and onion in a blender. Pour the puree into a jar, and add the dish soap and water. Let stand for 24 hours. Then strain out the pulp, and use a handheld sprayer to apply the remaining liquid to bug-infested plants, making sure to thoroughly coat the tops and undersides of all the leaves. (For related text, see page 82.)

Houseplant Repotting Mix

1 lb. of potting soil
1 lb. of professional potting mix
¼ cup of Epsom salts
¼ cup of bonemeal
1 tbsp. of instant tea granules

Thoroughly mix all of the ingredients, and then sprinkle it around the root mass of your transplants. *Don't* pack it in. (For related text, see page 317.)

Hurry-Up-the-Harvest Tonic

When I know Old Man Winter is waiting in the wings and my plants are still chock-full of unripe veggies, I give my garden a big drink of my Hurry-Up-the-Harvest Tonic.

1 cup of apple juice
½ cup of ammonia
½ cup of baby shampoo

Mix all of these ingredients in your 20 gallon hose-end sprayer jar, filling the balance of the jar with warm water. Then spray the Tonic on your garden to the point of run-off. (For related text, see page 195.)

Knock 'em Dead Insect Spray

6 cloves of garlic, chopped fine
1 small onion, chopped fine
1 tbsp. of cayenne pepper
1 tbsp. of liquid dish soap

Mix all of these ingredients in 1 quart of warm water and let sit overnight. Strain out the solid matter, pour the liquid into a sprayer bottle, and knock those buggy pests dead. (For related text, see page 211.)

Lawn Freshener Tonic

A good way to determine whether it's time to water is by walking on the grass. If it doesn't spring back to life, it's definitely thirsty. To help it along, strap on your aerating lawn sandals or golf shoes and take a stroll around your yard. Then follow up with this Tonic.

1 can of beer
1 cup of baby shampoo

½ cup of ammonia
½ cup of weak tea

Mix all of these ingredients in your 20 gallon hose-end sprayer and apply to the point of run-off. (For related text, see page 116.)

Lawn Fungus Fighter Tonic

If your lawn develops brown or yellow patches that eventually die out, fight back with this fix-it formula.

1 tbsp. of baking soda
1 tbsp. of instant tea granules
1 tbsp. of horticultural or
   dormant oil
1 gal. of warm water

Mix all of these ingredients together in a large bucket, then apply with a hand-held sprayer by lightly spraying the turf. Do not drench or apply to the point of run-off. Repeat in 2 to 3 weeks, if necessary. (For related text, see page 117.)

Lawn Saver Tonic

To repair a dog-spotted lawn, first lightly sprinkle gypsum over and around each spot (it dissolves accumulated salts like magic). Then overspray your lawn with 1 cup of baby shampoo or liquid dish soap per 20 gallons of water. One week later, overspray the turf with this Tonic.

½ can of beer
½ can of regular cola (not diet)
½ cup of ammonia

Combine these ingredients in your 20 gallon hose-end sprayer. Then spray your turf to the point of run-off. (For related text, see page 229.)

Lawn Snack Tonic

1 can of beer
1 cup of baby shampoo
½ cup of ammonia
1 tbsp. of corn syrup

Mix all of these ingredients in your 20 gallon hose-end sprayer. Fill the balance of the jar with water, and overspray your lawn to the point of run-off. (For related text, see page 109.)

Lethal Weapon

3 tbsp. of garlic-and-onion juice*
3 tbsp. of skim milk
2 tbsp. of baby shampoo
1 tsp. of hot sauce
1 gal. of water

Mix all of these ingredients together in a bucket, and pour into your 20 gallon hose-end sprayer. Spray on your vegetables and flowers every 10 days to prevent aphid problems. (For related text, see page 220.)

*Make garlic-and-onion juice by chopping 2 cloves of garlic and 2 medium onions. Blend in a blender with 3 cups of water, then strain and use the remaining liquid. Extra can be frozen for future use.

Meow-va-lous Tonics

Cats are very scent oriented. You can make them turn up their noses and head elsewhere by overspraying the perimeter of your yard with either of these two Tonics.

Tonic #1: Mix ½ cup of Tobacco Tea (recipe on page 354) or oil of mustard and ¼ cup of liquid dish soap in 2 gallons of warm water.

Tonic #2: Add 1 clove of garlic (crushed), 1 tbsp. of cayenne pepper, and 1 tsp. of liquid dish soap to 1 qt. of warm water, and puree the heck out of it. (For related text, see page 230.)

Mildew Relief Tonic

1 tbsp. of baby shampoo
1 tbsp. of hydrogen peroxide
1 tsp. of instant tea granules
2 cups of water

Mix all of these ingredients in a handheld mist sprayer and apply to rose leaves. Midafternoon on a cloudy day is the best time to apply it. (For related text, see page 96.)

Mole-Chaser Tonic

1½ tbsp. of hot sauce
1 tbsp. of liquid dish soap
1 tsp. of chili powder
1 qt. of water

Mix all of these ingredients, and pour a little of the mix into mole runways to make those moles run away! (For related text, see page 234.)

Mosquito Lemon Aid

Here's a great way to reduce the numbers of mosquitoes that call your turf home. Your yard will smell lemon fresh, but the mosquitoes will hate it!

1 cup of lemon-scented ammonia
1 cup of lemon-scented dish soap

Mix these ingredients in your 20 gallon hose-end sprayer and hose down everything in your yard 3 times a week, preferably early in the morning or late in the evening. (For related text, see page 222.)

Moss Buster Tonic

This powerful stuff will get moss and mold out of your lawn in a hurry.

1 cup of antiseptic mouthwash
1 cup of chamomile tea
1 cup of Murphy's Oil Soap

Mix all of these ingredients in your 20 gallon hose-end sprayer, and apply to the point of run-off every 2 weeks until the moss is history. For quick results, add 3 ounces of copper sulfate to 5 gallons of water and spray on the moss. (For related text, see page 121.)

Move On, Moles Tonic

Mix up a batch of this timely Tonic to rid your lawn of moles.

1 cup of liquid dish soap
1 cup of castor oil
2 tbsp. of alum (dissolved in hot water)

Mix all of these ingredients in your 20 gallon hose-end sprayer, and spray over any problem areas. (For related text, see page 128.)

Mulch Moisturizer Tonic

In the spring, when you add a fresh new layer of mulch, overspray it with this timely Tonic to give it a little extra kick.

1 can of regular cola (not diet)
½ cup of ammonia
½ cup of antiseptic mouthwash
½ cup of baby shampoo

Mix all of these ingredients in your 20 gallon hose-end sprayer, and give your mulch a nice long, cool drink. (For related text, see pages 30 and 314.)

Natural Plant Food

This tasty stuff will make your most finicky houseplant say "Yum, yum!"

1 tbsp. of liquid fish fertilizer
4 tsp. of instant tea granules
½ tsp. of liquid dish soap
1 gal. of warm water

Mix these ingredients in a jug. Then store it away until it's feeding time in the old plant corral. Label it! (For related text, see page 302.)

No, Mo' Nematodes Tonic

1 can of beer
1 cup of molasses

Mix these ingredients in your 20 gallon hose-end sprayer, and thoroughly soak any area where nasty nematodes are doing their dirty work. (For related text, see page 260.)

Organic Bulb Snack

When planting daffodils and other spring-flowering bulbs, drop 1 tablespoon of this mixture into the bottom of each planting hole.

10 lbs. of compost
5 lbs. of bonemeal
1 lb. of Epsom salts

Store leftover Bulb Snack in an airtight container to keep it nice and dry. (For related text, see page 161.)

Ornamental Grass Chow

Here's a fantastic formula for feeding your ornamental grasses that'll give them plenty of growing power.

2 lbs. of dry oatmeal
2 lbs. of crushed dry dog food
1 handful of human hair

Work a handful of this mixture into the soil, and then plant to your heart's content! (For related text, see page 171.)

Perennial Passion Powder

Your perennials will bloom like champs when you put this powerful powder onto their training table.

2 lbs. of dry oatmeal
2 lbs. of crushed dry dog food
1 handful of human hair
½ cup of sugar

Mix all of these ingredients in a bucket, then spread a trowelful around each of your perennial plants in early spring. (For related text, see page 306.)

Perennial Perk-Me-Up Tonic

This excellent elixir will get your newly divided perennials back on their feet in no time at all.

1 can of beer
1 cup of ammonia
½ cup of dish soap
½ cup of liquid fertilizer
½ cup of corn syrup

Mix all of these ingredients in a 20 gallon hose-end sprayer and saturate the ground around the perennials to the point of run-off. (For related text, see page 149.)

Pollution Solution Tonic

To give your lawn some relief from the dust, dirt, and pollution that accumulate over the winter, apply this mix with a handheld broadcast spreader as early as possible in the spring.

50 lbs. of pelletized lime
50 lbs. of pelletized gypsum
5 lbs. of Epsom salts

Spread this mix over 2500 square feet of lawn area. Then wait at least 2 weeks before applying any fertilizer to the area to give the mix a chance to go to work. (For related text, see page 131.)

Powdery Mildew Control Tonic

4 tbsp. of baking soda
2 tbsp. of Murphy's Oil Soap
1 gal. of warm water

Mix these ingredients together. Pour into a handheld mist sprayer, and apply liberally when you see the telltale white spots on your plants, or even before! (For related text, see page 155.)

Pruning Wound Bandage Tonic

½ cup of interior latex paint
½ cup of antiseptic mouthwash
1 tsp. of Total Pest Control

Mix all of these ingredients in a small bucket, and paint the liquid bandage on pruning wounds to keep bugs and thugs away. (For related text, see page 56.)

Rhubarb Bug Repellent Tonic

Here's a potent plant Tonic that will say "Scram!" to just about any kind of bug you can think of.

3 medium-size rhubarb leaves
1 gal. of water
¼ cup of liquid dish soap

Chop up the rhubarb leaves, put the pieces into the water, and bring it to a boil. Let the mixture cool, then strain it through cheesecloth to filter out the leaf bits. Then mix in the dish soap. Apply this terrific Tonic to your plants with a small hand sprayer and kiss your bug problems goodbye. This Tonic also helps reduce blight on tomatoes. (For related text, see page 202.)

Rise-'n'-Shine Clean-Up Tonic

This Tonic will roust your yard out of its slumber in spring, nailing any wayward bugs and thugs that were overwintering in the comfortable confines of your lawn and garden.

1 cup of Murphy's Oil Soap
1 cup of Tobacco Tea (recipe on page 354)
1 cup of antiseptic mouthwash
¼ cup of hot sauce

Mix all of these ingredients in your 20 gallon hose-end sprayer, filling the balance of the sprayer jar with warm water. Apply to everything in your yard to the point of run-off. (For related text, see page 106.)

Robust Rose Food

Feed your established rose bushes initially in the spring with this fabulous food. They'll love you for it!

5 lbs. of garden food
2 cups of bonemeal
1 cup of Epsom
　salts
1 cup of sugar
4 pulverized
　(dried) banana peels

Mix all of these ingredients together, and sprinkle a handful or two around the base of each plant. (For related text, see page 308.)

Root Pruning Tonic

1 can of beer
4 tbsp. of instant tea granules
1 tbsp. of shampoo
1 tbsp. of ammonia
1 tbsp. of hydrogen peroxide
1 tbsp. of whiskey

Mix all of these ingredients in 2 gallons of very warm water. Then pour a quart of the elixir into the soil at the spots where you've cut your shrubs' roots. (For related text, see page 77.)

Rose Ambrosia

If your roses could talk, they would have great things to say about this grand elixir, which gives them just what they need to grow strong and bloom like gangbusters.

1 cup of beer
2 tsp. of instant tea granules
1 tsp. of Rose/Flower Food
1 tsp. of fish fertilizer
1 tsp. of hydrogen peroxide
1 tsp. of liquid dish soap

Mix all of these ingredients in 2 gallons of warm water, and give each of your roses 1 pint every 3 weeks. Dribble it onto the soil after you've watered, so it will penetrate deep into the root zone. (For related text, see page 92.)

Rose Aphid Antidote

1 lemon or orange peel, coarsely
　chopped
1 tbsp. of baby shampoo
2 cups of water

Put these ingredients into a blender and blend on high for 10 to 15 seconds. Use a coffee filter to strain out the pulp. Pour the liquid into a hand-held mist sprayer. Before applying the Tonic, get out your hose, attach a high-pressure spray nozzle, and blast your plants with water to dislodge some of the aphids. About 10 minutes later, thoroughly spray buds and young stems with Rose Aphid Antidote. Repeat after 4 days, and your aphids should be history. (For related text, see page 96.)

Rose Clean-Up Tonic

Fall is the best time to set back the insects and diseases that plague roses. After your plants have shed their leaves and been pruned, but before you mulch or wrap them with winter protection, spray them thoroughly with this Tonic.

1 cup of baby shampoo
1 cup of antiseptic mouthwash
1 cup of Tobacco Tea (recipe on
  page 354)

Place all of these ingredients in your 20 gallon hose-end sprayer, and spray your plants well from top to bottom. (For related text, see page 92.)

Rose Revival Tonics

This dynamic duo will get your bare-root roses off and growing like champs. First, wash your newly purchased bare-root rose bushes, roots and all, in a bucket of warm water with the following added.

1 tbsp. of liquid dish soap
¼ tsp. of liquid bleach

Then before planting, soak your bare-root rose bushes in a clean bucket filled with 1 gallon of warm water for about half an hour, with the following added to it.

2 tbsp. of clear corn syrup
1 tsp. of liquid dish soap
1 tsp. of ammonia

(For related text, see page 89.)

Rose Start-Up Tonic

Here's the perfect meal to get your bushes off to a rosy start.

1 tbsp. of liquid dish soap
1 tbsp. of hydrogen peroxide
1 tsp. of whiskey
1 tsp. of Vitamin B_1 Plant Starter

Mix all of these ingredients in ½ gallon of warm tea. Then pour the liquid all around the root zone of each of your prize rose plants. (For related text, see page 93.)

Rot Go Tonic

This terrific Tonic will stop one of a tomato grower's worst nightmares: blossom end rot.

1 heaping shovelful of compost
1 tsp. of gypsum
1 tsp. of Epsom salts

Mix all of these ingredients in a bucket. Then, when you plant your tomato seedlings, add a trowelful to each planting hole. (For related text, see page 251.)

Scat Cat Solution

Protect your prized plantings from felines with this Tonic.

5 tbsp. of flour
4 tbsp. of powdered mustard
3 tbsp. of cayenne pepper
2 tbsp. of chili powder
2 qts. of warm water

Mix all of these ingredients together and sprinkle the solution around the perimeter of the areas you want to protect. (For related text, see page 230.)

Seed and Soil Energizer Tonic

This potion will get your seeds off to a rip-roaring start.

1 tsp. of liquid dish soap
1 tsp. of ammonia
1 tsp. of whiskey

Mix all of these ingredients in 1 quart of weak tea, pour into your mist-sprayer bottle, and shake gently. Then once each day mist the surface of beds planted with seeds. (For related text, see page 13.)

Seed Starter Tonic

Whether you start your seeds indoors or out, give them a good send-off with this timely Tonic.

1 cup of white vinegar
1 tbsp. of baby shampoo or liquid dish soap
2 cups of warm water

Mix all of these ingredients together in a bowl, and let your seeds soak in the mixture overnight before planting them in well-prepared soil. (For related text, see page 15.)

Seedling Starter Tonic

Don't let your bedding plants go hungry! While they're still in their six-packs, treat them to this nutritious mixture.

2 tsp. of fish fertilizer
2 tsp. of liquid dish soap
1 tsp. of whiskey

Mix all of these ingredients in 1 quart of water. Feed this brew to your adopted seedlings every other time you water them, and give them a good soak with it just before you set them out. (For related text, see page 17.)

Seedling Strengthener

Until seedlings have a little time to stretch their roots a bit, they can't make use of the ready and waiting fertilizer you've mixed into the soil. To tide them over, mist-spray bedding plants every few days with this elixir for 2 to 3 weeks after planting.

2 cups of manure
½ cup of instant tea granules
5 gal. of warm water

Put the manure and tea into an old nylon stocking, and let it steep in 5 gallons of water for several days. Dilute the brew with 4 parts of warm water before you use it. (For related text, see page 17.)

Shrub Pest Preventer

1 cup of baby shampoo
1 cup of antiseptic mouthwash
1 cup of Tobacco Tea (recipe on
    page 354)
1 cup of chamomile tea

Mix all of these ingredients in a bucket,
and then add 2 cups of it to your 20
gallon hose-end sprayer, filling the
sprayer jar with warm water.
Overspray your shrubs until they are
dripping wet whenever the temperature is above 50°F. (For related text, see
page 323.)

Shrub Stimulator Tonic

4 tbsp. of instant tea granules
4 tbsp. of bourbon, or ½ can of
    beer
2 tbsp. of liquid dish soap
2 gal. of warm water

Mix all of these ingredients together,
and sprinkle the mixture over all of
your shrubs in spring. (For related text,
see page 76.)

Skunk-Away Pet Bath

A cat or dog who's had a run-in with
the wrong end of a skunk needs help
pronto. You can deliver first aid fast
with the help of this potent potion.

1 qt. of 3% hydrogen peroxide
¼ cup of baking soda
1 tbsp. of liquid dish soap

Mix all of these ingredients in a bucket
and wash your pet with the solution.
Rinse thoroughly, then as soon as possible, follow up with another bath
using a moisturizing dog or cat shampoo. (For related text, see page 244.)

Skunk-Odor-Out Tonic

1   cup of bleach or vinegar
1   tbsp. of liquid dish soap
2½ gal. of warm water

Mix these ingredients and thoroughly
saturate walls, stairs, or anything else
your local skunk has left his mark on.
Caution: Use this Tonic only on nonliving things — not on pets or humans.
(For related text, see page 244.)

Sleepytime Tonic

When Old Man Winter is just
around the corner, you should tuck
your beds in with a thick blanket of
mulch. This mixture feeds the mulch
that slowly feeds your garden.

1   can of beer
1   can of regular cola (not diet)
1   cup of baby shampoo
½ cup of ammonia
¼ cup of instant tea granules

Mix all of these ingredients in a bucket,
pour them into your 20 gallon hose-
end sprayer, and saturate the mulch in
flower beds, around shrubs, and
beneath trees. (For related text, see
page 324.)

Slug It Out Tonic

1 can of beer
1 tbsp. of sugar
1 tsp. of baker's yeast

Mix these ingredients in a bowl, and let 'em sit for 24 hours. Then pour the mixture into shallow aluminum pie pans, and set the pans so the rims are just at ground level in various areas of your garden. You'll get lots and lots of slugs, and you'll know that they died very happy! (For related text, see page 222.)

Slugweiser

1 lb. of brown sugar
½ package (1½ tsp.) of dry yeast

Pour these ingredients into a 1 gallon jug, fill it with warm water, and let it sit for 2 days, uncovered. Pour it into slug traps. (For related text, see page 123.)

Soil Soother Tonic

1 can of beer
1 can of regular cola (not diet)
½ cup of liquid dish soap
½ cup of Tobacco Tea (recipe on page 354)

Mix all of these ingredients in your 20 gallon hose-end sprayer, and give the bed a good soaking. (For related text, see page 145.)

Spring Soil Energizer Tonic

If you already have an established flower bed that you replant each spring, wake it up by applying this fantastic formula 2 weeks before you start planting.

1 can of beer
1 cup of liquid dish soap
1 cup of antiseptic mouthwash
1 cup of regular cola (not diet)
¼ tsp. of instant tea granules

Mix all of these ingredients in a separate bucket, and fill your 20 gallon hose-end sprayer. Overspray the soil to the point of run-off. This recipe makes enough to cover 100 square feet of garden area. (For related text, see page 192.)

Spring Wake-Up Tonic

Springtime is the right time to get your lawn off on the right root, and there's no better way to do it than to apply this mix as early as possible.

50 lbs. of pelletized lime
50 lbs. of pelletized gypsum
5 lbs. of bonemeal
2 lbs. of Epsom salts

Mix all of these ingredients in a wheelbarrow, and apply the mixture with your handheld broadcast spreader no more than 2 weeks before fertilizing. This will help aerate the lawn while giving it something to munch on until you start your regular feeding program. (For related text, see page 109.)

Squeaky Clean Tonic

This is a more potent version of my All-Season Clean-Up Tonic, and no matter what bad-guy bugs are buggin' your plants, it'll stop 'em in their tracks.

1 cup of antiseptic mouthwash
1 cup of Tobacco Tea (recipe on page 354)
1 cup of chamomile tea
1 cup of urine
½ cup of Murphy's Oil Soap
½ cup of lemon-scented dish soap

Mix all of these ingredients in a bucket, then pour into your 20 gallon hose-end sprayer, and apply to the point of run-off. The Murphy's Oil Soap suffocates bugs on contact, and the lemon-scented dish soap contains a citrusy odor that bugs just abhor. (For related text, see page 315.)

Squirrel Beater Tonic

To keep those pesky squirrels from chewing up everything in sight, douse your prized plantings with this spicy Tonic.

2 tbsp. of cayenne pepper
2 tbsp. of hot sauce
2 tbsp. of chili powder
1 tbsp. of Murphy's Oil Soap
1 qt. of warm water

Mix all of these ingredients together, pour into a handheld sprayer, and liberally spray on all your plants. (For related text, see page 239.)

Stress Reliever Tonic

1 cup of baby shampoo
1 cup of antiseptic mouthwash
1 cup of Tobacco Tea (recipe on page 354)
¾ cup of weak tea
¼ cup of ammonia

Mix all of these ingredients in your 20 gallon hose-end sprayer and apply to the point of run-off. (For related text, see page 327.)

Summer Rejuvenating Tonic

When your annuals seem to be on the brink of exhaustion in late summer, pinch them back severely and give them a good dose of this potent pick-me-up.

¼ cup of beer
1 tbsp. of corn syrup
1 tbsp. of baby shampoo
1 tbsp. of 15-30-15 fertilizer

Mix all of these ingredients in 1 gallon of water, and slowly dribble the solution onto the root zones of your plants. Within 2 weeks, they'll be real comeback kids! (For related text, see page 136.)

Super Shrub Restorer

1 can of beer
1 cup of ammonia
½ cup of liquid dish soap
½ cup of molasses or clear corn syrup

Mix all of these ingredients in your 20 gallon hose-end sprayer. Drench shrubs thoroughly, including the undersides of leaves. If you have some left over, spray it on your trees and lawn. (For related text, see page 80.)

Super Shrub Soil Mix

2 bushels of compost
½ cup of Epsom salts
½ cup of bonemeal
1 tbsp. of medicated baby powder

Mix all of these ingredients together in a container, and work about a cup into each hole when you plant your shrubs. (For related text, see page 77.)

Super Shrub Tonic

You'll have the happiest, healthiest, bloomingest shrubs in town if you add this excellent elixir to their diet.

½ can of beer
½ cup of fish fertilizer
½ cup of ammonia
¼ cup of baby shampoo
1 tbsp. of hydrogen peroxide

Mix all of these ingredients in your 20 gallon hose-end sprayer jar. Then feed your flowering shrubs in very early spring and every 3 weeks throughout the growing season. (For related text, see pages 77 and 306.)

Super Slug Spray

1½ cups of ammonia
1 tbsp. of Murphy's Oil Soap
1½ cups of water

Mix these ingredients in a handheld mist sprayer bottle, and over-spray areas where you see signs of slug activity. (For related text, see page 141.)

Super Spider Mite Mix

4 cups of wheat flour
½ cup of buttermilk (not fat-free)
5 gal. of water

In a big bucket, make a slurry of the flour, buttermilk, and 2 cups of the water. Then add the rest of the water. Apply to both sides of mite-infested leaves with a handheld mist sprayer. (For related text, see page 188.)

Terrific Tree Chow

25 lbs. of Garden Food
1 lb. of sugar
½ lb. of Epsom salts

Feed your trees by drilling holes at the weep line (at the tip of the farthest branch), 8 to 10" deep, 18 to 24" apart in 2' circles. Fill the holes with 2 table-spoons of the above mixture, and sprinkle the remainder over the soil. (For related text, see page 55.)

Terrific Turf Tonic

Keep your lawn looking its best by washing it down once a month with this Tonic after you mow.

1 cup of baby shampoo
1 cup of ammonia
1 cup of weak tea

Mix all of these ingredients in your 20 gallon hose-end sprayer and fill the balance of the sprayer jar with warm water. Then apply it to your lawn to the point of run-off. (For related text, see page 313.)

Thatch Buster Tonic

1 cup of beer or regular cola
(not diet)
½ cup of liquid dish soap
¼ cup of ammonia

Mix all of these ingredients in your 20 gallon hose-end sprayer. Fill the balance of the jar with water, and spray the entire turf area. Repeat once a month during the summer, when grass is actively growing. (For related text, see page 108.)

Timely Tree Tonic

1 cup of beer
4½ tbsp. of instant tea granules
1 tbsp. of baby shampoo
1 tbsp. of ammonia
1 tbsp. of whiskey
1 tbsp. of hydrogen peroxide
1 tbsp. of gelatin

Mix all of these ingredients in 2 gallons of warm water Give each tree up to a quart of this Tonic about once a month through the summer for smooth sailing. (For related text, see page 55).

Tobacco Tea

½ handful of chewing tobacco
1 gal. of hot water

Wrap up the chewing tobacco in a piece of cheesecloth or panty hose, put it into the water, and soak it until the water turns dark brown. Fish out the cheesecloth and strain the liquid into a glass container with a good, tight lid. Then store the tea, and use it whenever a Tonic recipe calls for it.

Tomato Booster Tonic

2 tbsp. of Epsom salts
1 tsp. of baby shampoo
1 gal. of water

Mix these ingredients together, and liberally soak the soil around tomato plants as they flower to stimulate their growth. (For related text, see page 200.)

Transplant Tonic

When dividing perennials, soak the best rooted pieces in this Tonic for about 10 minutes just before replanting them.

1 can of beer
¼ cup of instant tea granules
2 tbsp. of liquid dish soap
2 gal. of water

When you're finished planting, use a small pail to scoop up any leftover Tonic and dribble it around your plants. (For related text, see page 321.)

Tree Chow Energizing Tonic

1 can of beer
1 cup of liquid lawn food
½ cup of liquid dish soap
½ cup of ammonia

Mix these ingredients in your 20 gallon hose-end sprayer, filling the balance of the jar with regular cola (not diet). (For related text, see page 55.)

Tree Planting Booster Mix

This magic potion will get your trees off to a flying start.

4 lbs. of compost
2 lbs. of gypsum
1 lb. of Epsom salts
1 lb. of dry dog food
1 lb. of dry oatmeal

Mix all of these ingredients together in a bucket. Work a handful or two into the bottom of the planting hole and sprinkle some over the top after planting. (For related text, see page 52.)

Tree Snack Mix

5 lbs. of bonemeal
1 lb. of Epsom salts
1 lb. of gypsum
½ cup of moth-
   balls

Mix all of these ingredients together, and spread in a broad band beneath your trees using a handheld spreader. (For related text, see page 55.)

Tree Transplanting Tonic

⅓ cup of hydrogen peroxide
¼ cup of instant tea granules
¼ cup of whiskey
¼ cup of baby shampoo
2 tbsp. of fish fertilizer

Mix all of these ingredients with 1 gallon of warm water in a bucket, and pour it into the hole when you transplant a tree or a shrub. (For related text, see page 52.)

Tree Wound Sterilizer Tonic

¼ cup of ammonia
¼ cup of liquid dish soap
¼ cup of antiseptic mouthwash

Mix all of these ingredients in 1 gallon of warm water, pour into a handheld sprayer bottle, and drench the spots where you've pruned limbs from trees or shrubs. (For related text, see page 56.)

Vegetable Power Powder

25 lbs. of organic garden food
5 lbs. of gypsum
2 lbs. of diatomaceous earth
1 lb. of sugar

Mix all of these ingredients together, and put them into a handheld broadcast spreader. Set the spreader on medium and apply the mixture over the top of your garden. Follow up immediately by overspraying the area with my Spring Energizer Tonic. (For related text, see page 192.)

Veggie Tonic #1

Even vegetable plants appreciate a little variety in their diet. My All-Season Green-Up Tonic is great stuff (see page 333), but every so often, use this Tonic as a change of pace, alternating it with Veggie Tonic #2.

1 can of beer
1 cup of ammonia
4 tbsp. of instant tea granules
2 tbsp. of baby shampoo

Mix all of these ingredients in your 20 gallon hose-end sprayer. Then spray all the plants in the garden to the point of run-off. (For related text, see page 190.)

Veggie Tonic #2

Alternate this potion with Veggie Tonic #1.

½ cup of fish fertilizer
2 tbsp. of whiskey
2 tbsp. of Epsom salts
2 tbsp. of instant tea granules
1 tbsp. of baby shampoo

Mix all of these ingredients in your 20 gallon hose-end sprayer. Then spray all the plants in the garden to the point of run-off. (For related text, see page 190.)

Weed Killer Prep Tonic

To really zing a lot of weeds in a large area, overspray them first with this Tonic.

1 cup of liquid dish soap
1 cup of ammonia
4 tbsp. of instant tea granules

Mix all of these ingredients in your 20 gallon hose-end sprayer, filling the balance of the sprayer jar with warm water. Then spray away! (For related text, see page 119.)

Whitefly Wipeout Tonic

1 cup of sour milk (let it stand out for 2 days)
2 tbsp. of flour
1 qt. of warm water

Mix all of these ingredients in a bowl and spray the mixture over any plants that are troubled by whiteflies. (For related text, see pages 142 and 219.)

Winter Walkway Protection Tonic

To keep the grassy areas around your walks and driveways in good shape during the winter, first sprinkle the lawn liberally with gypsum. Then apply this Tonic.

1 cup of liquid dish soap
½ cup of ammonia
½ cup of beer

Mix all of these ingredients in your 20 gallon hose-end sprayer, and then apply it over the gypsum. (For related text, see page 270.)

Winterizing Tonic

To head off trouble next spring, zap cutworms and other bugs with this Tonic.

1 cup of Murphy's Oil Soap
1 cup of Tobacco Tea (recipe on page 354)
1 cup of antiseptic mouthwash

Mix all of these ingredients in a 20 gallon hose-end sprayer, filling the balance of the jar with warm water. Saturate your lawn and garden, and they'll be rarin' to grow come spring. (For related text, see page 320.)

Index

Page numbers in *italics* denote Top Ten lists

Flour
and skunk control, 244
in tonics, 142, 188, 213,
231, 335, 349, 354,
357
Flower arrangements, 66, 316,
317
Flower Flea Fluid, 157 (recipe),
339 (recipe)
Flower fleas. *See* Leafhoppers
Flower Power Tonic, 134, 135
(recipe), 339 (recipe)
Flower Soil Prep Mix, 134, 135
(recipe), 144, 340 (recipe)
Flowering ground covers, *126*
Flowering shrubs, 66, *67*
Flowering trees, 47–48, 62
Focal points, gates as, 291, 295
Forsythia, 35, 65, 66, *67*, 107,
162, 306
Foundation plantings, 71
Four-lined plant bug, 210
Foxglove, 145, 146, *148*, 152,
246, 312
Fragrant plants, 48, 90, 162,
168, 181, 198
Freezes, 263
Fringe tree, 48, *48, 51*
Frost, 261–263
Fruit trees, ornamental, 47
Fuchsia, *138*
Fungi
as decomposers in soil, 7,
252
disease, 83, 98, 117, 127,
136, 143, 152, 155,
174–175, 177,
250–251, 253–255
fairy rings on the lawn, 130
Fungicides, 177, 253
Fung-onil, 253
Fungus Fighter Tonic, 152
(recipe), 174 (recipe), 251,
340 (recipe)
Fusarium, 255

G

Garbage can, to control ornamental grass spreading, 173

Garden design
bulbs, 161, 162–163, 165
fencing, 286, 290
gates as focal points, 291,
295
ground covers, 122, 124
lawn space, 101
ornamental grasses, 171
perennials, 145
roses, 88
shrubs, 68–69
size of plants. *See* Size of
mature plant
steps, 276
trees, 40–41, 43, 44, 47
use of surface tree roots, 59
walkways, 275
where to get ideas, 301–302
Garden journal, 29, 301
Garlic, *199*
as a pesticide, 141, 158, 198,
213
to repel animals, 128, 234,
245
in tonics, 85, 99, 169, 221,
229, 231, 245, 332,
333, 337, 338, 340,
342, 344
Garlic Tea Tonic, 99 (recipe),
157, 340 (recipe)
Gates, 291, 294–295
Gelatin, in tonics, 55, 319, 336,
355
General Foliage Plant Food, 303
(recipe), 340 (recipe)
Geranium, 16, *138*, 140–141,
219, 311
scented, 225, 319
Get-Up-and-Grow Tonic, 109,
110 (recipe), 340
(recipe)
Ginkgo, *42, 45, 51*
Gladiolus, 159, 160, *164*, 168
Glyphosate, 175
Golden star, *126*
Golden-rain tree, *48, 51*
Goldenrod, *151*
Golf ball, in sprayer buckets,
110
Gomphrena, *137*

Gopher-Go Tonic, 233 (recipe),
341 (recipe)
Gophers, 232–233
Grafted plants, 20
Granite meal, 25
Grape, 179, 209, 291
Grapefruit, as a bug trap, 215
Grass Clipping Dissolving
Tonic, 114 (recipe), 341
(recipe)
Grass Seed Starter Tonic, 118,
119 (recipe), 341 (recipe)
Grasses. *See also* Lawn;
Ornamental grasses
bahia, 120
Bermuda, 102, 103, *104,*
106, 114
blue. *See* Bluegrass
blue oat, *172*
buffalo grass, 102, *104*
centipede, 102, *104,* 120
colonial bent, *105,* 216
crabgrass, 107, 119, 306
feather reed, *172*
fountain, *172, 174*
maiden, 170, *172,* 176, 177
mondo, *125*
oat, *172*
pampas, 170, *172,* 175,
304
perennial ryegrass, 102, *105,*
114, 118
St. Augustine, 102, *104,* 120
silver spike, *172*
switch, *172*
zoysia, 102, *104,* 114
Gravel, 29–30, 281
Greenhouses, mini, 15
Ground covers, 23, 101, 103,
122–126, 124, 310
evergreen, 124, *125*
flowering, *126*
grass. *See* Lawn
problems and solutions, 130
Ground Cover Starter Mix, 122
(recipe), 123, 341 (recipe)
Groundhogs, 198
Grubs, 244
Guara, *151*
Gum, in mole tunnels, 128, 234

Gypsum, 229
    as soil amendment, 27, 194, 269, 270
    in tonics, 7, 53, 55, 110, 122, 131, 135, 192, 251, 311, 334, 340, 341, 347, 349, 352, 356, 357
Gypsy moths, 58, 224

H

Hackberry, 47
    common, 44
Hair
    as animal repellent, 240, 246
    in the compost pile, 191
    as nematode deterrent, 214
    in tonics, 171, 307, 346
Hair spray, 317
Hand clippers, 36
Happy Herb Tonic, 198 (recipe), 285, 341 (recipe)
Hardening off, 14
Harvesting, 316, 318
Hawthorn, *45*
Heat check, 142
Heather, *70*
Hedges, 33, 69, 81, 170, 175, 313
Heeling in, 21
Heirloom varieties, 257
Helen's flower, *151*
Helianthus, *151*
Heliopsis, *148, 151*
Hemlock, 36, 44
    Canada, *46, 266*
Herb Soil Booster Mix, 311 (recipe), 342 (recipe)
Herbicides, 103, 107, 119, 123, 129
Herbs, 198, *199*, 210, 215, 225, 285, 311, 319
Heuchera, *148*, 152
Holdfasts of vines, 179
Holly, 68, 69, 71, 83, 284
    Foster, *266*
    Japanese, 65, *74*, 83
Hollyhock, 158, 253, 312
Honey, for sticky bug trap, 208

Honeysuckle, 179, 187
    everblooming, *185*
Hornbeam, *45*
    European, *42*, 44
Horticultural oil, in tonics, 117, 221, 343
Hose guards, 171
Hoses, 75, 250, 315
Hosta, *148, 151*, 246, 303
Hot Bite Spray, 169 (recipe), 342 (recipe)
Hot Bug Brew, 82, 342 (recipe)
Hot green pepper, in tonics, 342
Hot sauce, in tonics, 107, 169, 221, 229, 234, 239, 245, 337, 342, 344, 345, 347, 353
Hot-water bottle, for a kneeling pad, 172
Houseplant Repotting Mix, 317 (recipe), 342 (recipe)
Houseplants, 302, 317, 319, 326, 327
Humus, 6, 190
Hurry-Up-the-Harvest Tonic, 195 (recipe), 343 (recipe)
Hyacinth, 159, 162, *164*
    Dutch, 163
    grape, 160, 162, 163, *164, 165, 166*
Hybrid varieties, 12
Hydrangea, *67*, 83, 84, 221, 246
    climbing, 179, *185*
Hydrogen peroxide, in tonics, 53, 55, 77, 90, 92, 97, 107, 153, 165, 198, 244, 303, 307, 335, 337, 340, 341, 344, 348, 349, 351, 353, 354, 355, 356
Hyssop, 198

I

Imidacloprid, 127, 209
Impatiens, 16, 124, 133, 135, *137, 138*, 143, 208, 311
Indoor seed sowing, 14–15
Injuries, saving your back, 23
Interior latex paint, in tonics, 56, 347

Iris, 246
    bearded, 161, *164*, 166, 167
    Dutch, *164, 166*
Iris borers, 167
Iron
    as an essential nutrient, 59, 61, 83, 86, 191, 303
    in tonics, 303, 341
Iron sulfate, in tonics, 87, 339
Ivy, 122, 124, *125*, 130
    Boston, 179, *185*
    English, 59, 124, 130, 250

J

January tasks, 301–303
Japanese beetle, 97, 127, 158, 198, 209
Jasmine, 179
    Confederate, *185*
Joe-pye weed, *151*
July tasks, 316–317
June beetle, 127
June tasks, 314–315
Juniper, 36, 68, *74*, 78, 87, 176
    Chinese, *73*
    columnar, 71
    creeping, 65, *70*, 122, *125*

K

Kale, *196*
Kiddie pool, 318
Kiwi, 193
Kneeling pad, 172
Knock 'em Dead Tonic, 208 (recipe), 343 (recipe)
Kool-Aid, grape, 248

L

Lacebugs, 85
Lacewing, 154
Ladybeetles, 96, 154, 220
Ladybugs. *See* Ladybeetles
Lady's mantle, *150*
Lamb's ears, *125*
Lamium, 122, *126*
Lampshades, 263
Lantana, *137*

Larkspur, 132, 218
Laundry soap, dry, in tonics, 117, 339
Laurel, mountain, 85
Lavender, 311, 319
  English, *199*
Lawn, 100–121, 117
  aeration, 3, 116, 216, 253, 269
  cool-season grasses, 102, *105,* 120, 320
  dethatching, 103, 108, 216, 253
  disease, 104, 117, 127
  fertilizing. *See* Fertilizer, lawn
  five fine ways to shrink, 101
  grass clippings, 8, 114
  Milky Spore for, 97, 127, 158, 209
  mowing, 102, 103, 111, 113–114, 121
  pests, 97, 104, 127
  problems and solutions, 127–129, 131
  reseeding, 118, 216, 320
  for shady areas, 120, 121
  traffic considerations, 104, 105, 121, 172
  types of grasses, 102–105
  warm-season grasses, 102, *104,* 106, 120, 321, 327
Lawn Freshener Tonic, 116 (recipe), 343 (recipe)
Lawn Fungus Fighter Tonic, 117 (recipe), 253, 343 (recipe)
Lawn Saver Tonic, 229 (recipe), 343 (recipe)
Lawn Snack Tonic, 109, 110 (recipe), 117, 344 (recipe)
Lawn sprayer, 110
Lawnmower, sharpening blades, 113
Leaf mold, 6
Leaf spot, 152, 177, 250–251
Leafcutter bees, 99
Leafhoppers, 157, 221, 256
Leafminers, 153, 202, 216

Lemon peel, in tonics, 97, 348
Lemon-scented ammonia, in tonics, 223, 345
Lemon-scented dish soap, in tonics, 223, 345, 353
Lethal Weapon, 220, 221 (recipe), 344 (recipe)
Lettuce, 191, 193, *196,* 202, 237, 309, 323
Leucothoe, drooping, *73, 74*
Lighting, 69, 244, 254, 275, 276, 307, 323
Ligustrum, *266*
Lilac, 35, *67,* 68, 85, 252
Lily, 159, 162, *164,* 166, 246, 257
  Asiatic hybrids, 166
  Oriental, 162, 168
  spider, 160
  tiger, 169
Lily lice, 168
Lime
  as soil amendment, 6, 184, 194
  in tonics, 87, 110, 131, 135, 184, 311, 336, 339, 340, 342, 347
Linden, *42*
Linoleum, as seedling collar, 214
Liquid dish soap, 219, 229
  bottle as a bug trap, 208
  secret behind, 330
  in tonics, 8, 13, 15, 17, 27, 55, 56, 76, 80, 85, 89, 90, 92, 108, 112, 114, 128, 135, 145, 149, 153, 157, 177, 192, 201, 202, 223, 229, 231, 233, 234, 235, 244, 271, 303, 305, 315, 319, 321, 323, 332, 333, 334, 336, 337, 338, 339, 341, 342, 343, 344, 345, 346, 347, 348, 349, 350, 351, 352, 353, 355, 356, 357
Liquid Iron, 59, 83, 86, 339
Liquid Mole Repellent, 128

Liriope, 124, *125*
Loam, 3
Lobelia, *137, 138,* 142
Locust, black, *42*
Loosestrife, 146
Loppers, 36
Low-care ornamental grasses, 170–177
Lungwort, *148*

M

Maggots, 194
Magnesium, 27
Magnolia
  'Little Gem', *46*
  star, 65, *67*
  sweet bay, *46, 48*
Mail order. *See* Catalog shopping
Mailing tube, as seedling collar, 214
Manganese, 191
Manure
  as caterpillar repellent, 214
  as soil amendment, 6, 8, 25, 228, 260
  in tonics, 17, 27, 184, 336, 350
Manure Tea, 27 (recipe), 336
Maple, 44, 59, 304
  Japanese, 44, *51*
  red, *42, 45*
  trident, *42*
March tasks, 305–307
Marigold, 34, 133, *138,* 143, 311, 319
  French, *137,* 142, 223, 260
Marjoram, sweet, 319
Masonry, 277, 279–281
May tasks, 310–313
Mealybugs, 186–187, 302
Melampodium, 135, *137*
Melon, 191, 193, *197,* 310
Meow-va-lous Tonics, 231 (recipes), 344 (recipe)
Merit, 127, 209
Mesh, plastic, 248
Mexican bean beetle, 205, 209

Powdery mildew, 96–97, 140, 155, 252
Powdery Mildew Control Tonic, 155 (recipe), 252, 347 (recipe)
Privet, golden, *73*
Problems and solutions. *See also* Disease; Pests
  annuals, 140–143
  bulbs, 167–169
  fences and walls, 296–298
  lawns and ground covers, 127–131
  ornamental grasses, 174–177
  perennials, 152–158
  roses, 96–99
  shrubs, 82–87
  spring rains, 269
  trees, 58–63
  vegetables, 200–201
  vines, 186–188
  walkways, 282–285
Pruning, 33–36, 120, 304
  annual transplants, 134
  bare-root plants, 22
  and disease, 34, 79, 82
  don't overprune, 78
  hedges, 33, 81, 313
  ivy, 130
  ornamental grasses, 173, 174, 304
  to promote bloom, 34, 312
  renewal, 79, 80
  roots, 77
  roses, 93, 308
  shrubs, 77–80, 85, 284, 306, 313
  tomatoes, 200
  trees, 56–57, 304, 325
  use for cut branches, 229, 236
  vines, 183
  walkways, 284
Pruning tools, 36, 284, 313
Pruning Wound Bandage Tonic, 56 (recipe), 79, 304, 347 (recipe)
Pumpkin, 243
Pyrethrin, 97, 154
Pyrethrum, 216

Q

Queen Anne's lace, 215

R

Rabbits, 23, 194, 236–237
Rabies, 241
Radish, 193, *196,* 309
Rain, flooding and mud, 268–269, 285
Raking, 29, 106, 108, 253, 322, 324
Raspberries, 21, 257
Raspberry mosaic virus, 257
Recordkeeping. *See* Garden journal
Redbud, *48, 51*
Redwood, dawn, *42*
Resistant plants, 189, 252, 255, 257, 267
Rhododendron, 65, *67,* 69, 83, 85, 86–87, 307
Rhubarb, 194, 202, 347
Rhubarb Bug Repellent Tonic, 202 (recipe), 347 (recipe)
Ringworm, 241
Rise-'n'-Shine Clean-Up Tonic, 106, 107 (recipe), 347 (recipe)
Robust Rose Food, 308 (recipe), 348 (recipe)
Rock garden plants, 296–297
Roofing shingles, 265
Root development, 17, 18, 40, *42,* 59
Root maggots, 218
Root Pruning Tonic, 77 (recipe), 348 (recipe)
Root rot, 83, 136
Rootbound plants, 16
Roots
  bulb, 161
  depth, and watering, 28
  holdfasts of vines, 179
  mangled, on mail-order plants, 22
  with nematodes, 259
  and planting, 53, 75, 305
  pruning, *77*

  vine, 179
Rose, 34, *67,* 88–99, 228, 246
  bare-root, 21, 89
  climbing, *95,* 179, 291
    'America', *95*
    'Belle of Portugal', *95*
    'Blaze Improved', *95*
    'Golden Showers', *95*
    'Iceberg, Climbing', *95*
    'Joseph's Coat', *95*
    'Lady Banks', *95*
    'Leontine Gervais', *95*
    'Madame Alfred Carriere', *95*
    'Zephirine Drouhin', *95*
  diseases, 96–97, 98
  floribunda, *94*
    'Angel Face', *94*
    'Auguste Renoir', *94*
    'Betty Prior', *94*
    'Europeana', *94*
    'Guy de Maupassant', *94*
    'Iceberg', *94*
    'Intrigue', *94*
    'Playgirl', *94*
    'Singin' in the Rain', *94*
    'Toulouse Lautrec', *94*
  fragrance, 90
  hybrid tea, 89, 91
    'Dainty Bess', *91*
    'Double Delight', *91*
    'Fragrant Cloud', *91*
    hybrids, *70*
    'Just Joey', *91*
    'McCartney', *91*
    'Midas Touch', *91*
    'Mister Lincoln', *91*
    'Pascali', *91*
    'Peace', *91*
    'Scarlet Meidilland', *70*
    'Tropicana', *91*
  Lenten, *148*
  mulch, 93, 98
  pests, 96, 97, 99, 158, 209, 221
  planting, 89, 90
  problems and solutions, 96–99
  pruning, 34, 35, 93, 308
  seven super steps, 92–93